BarnaTrends

2017

What's New and What's Next at the Intersection of Faith and Culture

BakerBooks

a division of Baker Publishing Group
Grand Rapids, Michigan

© 2016 by Barna Group

Published by Baker Books
a division of Baker Publishing Group
P.O. Box 6287, Grand Rapids, MI 49516-6287
www.bakerbooks.com

Library of Congress Cataloging-in-Publication Data is on file at the Library of Congress, Washington, DC.

ISBN 978-0-8010-1863-3

Cover Design: Chaz Russo

Table of Contents

Barna Trends is an annual guide to the latest cultural, religious, and political trends, designed to help you navigate a complex and ever-changing world.

Barna Trends 2017 Was Created by:
Roxanne Stone Editor-in-Chief
Alyce Youngblood Editorial Manager
Chaz Russo Creative Director
Cory Maxwell-Coghlan Senior Writer
Pam Jacob Senior Research Director
Brenda Usery Production Manager
Douglas Brown Copy Editor
David Kinnaman President

Contributors & Writers:
Audrey Assad, George Barna, Jefferson Bethke, Christine Caine, Bonnie Camarda, Joyce Chiu, Andy Crouch, Claire Diaz-Ortiz, Nicole Baker Fulgham, Brad Griffin, Scott Harrison, Aly Hawkins, Brooke Hempell, Kathy Khang, David Kim, Bryan Loritts, Gabe Lyons, Mark Matlock, Jedd Medefind, Carol Howard Merritt, Jake Mulder, Sarah Ngu, Kara Powell, Megan Pritchett, Sarah Joy Proppe, Gareth Russell, Preston Sprinkle, Jon Tyson, Tyler Wigg-Stevenson, Jun Young

Designs By:
Annette Allen, Grant England, Michael Forrest, Amy Roberts, Chaz Russo, Rob Williams

The Barna Team Also Includes:
Cassie Bolton, Amy Brands, Matt Carobini, Joyce Chiu, Inga Dahlstedt, Bill Denzel, Aly Hawkins, Brooke Hempell, Traci Hochmuth, Rick Ifland, Pam Jacob, Elaine Klautzsch, Steve McBeth, Josh Pearce, Megan Pritchett, Gareth Russell, Caitlin Schuman, Todd Sorenson, Todd White

Barna Group is a visionary research and communications company headquartered in Ventura, California, with locations in New York, Atlanta and London. Widely considered to be a leading source for actionable insights on faith and culture, Barna Group has conducted more than one million interviews over the course of hundreds of studies. Since it was founded by George and Nancy Barna in 1984, Barna Group has carefully and strategically tracked the role of faith in America, developing one of the nation's most comprehensive databases of spiritual indicators.

Barna Research
When you're trying to determine the next step to take, you need a trusted guide. Barna can help provide a clear view of your key audiences and actionable insights through custom research, consulting, and resources. To find out more, visit barna.com/services.

Barna
P.O. Box 1030
Ventura, CA 93002
805-639-0000
www.barna.com

Stay Connected with Barna
🐦 @BarnaGroup
📘 @BarnaGroup
▶ Barna Group

Make Something

An Introduction by David Kinnaman, President of Barna Group

Knowledge is power. You've no doubt heard the phrase.

True power, however, comes not merely by having the right information, but by knowing what to do with it. In other words, discernment is power.

Take the book of Proverbs. Reading Solomon's Twitter-like stream of ancient advice for living wisely is a great start, but his guidance becomes wisdom—not just information—only when it's appropriately applied to our sustained efforts to live wisely. When we make something of the information.

The recent growth of the sharing economy provides a timely example of entrepreneurs and leaders making something of information. Companies like Uber, Lyft, Postmates, and Airbnb observed a shift toward a hyper-connected culture that prioritizes community, choice, and mobility. They built networks and technology to meet those needs. They *made something.*

Barna Trends is a collection of the best research and insights our company has amassed over the last year or so. The goal of this compilation, consistent with Barna's vision as a company, is to help spiritual influencers understand the times and know what to do. There is plenty of information here (we are, after all, data geeks). But you'll also find in-depth analysis, personal stories, cultural critique, and ideas for living and leading wisely in the future—all offered to help you make something of the information.

In the pages of *Barna Trends*, you will encounter our team pursuing George Barna's founding vision: to provide current and accurate information, in bite-sized pieces, to facilitate effective decision-making. Along the way you'll read analysis and reflections on a range of topics from the talented Barna team and experts from various geographies and demographics.

We hope this project reveals opportunities in your context that you hadn't noticed before. As you read, you might practice looking beyond the trends by asking yourself, *So what?* Or, more specifically, *What does this mean for how I live and lead, in the place I live and lead? How can I make something of this information?*

In our work we sometimes see an unfortunate phenomenon: spiritual influencers who want to understand the trends but bring narrow motivations to the process of discernment. Maybe they hope to keep their particular vision of the world alive, so they look for information that confirms their preconceptions and biases. Perhaps an entrepreneur looks for confirmation of his business model. A ministry leader scours the data only to bolster her pet project. Or a preacher looks for the right statistic to drive home his point, failing to wonder if the argument itself is true.

We hope you bring a broader set of goals to *Barna Trends*. As you digest the data, our prayer is that you use it to make something in and for the world where God has placed you.

How to Use This Book

The research presented in *Barna Trends* is packaged to suit a variety of reading experiences: personal interest, group discussion, sermon preparation, academic study, market research, and so on. To ensure readers can easily filter through and absorb the information, *Barna Trends* is divided into three broad sections: Culture, Life, and Faith. These sections speak to different, yet interwoven, parts of the reader's world.

- **Culture** covers mindsets and movements within the broader public, from the internet to the voting booth.
- **Life** has a more personal lens, taking a closer look at our workplaces, homes, schools, and daily routines.
- **Faith** focuses on the state of our spiritual lives, individually and collectively, in America and around the world.

Each of these topics is divided further into additional subcategories, shaped by the most relevant research

Interested in other projects from Barna Group? More information about Barna's research, services, speaking, books, and resources is available at barna.com

Barna has to offer. We've sought to share our findings in creative ways that best engage the reader, from feature-length reports and fast facts to eye-catching infographics and personal columns.

Some of the unique pieces you'll read include:

Barna Takes—personal observations and predictions from the Barna team and trusted experts and friends.

At a Glance—concise, easily digestible blurbs and quotes to introduce you to the themes covered in each section.

America by the #s—quick snapshots of national trends.

Generations—special pages set aside to explore how generational perspectives and differences are revealed by research.

Broken down in this way, we hope that *Barna Trends* will inform and enrich you. Taken as a whole, we believe it paints a vivid picture of where we are—and where we are going.

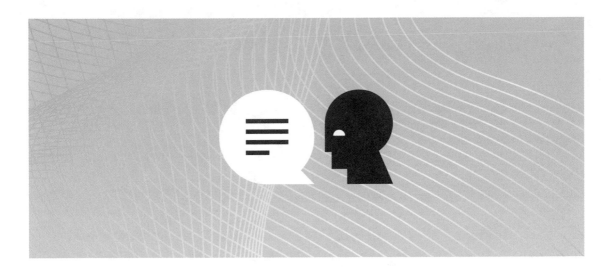

Presenter's Packs & Resources

Throughout the pages of *Barna Trends*, you will see the icon above. This mark indicates that the content you are reading is related to one of Barna's presenter's packs. **Presenter's Packs** are digital downloads of professionally designed PowerPoint slides—including many of the graphics in this book—to help you grasp and share data with your colleagues, congregation, or community. (You can find more information about how to download these resources on page 221.)

However, before you present these findings to others—in fact, before you even begin the first section—we want to make sure you're equipped to understand the language of Barna research. We've bookended *Barna Trends* with a number of resources to aid your reading and learning experience.

We get a lot of questions like, *Who are notional Christians? What does it mean to be "Bible-minded"? So, when were Millennials born?* Which is why, right here at the beginning, we have provided a handful of key terms and definitions that are foundational to our reporting. Just turn to the next page (page 10) to look through this introductory **Glossary**.

At the end of the book, there is a breakdown of the **Methodology** used for the surveys and studies that make up *Barna Trends* (page 230). This will give you a bit more context for the data, including the types of audiences surveyed, how many people have been surveyed, and when surveys took place. You'll also catch brief summaries of this kind of research information throughout the book; for example, you may see a note alongside a chart, infographic, or feature that looks something like this: *n=1,000 | December 2016*. In this particular case, it means the corresponding data is from the survey responses of 1,000 individuals in December of 2016. These notes will share important details about the timing, scope, and focus of each study. Unless otherwise stated, all percentages in *Barna Trends* refer to nationally representative samples of U.S. adults.

The concluding pages of *Barna Trends* also include an **Index** (page 233). We realize there is a lot of information to read and retain. Our goal is that it would be engaging *and* efficient, not confusing or overwhelming. Sometimes you may just want to learn more about a subject of immediate interest to you, or you might need to quickly refresh your memory on a particular statistic for a sermon or presentation. To help you better navigate the content, we've compiled a thorough list of some of the major themes and topics of *Barna Trends*.

Finally, if you're looking for additional information, definitions, or commentary, visit barna.com or follow Barna Group on social media for updates about our current and upcoming projects.

Glossary—Theolographics

Self-identified Christians (sometimes called "all Christians" or just "Christians") choose "Christian" from a list of religious affiliations.

Other faith choose a faith other than Christianity from a list of religious affiliations.

No faith choose "atheist," "agnostic," or "none" from a list of religious affiliations.

Born again Christians are self-identified Christians who have made a personal commitment to Jesus that is still important in their lives today and believe that, when they die, they will go to heaven because they have confessed their sins and accepted Jesus Christ as their Savior.

Non–born again (or notional) Christians are self-identified Christians who do not qualify as born again.

Practicing Christians are self-identified Christians who say their faith is very important in their lives and have attended a worship service within the past month.

Practicing Catholics are practicing Christians who describe themselves as Catholic.

Practicing mainline Protestants are practicing Christians who attend a church affiliated with a mainline Protestant denomination: American Baptist Churches USA, the Episcopal Church, Evangelical Lutheran Church of America, United Church of Christ, United Methodist Church, and Presbyterian Church USA.

Practicing non-mainline Protestants are practicing Christians who attend a non-mainline church: charismatic/Pentecostal churches, churches in the Southern Baptist Convention, churches in the Wesleyan-Holiness tradition, and non-denominational churches, among others.

Non–practicing Christians are self-identified Christians who do not qualify as practicing.

Unchurched adults are those who have not attended a church service, other than a special event such as a wedding or funeral, in the past six weeks.

An **orthodox view of God** is the belief that God is the all-powerful, all-knowing, perfect creator of the universe who rules the world today.

Evangelicals meet nine criteria, which include having made a personal commitment to Jesus Christ that is still important in their life today and believing that, when they die, they will go to heaven because they have confessed their sins and accepted Jesus Christ as their Savior. The seven other conditions include saying their faith is very important in their lives; believing they have a personal responsibility to share their religious beliefs about Christ with non-Christians; believing that Satan exists; believing that Jesus Christ lived a sinless life on earth; asserting that the Bible is accurate in all that it teaches; believing that eternal salvation is possible only through grace, not works; and describing God as the all-knowing, all-powerful, perfect deity who created the universe and still rules it today. Being classified as an evangelical is not dependent on church attendance or denominational affiliation, and respondents are not asked to describe themselves as "evangelical."

Bible readers read the Bible at least three to four times a year outside of a worship service, Mass, or church event.

Bible-minded people believe the Bible is accurate in all the principles it teaches and have read the Scriptures within the past week.

Bible-engagement definitions are based on data collected for American Bible Society's annual "State of the Bible" study. Barna created a four-part typology based on people's view of and level of engagement with the Scriptures: Bible engaged, Bible friendly, Bible neutral, and Bible skeptic.

Bible engaged means that people have a "high" view of the Scriptures and read the Bible four or more times per week. They view the Bible as a) the actual or b) the inspired Word of God with no errors, or as c) the inspired Word of God with some errors. They must also read, use, or listen to the Bible four times a week or more to be considered Bible engaged.

Bible friendly people also have a "high" view of the Scriptures but read them less frequently. They are similar to the Bible engaged in their definitions of the Bible, but read it fewer than four times in a week.

Bible-neutral people have a lower, but not negative, view of the Bible. This person chooses neither of the top two definitions of the Bible (i.e., the "highest" views) nor the most skeptical statement. They tend to pick "middle options" and rarely or never read the Bible.

Bible skeptics believe the Bible is just another book of teachings written by men. The Bible skeptic selects the statement in the survey that reflects the "lowest" view of the Bible and rarely or never reads the Bible.

Glossary—Demographics

Generations
Teens were ages 13 to 17 when the research was performed.
Millennials were born between 1984 and 2002 (adults 18 and older only).
Gen-Xers were born between 1965 and 1983.
Boomers were born between 1946 and 1964.
Elders were born prior to 1946.

Ethnicity is based on respondents' self-descriptions of their ethnicity. Those who describe themselves as Hispanic plus another ethnicity are coded as Hispanic only. To ensure adequate sample sizes, Barna usually segments the population only by the three largest ethnic groups:
White/Caucasian
Black/African American
Hispanic/Latino

Region
Northeast are residents of CT, DE, MA, MD, ME, NH, NJ, NY, PA, RI, VA, VT, WV, and Washington, DC.
Midwest are residents of IA, IL, IN, KS, KY, MI, MN, MO, ND, NE, OH, SD, and WI.
South are residents of AL, AR, FL, GA, LA, MS, NC, OK, SC, TN, and TX.
West are residents of AK, AZ, CA, CO, HI, ID, MT, NM, NV, OR, UT, WA, and WY.

Political Affiliation and Ideology
Democrats are registered as a Democrat at their current address.
Independents are registered as non-partisan at their current address.
Republicans are registered as a Republican at their current address.
Conservatives identify as "mostly conservative" when it comes to political issues.
Liberals identify as "mostly liberal" when it comes to political issues.

Trending in ...
Culture

Let's start with the big picture: a frank, factual overview of how people learn about, perceive, and interact with the world around them.

This first section covers public topics that frequently provoke conversation— "hot-button," "controversial," whatever adjective you prefer—which is why it's so vital to have an informed grasp of them. In these opening pages, Barna presents timely, innovative studies of some of today's most important cultural movements, as well as the internal mindsets and motivations that guide them.

In CULTURE, Barna looks at trends such as:
- the tension and polarization of American politics
- how mobile technology and social media have already changed *everything*
- perceptions of the Black Lives Matter message
- America's new moral code: self-fulfillment
- what people really think of immigration policies

 Media

 Politics

 Perspectives

 Generational Culture

Featuring:

Claire Díaz-Ortiz, Cory Maxwell-Coghlan, Roxanne Stone, Andy Crouch

At a Glance: Culture

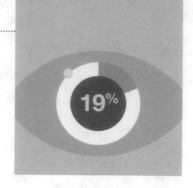

The Truth About How People See Global Warming

Though some groups still contest the science, most Americans in 2016 believe that climate change is real—and that humans bear responsibility for it.

When asked, "Do you believe humans have caused climate change and/or global warming?" 42 percent say "absolutely" and 29 percent say "possibly." One in five (21%) say it either "probably" or "definitely" does not fall on humanity's shoulders.

The more time you spend in school, the more likely you are to agree. Though a majority from all education levels affirm that climate change and/or global warming is a product of human activity, those with some college (41%) or a college degree (50%) are more certain, saying it's absolutely so.

Among faith segments, 43 percent of practicing Christians and more than half (52%) of those with no faith absolutely believe humans have played a role in climate change.

Some faith groups, however, are very unlikely to agree with this statement; 42 percent of evangelicals and 44 percent of practicing mainline believers say no, humans have "definitely not" caused global warming—the highest percentages to give this answer among all segments of this survey.   *n=1,097 | April 7-14, 2016*

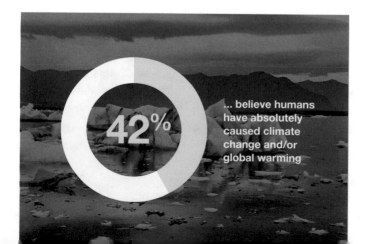

42% ... believe humans have absolutely caused climate change and/or global warming

An Eye or a Cheek?

Nineteen percent of American adults believe "an eye for an eye" should be the primary philosophy of punishment in our society, compared to 12 percent of practicing Christians. Jesus' own expression, "turn the other cheek," is a less popular philosophy of punishment, preferred by 5 percent of all adults and 7 percent of practicing Christians.

n=1,404 | June 25-July 1, 2013

Adopting Across Ethnicities

Should people adopt a child of a different race or ethnicity than their own? Most (61%) think it's fine. Thirty-two percent agree that it's OK but add that the decision to adopt should come with lifestyle changes. Just 6 percent think it's not a good idea for families to bring in a child of a different race or ethnicity.

America by the #s: Should the U.S. Welcome Refugees?

A slight majority of Americans feel that the nation should welcome refugees in times of crisis. Fifty-one percent of all adults either strongly or somewhat agree. Twenty-two percent somewhat disagree and 19 percent strongly disagree that the U.S. should take this approach. Seven percent say they are not sure.

Nonwhite Americans are more likely than white respondents to support welcoming refugees. Hispanic adults are the most likely to strongly agree (32%), though for both Hispanic and Asian respondents, a total of 65 percent either strongly or somewhat agreed.

n=1,097 | April 7-14, 2016

Too Much Information

Although few of us might choose to go back to an age without Google, we often feel overwhelmed by what the online world makes available to us. More than seven out of 10 adults (71%) admit to being overwhelmed by the amount of information they need to stay up to date—and they do not even entirely trust what information they *do* get online. American adults (55%) admit to only believing about half of what they read online. More than half of Americans (54%) actually think they have too much information (even 56% of Millennials feel this way), and one in six (59%) say all that information can get in the way of making a decision.

> People have always struggled with violence in many different cultures all around the world. But it seems particularly difficult right now, in this time, in this place, mainly because we have a culture that seems to be *nurturing* violence. . . . This system of greed uses people, dehumanizes people in such a way that people are violated. They are not seen as humans, but rather a means to profit. . . . We need to be aware, to be able to open our eyes to the faces of people who are affected—those who have been driven out into the streets, those who are living with unfair working conditions, those who make our lives easier because of the violence that they face."
> —*Carol Howard Merritt, pastor, coauthor of the Barna FRAME* Fighting for Peace

" Our devices are wireless, but as a people we're more tethered than ever. More than half of Millennials say they check their phones first thing in the morning and right before bed. Forty-five percent of Americans say they struggle to go one day without internet access. Thirty percent of Millennials say they love their cell phone. A quarter of Americans check their phone at least once an hour. Half of Millennials say that their gadgets actually get in the way of their relationships. . . .

"There are a lot of aspects to a hyperlinked life, and there are three that we found were most interesting. First, being always on and plugged into our devices. Second, our growing dependency on the data that's provided through these devices. Finally, there's this 'appification' of life—basically, what we mean is there's now an app for anything. We've appified friendship, we've appified prayer, we've appified health. And when that happens, it changes the way we think about life."

—*Jun Young, principal at Zum Communications, coauthor of the Barna FRAME* The Hyperlinked Life

A Nuclear Question

When it comes to the government taking violent action, there's a big difference between what people personally believe and what they think Jesus would believe—even among Christians.

Nearly one-quarter of adults (23%) agree with the statement "Nuclear weapons are absolutely necessary to keep our enemies from attacking us." Roughly the same percentage of practicing Christians (24%) also affirm this idea. However, reframe the question to ask if Jesus would say that nuclear weapons are a necessary evil, and just 2 percent agree.

Thirty-eight percent of all adults, including 40 percent of practicing Christians, think "the government should have the option to execute the worst criminals." Would Jesus agree? Only 5 percent say yes.

One in four among adults (26%) and practicing Christians (25%) also feel that they "have a patriotic duty to support the wars our country fights." They aren't so sure Jesus would; 7 percent say he would feel this responsibility.

Waiting on Online Dating

Online dating seems to be gaining popularity, but recent Barna research shows that active online daters are still a minority across all generations. Five percent of all adults use online dating methods regularly, 14 percent have tried it once or twice, and 9 percent previously online dated but don't anymore. The majority of adults (56%) say they would never online date, though 16 percent are open to giving it a shot.

Match.com is the most popular online dating site, used by 34 percent of adults. Other favorites include OK Cupid (20%) and eHarmony (19%). For all the buzz about platforms like Tinder, just 11 percent use the app. However, Millennials are the most likely to be swiping left and right (30%); only OK Cupid is used more than Tinder among Millennials (35%).

Where Do We Go from Here?

Seventy-two percent of registered voters indicate they believe the United States is headed in the wrong direction. This sentiment is fairly pervasive—with the exception of liberals. When it comes to political ideology, nine out of 10 conservatives (87%), and seven out of 10 moderates (69%) agree America is headed in the wrong direction. However, less than half of all liberals (45%) agree with the rest—the majority of liberals believe the nation is actually headed in the right direction (55%).

A plurality of voters (45%) state they would prefer a federal government that is "less active and far-reaching than we currently have." About one-third of the voters (34%) opt for keeping things the way they are now. The remaining one-fifth (21%) want the federal government

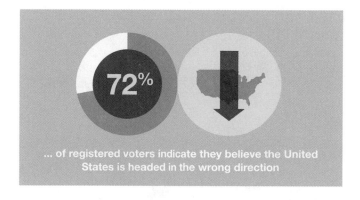

72%

... of registered voters indicate they believe the United States is headed in the wrong direction

to become "more active and far-reaching." Not surprisingly, seven out of ten conservatives (70%) support a smaller, less active government. Unexpectedly, a plurality of moderates (44%) join in that chorus. It's just as surprising that liberals are divided equally between sticking with the government we have today (40%) and expanding to a more active and far-reaching form (39%).

Examining the faith segments, evangelicals are the only niche for which a majority express a governance preference: 64 percent desire a less active, less far-reaching federal system. A plurality of non-evangelical born agains (47%), notionals (44%), and skeptics (41%) echo that perspective. People aligned with non-Christian faiths are the only segment for which a plurality (45%) wants to stick with what we have now.

n=1,097 | April 7-14, 2016

America by the #s: Ideas of Religious Freedom

Nine out of 10 adults agree that "True religious freedom means all citizens must have freedom of conscience" (90% in 2012 and 84% in 2015), according to data from Barna and Alliance Defending Freedom. Although almost three-quarters of Americans (72%) believe that "no one set of values should dominate the country," the deep divisions between Christian groups and others are stark. For example, only a quarter of evangelicals (25%) agree that no one set of values should dominate the country, but that figure is almost nine in 10 among those who claim no faith (89%).

When asked whether "traditional Judeo-Christian values should be given preference in the U.S.," a quarter of the general population agrees, but the difference between them and practicing Christians is significant. For example, one in five Millennials (21%) agree with prioritizing Judeo-Christian values, but this number more than doubles among practicing Christian Millennials (55% of whom agree with the statement). This trend continues with Gen-Xers (26% among the general population compared to 51% of Gen-X practicing Christians) and Boomers (29% compared to 46%).

n=1,200 | August 7–September 6, 2015

9 out of 10 adults agree: "True religious freedom means all citizens must have freedom of conscience"

Violent Concerns

When asked what their top concerns are when it comes to violence, 36 percent of American adults say bullying at school. More than a third are also worried about gangs (34%) or domestic violence (33%). Other concerns include foreign wars (32%), violence in entertainment (19%), police brutality (10%), and the death penalty (5%).

Digital Detox

Do you take regular breaks from social media? A striking majority of adults (60%) say they never unplug. One in five (21%) might for a while, 17 percent are on a permanent break, 11 percent pause for parts of the day, and 5 percent disconnect for one day a week.

Alternatives to Abortion

Among pro-life and pro-choice groups, the debate extends beyond which label you identify with. People also have different perspectives about which policies to promote. A recent Barna survey asked Americans to name the top way to prevent abortions. Here's what they had to say:

What would you say is the best solution to reduce abortions?

Promote contraceptive use - 33%
Promote family planning - 16%
Promote abstinence education - 12%
I do not believe it is necessary to work to reduce abortions - 11%
Offer adoption services - 9%
Make them illegal - 8%
Not sure - 8%
Other - 4%

Voters are perhaps as upset with themselves as they are with the system and its inhabitants. They know something substantial must be done, but either they don't know what that prescription is or they don't have the courage to pursue it. The prevailing sentiment is that we are beyond the point of tinkering. . . . Many resonate with the sense that America has lost its mojo. And they realize restoring it at this point will be much harder than simply maintaining it might have been."
—*George Barna, founder of Barna Group, special analyst for the 2016 election polling*

Most Are Frustrated by Federal Government

There appears to be a deep well of negative emotion across the nation. A large majority of voters (82%) admit to being "frustrated" with the federal government. That emotional unrest spans all segments of the population. It largely transcends ideology, characterizing the views of 87 percent of conservatives, 82 percent of moderates, and even three-quarters of liberals (74%). Frustration is common across all of the five faith segments Barna tracks, ranging from a high of 87 percent among evangelicals to a low of 76 percent among voters aligned with a non-Christian faith.

Perhaps the most notable outgrowth of these perceptions and emotions is that a majority of voters (56%) describe themselves as feeling "angry" toward the federal government. This anger is widespread, ranging from 63 percent among evangelicals and 61 percent among skeptics to 57 percent among notionals, 50 percent among non-evangelical born again Christians, and 43 percent of the people aligned with other faiths.

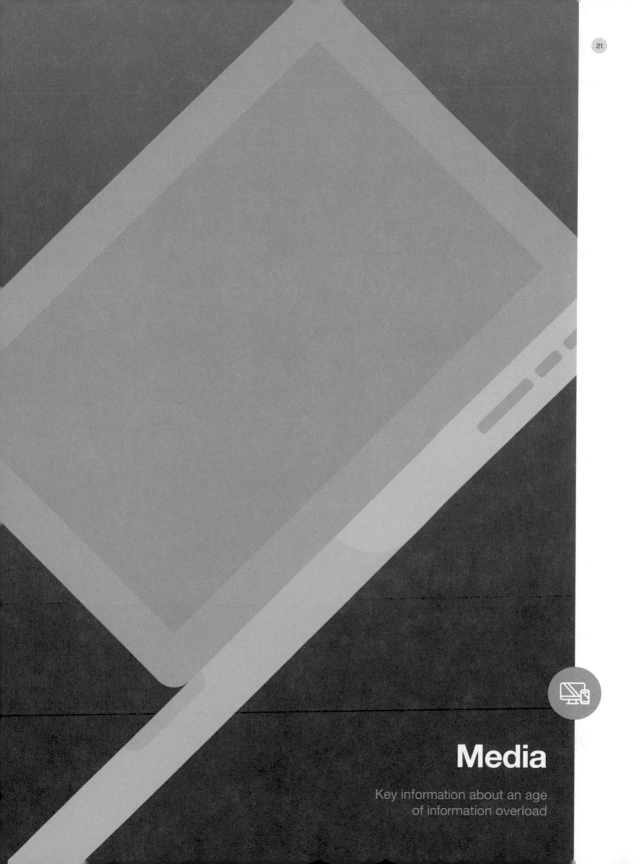

Media

Key information about an age
of information overload

"Where Did You Learn That?"

In just a single day on the internet, two million blog posts are written, 860,000 hours of YouTube videos are uploaded, and five billion pieces of content are shared on Facebook. It's difficult to ignore the increasing amount of content—and platforms—vying for our attention. So where exactly do Americans go to learn something new or to get new information in the digital age?

By far the most common media source for new information is the web. Six out of 10 (61%) American adults use an internet website daily or more often (this includes "at least daily," "a few times each day," and "ongoing throughout the day") to learn something new. Around half go to their mobile or smartphone (52%), or head to social media sites like Facebook or Twitter (49%). So the web—internet sites, social media, and smartphones—appears to be the most common destination for acquiring new information.

Even in a cyber age, television still remains hugely popular as a source of knowledge. Half of all American adults watch cable TV (50%) or network TV (49%) daily or more. Though more adults use the web throughout the day (27%) compared to network or cable TV (18%), the overall numbers of daily use are comparable.

Radio and newspapers do not enjoy the popularity of TV or the web, but they remain fairly common with almost four in 10 (37%) adults listening to the radio, and almost three in 10 (28%) reading the newspaper daily or more. The least common daily media sources for new information are books (17%), magazines (12%), and ebooks (9%). Though less common as a daily source, books and magazines have the highest proportion of users when it comes to monthly use (19% for both). Although people aren't reading books or magazines daily, they still constitute a portion of their monthly routine.

How often do you personally use each of the various media to learn something new or to get new information?

(% who chose "at least daily," "a few times each day," and "ongoing throughout the day")

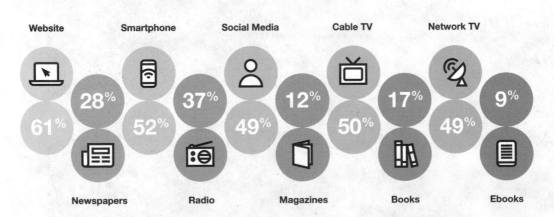

Website 61%   Newspapers 28%
Smartphone 52%   Radio 37%
Social Media 49%   Magazines 12%
Cable TV 50%   Books 17%
Network TV 49%   Ebooks 9%

n=1,011 | January 28–February 4, 2016

Digital Devices Make Porn Prolific (and Personal)

Compared to 150 years ago, porn's 21st-century iteration is more complex. For one thing, ease of access has never been greater—a fact mostly attributable to the explosive growth and widespread dissemination of new communication technologies during the past two decades.

A Barna study in partnership with Josh McDowell Ministry shows that the proliferation of high-speed internet and internet-enabled devices has fundamentally altered the ways people view and interact with pornography. These technological realities have "indiscriminately allowed people of all ages to encounter

and consume sexually explicit content," Sean McDowell says. The web has by far eclipsed all other avenues for accessing pornography. Among those who report having viewed porn, seven out of 10 adults (71%) and 85 percent of teens and young adults have done so using online videos. Six in 10 adults (59%) and two-thirds of teens and young adults (65%) view porn mostly online. Magazines and video rentals are passé.

Smartphones offer new and dynamic means of accessing and distributing pornography. Apps and text are an increasingly popular option, especially among teens and young adults. While just 12 percent of adults 25 and older view porn mostly on their phone, teens and young adults are three times more likely to do so (38%).

The proliferation of digital tools has blurred the lines between porn producers, distributors, and consumers. The affordability of video equipment and the abundance of user-friendly online platforms and services have allowed consumers to become producers, creating and distributing their own pornography.

The historically passive consumer has evolved into today's active producer—a result not only of changing technology, but also of shifting social norms of self-expression. Blogging, online dating, text messaging, and social media have become vehicles of "oversharing" in the internet age, a phenomenon that muddles the boundary between public and private life and has had a profound impact on the shape of pornography today.

The Ways People View Porn, by Age

- teens 13-17
- young adults 18-24
- older Millennials
- Gen-Xers
- Boomers

% among U.S. teens, young adults, and adults 25+ who actively seek out porn

online videos
85% 77%
85% 56%
79%

online pictures
57% 34%
52% 42%
40%

images in an app
11% 9%
15% 7%
9%

graphic novels
6% 8%
10% 7%
10%

magazines
2% 6%
9% 10%
0%

images sent via text
7% 2%
17% 3%
3%

on-demand videos
3% 8%
8% 11%
10%

rented/purchased DVDs
1% 16%
7% 13%
13%

n=2,001 (1,188 age 25+, 813 age 13–24) | July–August 2015 | © Josh McDowell Ministry

How Women Use Social Media

Most women have a Facebook account and spend more time on that site than any other (excluding Tumblr)

Facebook
Instagram
Pinterest
Twitter
Snapchat
Tumblr

Network	Have account	Time per visit
Facebook	81%	:30+
Instagram	26%	>:05
Pinterest	37%	:10-:19
Twitter	37%	>:05
Snapchat	10%	>:05
Tumblr	10%	:30+
Google+	23%	>:05

n=455 women | April 29-May 1, 2015 | Proverbs 31 Ministries

Women are most likely to check their social media either first thing in the morning or right before going to bed

First thing in the morning

50%

Right before going to bed

46%

The strongest motivations for social media use include curiosity, habit, and pleasure

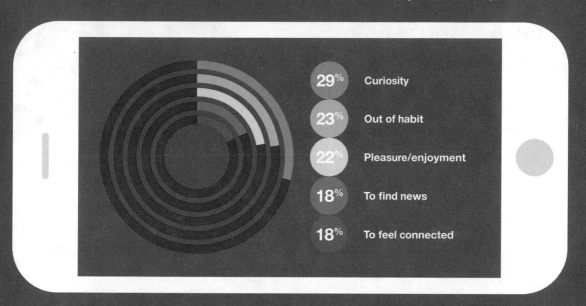

29% Curiosity

23% Out of habit

22% Pleasure/enjoyment

18% To find news

18% To feel connected

After using social media, most women report positive feelings

81% Connected to friends

58% Encouraged

49% Bored

43% Rejuvenated or energized

35% Like I want to change something about my life

24% Like I'm missing out on something (or fear of missing out)

21% Lonely

17% Jealous of other people's lives

Overall, the benefits of connection through social media outweigh the negative impacts of time wasting and distraction

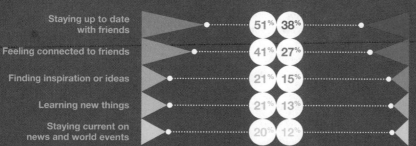

Staying up to date with friends	**51%** **38%**	Wasting time
Feeling connected to friends	**41%** **27%**	Getting distracted from work or things I need to do
Finding inspiration or ideas	**21%** **15%**	Judging other people
Learning new things	**21%** **13%**	Not being "present" to those physically around me
Staying current on news and world events	**20%** **12%**	Comparing myself to other people

A Q&A about Digital Overwhelm

with Claire Díaz-Ortiz

Claire Díaz-Ortiz is an author, speaker, and technology innovator who has been named one of the 100 Most Creative People in Business by Fast Company. *She was an early employee at Twitter, where she was hired to lead corporate social innovation. Her books include* Twitter for Good *and the Barna FRAME* Greater Expectations.

Barna research increasingly shows that people rarely "turn off." What kind of effect do you see this having on individuals and the public as a whole?

Every day, we wake up to our iPhones, and we go to sleep to our iPhones, and in the middle we sometimes don't even remember to live. We spend hours of our week simply online, and not necessarily being productive or making meaningful connections or relationships with those around us. We are in a state of digital overwhelm, and we need to figure out how to get out of that.

One of the problems about living our lives online is that we are essentially under constant attack. If we think of what our ancestors would do—when they would wake up in the morning, go hunt something, drag it, and bring it home—they were experiencing adrenaline rushes as a result of their fight or flight response. The problem is, today, we feel that when we check our email. We check our email, thinking that there's that one-in-a-million chance that something really amazing is inside. Maybe you won the lottery, or you got a job promotion. Something great could be there, so we consistently check email, Facebook, or Twitter in efforts to find that next high, essentially. We're seeking the digital high, and as a result we're burnt out and stressed out.

What are some practical ways that people can resist the pull of the digital high?

I believe that one of the best ways that we can set ourselves up for success in a life of potential digital overwhelm is to create a positive, powerful morning routine. Of course, the idea behind a morning routine is to do the most important thing first, as soon as you wake up, so that you can then tackle your day.

There are a few key tips that I always recommend when I'm talking to people about how to make schedules that really work for them.

The first thing that you should really consider doing is, when you wake up and when you go through your morning routine, take out a piece of paper and write out everything that's really on your mind. This isn't everything that you need to do today, but it's everything that's on your mind and that's weighing on you. Getting those things out on paper is a great first step.

Another key scheduling tip is to make sure that you have a plan. Once you see all those things that you need to potentially be doing, pick a few of those things that you should be doing today and put them into blocks of time when you should be doing them.

Another key tip is to work in blocks. Spend two hours writing if you're a writer, spend two hours doing podcasts if you're podcasting—and don't do 15 minutes of each and keep switching between. Work in blocks as much as possible.

Finally, another key tip is to make sure that a percentage of your work takes place off-line. Very few people need to be online for everything they do in a day so you want to make sure that you can be off-line as much as possible to free yourself from distractions and to get done what you need to get done.

Obviously, the internet and social media also bring us a lot of good things. What do you feel are the unique benefits of turning off?

We all want better lives, we want to feel closer to God, we want to be in more relationship with our family and friends, and we want to be more inspired on a daily basis, in our work and in our personal lives.

But we're going about it all wrong. We're trying to find happiness, we're trying to find success, and we're trying to find peace online, when really that peace can be found off-line, in spending some time in our real lives.

One of the problems with our online lives is that we end up working all the time, and ultimately I believe that the best creation happens off-line. After years of working in Silicon Valley, I find that the period starting Friday evening and ending about Saturday at lunch is dead time. I don't get the 200 emails I typically get in a day, and it's really a good time to potentially take off.

Think about your own life and think about what that time frame might be. See if you can grab it for yourself and take it as a digital Sabbath of sorts, so that you're not online and instead you're rejuvenating your soul.

The Complications of Being Connected

Cory Maxwell-Coghlan,
Barna Group,
Senior Writer &
Managing Editor, Web

The explosive growth of digital technology and mobile devices has fundamentally altered the way we communicate and engage with each other. Social media sites mediate our online presence and set new rules for digital interactions. But the question remains: Has social media made our lives better or worse?

The *raison d'être* of social media is connection. This is the primary function of sites like Facebook, and the tagline confirms it: "Connect with friends and the world around you on Facebook." So it comes as no surprise that connecting with friends and family is a primary motivation and outcome of using social media. In two

different studies, Barna found that most parents (54%) feel more connected to friends and family, and eight in 10 women (81%) report feeling connected to friends through social media.

Though it appears people are experiencing social media in mostly positive ways, it also has its downsides. People can become absorbed with comparison (which can affect mood and self-esteem) or checking accounts incessantly; half of women check their social media either first thing in the morning (50%) or right before going to bed (46%). Connections established or maintained online can also be fraught with complications; you're likely well aware of how social media can create a false sense of intimacy. This is not to mention the reality of cyber-bullying and harassment made possible through these new digital means.

As social media's influence expands, so do its gray areas. Businesses are taking advantage of social media by making their presence known in digital spaces where their customers spend time. Issues of privacy remain central here, especially with the use of metadata for targeted advertising or the real dangers of exposure in the age of oversharing. Political movements and candidates are also leveraging their social media platforms in unprecedented ways.

However, throughout our research on social media and technology, the clearest concern so far relates to time-wasting and distraction. Wasting time (42%) and being more distracted (40%) are the main reasons why technology and social media have made the lives of parents more difficult, and among women, the greatest negative impact of social media is wasting time (38%). This becomes a real issue of productivity in the workplace.

The potential of social media is endless, and we are—for the most part—experiencing it in positive ways. Still, we must be proactive in the days to come by speaking to both the challenges of social media and its redemptive possibilities.

Exploring the Digital Family Dynamic

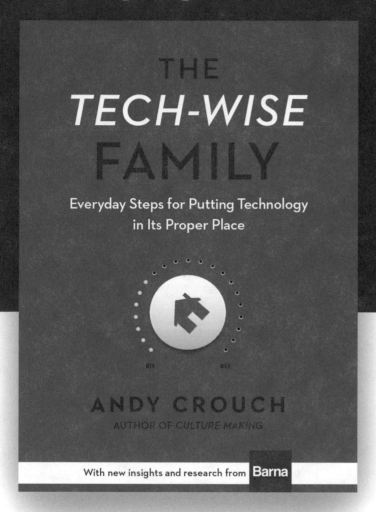

THE

TECH-WISE

FAMILY

Everyday Steps for Putting Technology
in Its Proper Place

ANDY CROUCH
AUTHOR OF *CULTURE MAKING*

With new insights and research from **Barna**

Provides a framework for tough questions like

- What are some important family values to embrace in the digital age?

- Does our use of technology move us closer to the values we've embraced?

- Are familial relationships suffering as a result of technology's distractions?

- Has "real life" taken a backseat to virtual life?

Making wise choices about technology in the context of family is more than just setting internet filters and screen time limits for children. It's about developing wisdom, character, and courage in the way we use digital media, rather than accepting technology's promises of ease, instant gratification, and the world's knowledge at our fingertips. And that's true for everyone in the family, not just the kids. Drawing on in-depth original research from Barna, Andy Crouch (executive editor of *Christianity Today* and the author of *Playing God* and *Culture Making*) shows how the choices we make about technology have consequences we may never have considered. For anyone who has felt their family relationships suffer or their time slip away amid technology's distractions, this book will provide a path forward to reclaiming "real" life in a world of digital devices.

BakerBooks
a division of Baker Publishing Group
Grand Rapids, Michigan

Purchase wherever
books and ebooks
are sold

Politics

What drives and divides the Left
and the Right in the United States

The American Voter

Presidential elections tend to focus disproportionately on polling numbers—who's ahead, who's behind, and so on. The 2016 election season was no exception—though, in many ways, it was full of the unexpected. As George Barna, founder of Barna and special analyst for 2016 election polling, said, "Nobody expected 17 candidates to seek the GOP nomination. Nobody expected Donald Trump to be taken seriously by Republican voters, much less to emerge as the man to beat. Nobody expected the last two credible Republican candidates to be those representing the Washington outsiders. Nobody expected a democratic socialist to give Hillary Clinton serious competition. Nobody expected so many evangelicals to back a Republican candidate whose lifestyle has consistently conflicted with their values. Nobody expected the televised debates to draw such record-breaking audiences. And the list goes on."

Looking beyond the race in the polls, what are the key priorities and motivations among voters and their ballot decisions? How do they change over time? And what was special about this election?

Person or Policy?

Early in April 2015, Barna asked voters how they would be evaluating candidates. At that time, there were 15 candidates running for the Republican

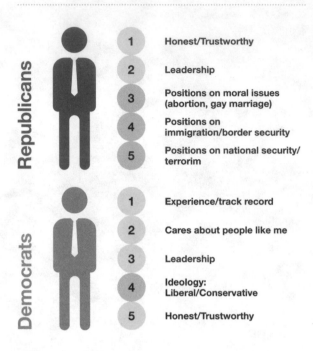

Republicans & Democrats: Top 5 Factors ● personal ● policy

Republicans

1. Honest/Trustworthy
2. Leadership
3. Positions on moral issues (abortion, gay marriage)
4. Positions on immigration/border security
5. Positions on national security/terrorim

Democrats

1. Experience/track record
2. Cares about people like me
3. Leadership
4. Ideology: Liberal/Conservative
5. Honest/Trustworthy

n=629 adult registered voters | January 28–February 4, 2016

nomination and five candidates on the Democratic side. What took precedence was a candidate's "stand on key issues," chosen by 71 percent of all voters, followed by "character" (41%). Policy factors were more on voters' radar than personal factors, such as a candidate's personality, experience, education, and character.

As the selection of presidential candidates began to narrow and become more differentiated over time, Barna surveyed again. In January 2016, there were 10 Republican candidates and three Democratic candidates left in the running. Barna asked a similar sample of voters who they would most likely support in the election and what their primary reason was for doing so. Interestingly, the top four reasons voters selected were unrelated to policy stances, and all focused primarily on candidate attributes. In aggregate, while policy positions were selected by 39 percent of voters as their most important reason, personal characteristics of the candidate were selected by 49 percent of voters (the rest cited a reason not listed).

This general pattern of prioritizing personal characteristics over policy stances holds true even within party lines. Democrat and Republican voters were both more likely to select a "personal factor" as their most important reason than a "policy factor," although Republicans did prioritize certain issues slightly more than Democrats.

The top two characteristics chosen by Democrats were "experience/track record" and "cares about people like me," while Republicans chose "honest/trustworthy" and "leadership."

This preference shift over time from "policy" to "personal" may be due in part to the fact that voters simply become more familiar with the individual profiles of each candidate as the campaign rolls on, and are thus able to weigh personal factors more accurately. This suggests that while voters may use policy distinctions in order to initially screen or assess a wide field of candidates, their final decision is based more on the personal attributes, not the policy stances, of a candidate.

Another possible reason for this shift from "policy" to "personal" is the disproportionately personality-driven nature of this particular election cycle. Few can deny the way in which Donald Trump's unique style fundamentally shifted the overall tone of the debates, conventions, and campaign messaging—on both sides. Though Trump has run his campaign on a few key policy promises (building a wall, a temporary ban on Muslims, etc.), his campaign has focused more on his personal suitability to manage the country from the Oval Office. The attacks on his political rivals held a deeply personal note, forcing them to respond in kind and further entrenching the personality-focused rhetoric that prevailed this election cycle.

Barna's survey in April 2016 also found historic low levels of favorability for the two major-party candidates: Donald Trump and Hillary Clinton. While favorability ratings do not directly correspond to people's likelihood of voting for a person, the overwhelmingly negative impressions held of both major candidates reflected the broader discontentment among the voting public, and may hint at why this election saw a disproportionate focus on character and personality. Hillary Clinton received favorable ratings from just 38 percent of the registered voters and unfavorable ratings from 60 percent. Donald

Kentucky has the highest percentage of practicing Christians registered as Democrats (47%). Kansas holds the top spot for practicing Christians registered as Republicans (46%).

n=978 | April– May, 2015; n= 920 registered voters | April 7–14, 2016

Trump fared even worse at the time; just 29 percent were favorable toward him and 69 percent unfavorable.

These shifts suggest, once again, that voter preferences among Americans are not set in stone, but rather can be affected by the candidates in a given election season.

Evangelicals' Priorities

Beyond differences across party lines, it's worth highlighting the candidate factors that evangelicals prioritize, given their important role in the election and their unique voting preferences. According to the 2016 survey, evangelicals buck the norm in multiple ways. They hold a candidate's experience and track record in much lower esteem than the average adult voter (2% versus 11%). Instead, they value a candidate's character (26% versus 6%) and positions on moral issues, such as abortion and gay marriage, more than the norm (19% versus 5%).

It seems that evangelicals are open to new, even inexperienced, candidates, so long as they feel that the candidate represents and embodies their values and ideologies, particularly when it comes to social issues.

Key Concerns of Voters

When it comes to the key policies and issues, which matter most to voters? Overall, the 2016 survey seems to indicate that the economy is top of mind for voters; moral issues take second place, followed

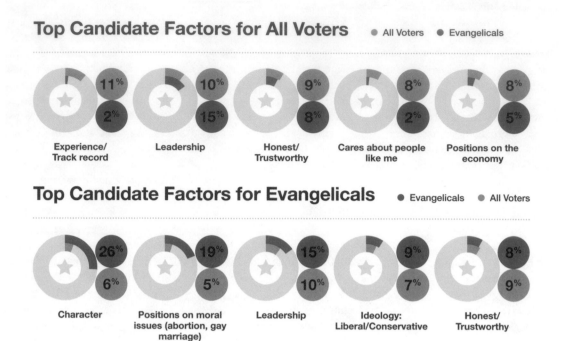

Top Candidate Factors for All Voters ● All Voters ● Evangelicals

11%	10%	9%	8%	8%
2%	15%	8%	2%	5%
Experience/ Track record	Leadership	Honest/ Trustworthy	Cares about people like me	Positions on the economy

Top Candidate Factors for Evangelicals ● Evangelicals ● All Voters

26%	19%	15%	9%	8%
6%	5%	10%	7%	9%
Character	Positions on moral issues (abortion, gay marriage)	Leadership	Ideology: Liberal/Conservative	Honest/ Trustworthy

n=629 adult registered voters | January 28–February 4, 2016

closely by immigration and national security.

Breaking it down by ethnicity, class, party affiliation, faith, age, and other groups, Barna found that Hispanics were, by far, the most concerned with the economy. Twenty percent of Hispanic voters surveyed selected a candidate's position on the economy as their most important factor in candidate selection, the highest-ranking factor in total for that group. Within the list of policy factors, independents prioritized a candidate's position on the economy, and so did Millennials and voters with children under age 18.

Evangelicals are the group that is most sensitive to a candidate's stance on moral issues (i.e., abortion and gay marriage) There were other groups that listed "moral issues" as their top policy

factor, but the percentage difference between "moral issues" and their second most important policy factor was too small (<3%) to be statistically significant.

One-fifth of evangelical voters (19%) chose a candidate's position on moral issues as the most important factor in their selection of a candidate. As a point of reference, the second most popular policy factor, the economy, was only selected by 5 percent of evangelicals. It's important to note the survey did not ask what stance the voter took on these issues, just whether it was the most important factor for them in their candidate choice.

Certain issues rise and fall in popularity over time. Candidates' positions on gun policies have received a boost in attention from Republicans (76% in 2015 compared to 84% in 2016). This bump in priority can be explained by the recent headlines about shootings.

The profile of the American voter is a heterogeneous one. It changes both laterally—across demographic and ideological lines—and over time as the election season progresses. Voters do have core interests and priorities, but they are not entirely static, as voters are responsive to what they are observing in their political and national landscape.

Patriotism in America

If you feel true to the "red, white, and blue," well, you're in good company. More than half (52%) of the general American population say "being an American" makes up a lot of their personal identity. The only factor that more adults (62%) strongly identified with was family. It's clear that patriotism is still a core value in the United States.

However, conflating personal identity with being an American is a factor on which various groups significantly diverge. Religious groups such as practicing Catholics (74%), practicing mainline (71%), practicing Christians (66%), and evangelicals (65%) are more likely to do so, while those with no faith (33%) are less likely. Both the unemployed (57%) and those whose income exceeds $100,000 (56%) also feel proudly American, while the employed (48%) and college graduates (47%) aren't as prone to identify with their American roots. Among political parties, Republicans are much more likely than average to say being an American is central to their identity (65%), while Democrats (42%), registered Independent voters (41%), and unregistered voters (27%) are less likely than average to do so.

Remarkable differences also appear between generational groups, with a steep drop of almost 50 percentage points between Elders (80%) and Millennials (34%) who feel very defined by their American citizenship. The sharpest immediate decline between one generation and the next occurs between Boomers and Gen-Xers. The generation that came of age during Watergate and the turbulent Vietnam War era still says, on the whole, that being an American makes up a lot of their identity (66%). But their children—the generation of globalization, MTV, and the Monica Lewinsky scandal—are far less inclined to claim it as a significant factor: Only 37 percent of Gen-Xers say being an American makes up a lot of their personal identity.

How much is "being an American" a part of your personal identity?

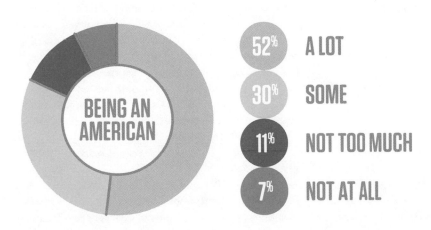

BEING AN AMERICAN

52% A LOT

30% SOME

11% NOT TOO MUCH

7% NOT AT ALL

n=1,000 | February 3–11, 2015

A Divided Nation

Cory Maxwell-Coghlan,
Barna Group,
Senior Writer &
Managing Editor, Web

Another election year has brought to light the deep ideological tensions dividing the nation. The growing gap between liberals and conservatives has come to define the American political landscape, and seems unlikely to change any time soon.

These tensions come to the fore on a number of issues. For example, Barna asked American adults whether they believe immigrants and refugees take jobs from Americans. Their answers demonstrate this stark divide: Seven out of 10 conservatives (70%) either strongly or somewhat agree with this statement compared to only one-quarter of liberals (27%). Another example is race. When asked how they feel about the Black Lives Matter movement, only 12 percent of conservatives say they support their message, compared to half of all liberals (50%). The list of issues in which this divide is evident goes on: healthcare, the environment, abortion, and same-sex marriage.

These kinds of conflicts are not new—we've been here before. The disputes over everything from the institution of slavery to the Vietnam War all led to polarization of the American public. But today's disagreements feel uniquely inflammatory, and there are a number of theories as to why: growing economic inequality, Southern conservative realignment, gerrymandering, a partisan primary process, private campaign financing, and a changing media environment, to name a few. These all play a role in creating a political climate in which polarization flourishes.

One characteristic feature of this election cycle—and a contributing factor to partisanship—has been a divisive political rhetoric that relies on anger and fear to demonize the other side. Voters look across the aisle with suspicion and hostility, seeing the "other" as the enemy. Neither side is innocent of this, but as Christians working to heal and restore a divided nation, we must not fall victim to an "us vs. them" mentality—a false good-evil dichotomy that blinds us not only to our own shortcomings, but to the truth that can be learned from our political rivals.

We must reject the tendency to scapegoat and glorify, naming one side as villain and the other as savior. Instead, we must have the humility to accept that there is no square inch of God's creation that has been unstained by sin and corruption. How would our political climate change if people were open to learn and to believe that—especially when it comes to politics—there are no easy answers?

American Christians are all fallible—liberal or conservative—but remain instruments of God's grace in this world. When we grasp this truth and enter the political sphere with humility and grace, challenging destructive and divisive narratives, we may begin to reunite a divided nation.

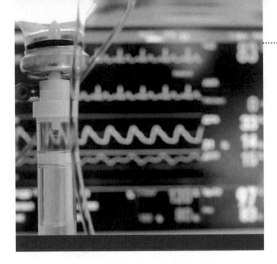

Defining Life and Death in America

What do Americans believe about life and death? When asked their opinions on the major topics of abortion, the death penalty, and euthanasia, American adults appear relatively tolerant of death. When it comes to abortion, the majority of adults believe abortion should be either legal in all cases (30%) or legal in most cases (34%). Smaller percentages believe it should either be illegal in most cases (23%) or illegal in all cases (13%). Looking at the death penalty, almost three-quarters (73%) of Americans believe it should be allowed. This group is made up of those who believe it should either be allowed only in extreme circumstances (37%) or believe it should be legal in all states (36%). Only 13 percent of adults believe it should be abolished, while an equally small percentage (14%) don't have an established view on the topic. Finally, when it comes to terminal illness, another significant majority (70%) believe each person should be allowed to end their life through euthanasia. More than two-fifths (41%) believe that "yes, absolutely" someone should be able to make that choice, and another one-third (29%) say "yes, possibly." Again, small minorities say "no, probably not" (6%) or "no, definitely not" (9%), with only 15 percent being unsure of what they believe.

n=1,097 | April 2016

The Threat of Terror

Since 9/11, the threat of terrorism has become a major preoccupation in the United States. In light of recent domestic and international events, Barna asked American adults to define terrorism. They are pretty evenly split among "any act of violence against civilians" (31%), "any illegal or threatening act (violent or not) with a political or religious agenda" (30%), and "an act of violence used to intimidate and/or effect political or religious change" (27%). This maps fairly well onto conventional definitions, though it shows a broader propensity to define any major act of violence as "terrorism." Most Americans believe they are either "not really" (52%) or "not at all likely" (20%) to be a victim of terrorism. However, almost a quarter believe it is "somewhat likely" (23%)—a sense likely spurred by recent global attacks and surrounding media coverage. When asked what they believe is the best solution to the threat of terrorism, the top responses were a mix of national security, immigration, and foreign policy solutions: "greater national security and surveillance/intelligence technologies" (23%), "better foreign policy/better relationship with countries around the world" (19%), and "stricter immigration policies and border control" (18%).

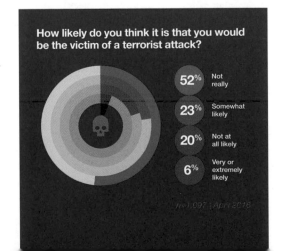

How likely do you think it is that you would be the victim of a terrorist attack?

52% Not really

23% Somewhat likely

20% Not at all likely

6% Very or extremely likely

n=1,097 | April 2016

Legal Same-Sex Marriage: How People Feel About It and What's Next 💬👤

When the U.S. Supreme Court legalized same-sex marriage in 2015, reactions were mixed. Then and now, Americans hold widely varying views on the morality, constitutionality, and impact of legal marriage for all, without regard to gender or sexual orientation.

In a nationally representative study conducted after the historic ruling, Barna identified key markers, like age and faith practice, that influence people's views on this still-contentious issue.

First, practicing faith is a stronger indicator of a person's views than his or her religious identity. Looking at the variances between practicing and non-practicing Christians, researchers can identify ways in which those who are more personally observant of their faith differ from those who are "legacy" or "cultural" believers. And when it comes to same-sex marriage, practicing Christians—those who say their faith is very important and have attended one or more church services during the past month—differ significantly from those who self-identify as Christian but do not regularly attend church or prioritize their faith. For example, practicing Christians (28%) are less likely than self-identified, non-practicing Christians (43%) to say they favor the Supreme Court ruling.

Second, practicing faith is a stronger indicator of a person's views than his or her age. In the general U.S. population, age has been and continues to be a defining fault line when it comes to same-sex marriage. Younger practicing Christians, however, have more in common with their older counterparts in the faith than they do with their peers in the general population. One-third of practicing Christians under 40 favor the ruling (35%), compared to six in 10 among all adults in their age cohort (61%)—a gap of 26 percentage points. By comparison, there is only a nine-point gap between younger practicing Christians and those 40 and older (26%).

Many Christians sense divisions within their religious tribe over this issue, and nowhere is the divide more obvious than between practicing and non-practicing Christians under 40. On nearly every question, deep divides emerge between these two groups of younger Christians. While only one-third of practicing Christians under age 40 (35%) are in favor of the Supreme Court's decision, three-quarters of non-practicing Christians under 40 support the ruling (73%).

Similarly, just one in six young non-practicing Christians say they are not in favor of the legal decision (18%), compared to more than half of practicing Christians under 40 (58%). The two groups' only agreement is in their shared belief that Christians can support legal marriage for same-sex couples while also affirming the church's traditional definition of marriage between one man and one woman (55% of practicing Christians under 40 vs. 58% of non-practicing Christians under 40).

There has been some speculation that significant numbers of young people have abandoned church involvement because of the Church's traditional teaching on sexuality, especially related to same-sex relationships. While this study doesn't confirm such a finding, it certainly shows that inactive Christians are skeptical about the church's authority on matters of sexuality and sexual orientation.

The cultural fault line between younger practicing Christians and younger lapsed and dechurched Christians is likely to widen in the coming years—particularly as younger churchgoers become a smaller slice of the overall population.

The Impact of Same-Sex Marriage

When Americans consider the impact of same-sex marriage on society, they express varying levels of concern.

More than half of all adults say they are at least somewhat concerned that religious freedom will become more restricted in the next five years (56%), a concern that is more pronounced among adults over 40 (62%) than among younger Americans (45%). Once again, younger practicing Christians (65%) are more closely aligned

Expectations of a Same-Sex Marriage Society

● all adults   ● Protestant non-mainline   ● Protestant mainline   ● Catholic   ● other faith
● no faith   ● evangelical (Barna defined)   ● practicing Christian

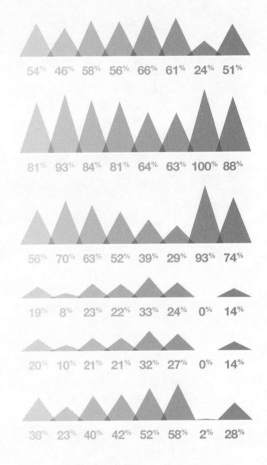

Agree that Christians can support legal marriage for same-sex couples and also affirm the church's traditional definition of marriage between one man & one woman

54% 46% 58% 56% 66% 61% 24% 51%

Agree that religious groups must remain free to teach and practice the traditional definition of marriage

81% 93% 84% 81% 64% 63% 100% 88%

Concerned that religious freedom will become more restricted in the next five years (very plus somewhat)

56% 70% 63% 52% 39% 29% 93% 74%

Believe religious institutions should be legally required to perform same-sex weddings

19% 8% 23% 22% 33% 24% 0% 14%

Believe clergy members should be legally required to perform same-sex weddings

20% 10% 21% 21% 32% 27% 0% 14%

Say that private business owners should be legally required to provide services for same-sex weddings

38% 23% 40% 42% 52% 58% 2% 28%

n=1,012 | June 27–28, 2015

with their older sisters and brothers in the faith (77%) than with younger non-practicing Christians (35%) in their concerns over religious freedom.

Considering the significant minority of Americans (20%) who say religious institutions and clergy members should be legally required to perform same-sex marriages, concerns about religious liberty protections may be warranted. The percentage is higher among younger non-practicing Christians (31%). Similarly, nearly half of Americans under 40 (44%) and half of young non-practicing Christians (49%) contend that private business owners should legally be made to provide services to same-sex weddings.

The prevalence of these views, even among young practicing Christians (33%), may represent future challenges to the ways people of faith exercise their religious commitments.

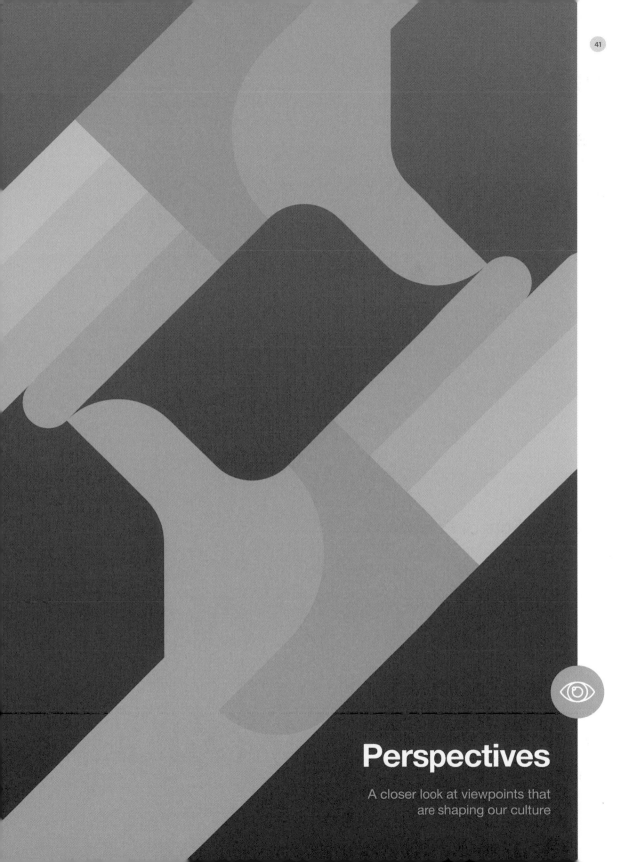

Perspectives

A closer look at viewpoints that
are shaping our culture

People of Faith Feel Sidelined in Society 💬👤

Cultural tensions are rising, whether in politics, race relations, or even everyday conversations with people who disagree with each other. But on top of the tensions felt by every American, people of faith feel added pressure. More than half of all practicing Christians report feeling misunderstood (54%) or even persecuted (52%) in society today. Millions of others use terms like "marginalized" (44%), "sidelined" (40%), and "silenced" (38%).

Among practicing Christian Millennials the negative perceptions are more pervasive: They are more likely than other groups to say they feel not only misunderstood (65%) and persecuted (60%), but also marginalized (48%), sidelined (59%), and silenced (46%). And nearly half of practicing Christian Millennials admit to being afraid to speak up (47%).

Part of the difficulty for these young adults is the negative perceptions of their non-Christian Millennial peers when it comes to Christians and Christianity (documented by Barna president David Kinnaman and Q founder Gabe Lyons in *unChristian* [Baker, 2009]). There is also growing doubt among Millennials about the Bible's authenticity and authority, revealed by Barna's research with the American Bible Society, which adds even more pressure to young believers' interactions with non-Christians.

But Christians are not the only people of faith feeling alienated from the cultural mainstream. Adherents to religions other than Christianity report similar perceptions. Nearly six in 10 feel misunderstood (57%), and millions more admit to feeling persecuted (45%), sidelined (36%), and silenced (34%)—probably for the same reason many Christians feel alienated: the growing cultural power of nonreligious people.

According to research from David Kinnaman's book *Good Faith*, more than two out of five adults believe that "people of faith" (42%) and "religion" (46%) are part of the problem facing our nation. If this opinion continues to gain popularity, more people of faith are likely to report feeling excluded from the cultural center.

The Conflicts of Faithfulness

● U.S. adults
● Evangelicals
● Practicing Christians
● Practicing Christian Millennials
● Other faiths

Thinking about your faith, how do you feel, personally, in society today?
Base: people who consider themselves a "person of faith"
% "very" + "somewhat" accurate

	Misunderstood	Persecuted	Marginalized	Sidelined	Silenced	Afraid to speak up	Afraid to look stupid
U.S. adults	41%	33%	31%	29%	28%	23%	19%
Evangelicals	65%	60%	53%	48%	50%	32%	21%
Practicing Christians	54%	52%	44%	40%	38%	31%	23%
Practicing Christian Millennials	65%	60%	48%	59%	46%	47%	38%
Other faiths	57%	45%	33%	36%	34%	22%	19%

n=1,200 | August 7–September 6, 2015 | Conducted for Good Faith (Baker Books, 2016)

Disenfranchised Youth

Roxanne Stone,
Barna Group,
Editor-in-Chief

In our research on younger generations, particularly Millennials, we continue to see a theme of disconnection. Young adults are waiting longer to get married, having children later, and switching jobs frequently (often also changing where they live). They are less trusting of government, of church, and even of colleges and universities than their older counterparts. In other words, there are very few institutions—either social or economic—binding Millennials.

Another aspect of this disconnection is their relative reluctance to claim any external factor as part of their identity. When it comes to identifying as an American, for example, there is nearly a 50-point drop between the oldest generation, Elders, and the youngest. Four out of five Elders say that being an American makes up a lot of their personal identity, but only one-third of Millennials (34%) say the same. But Millennials aren't only distancing themselves from country, they are less likely than older generations to claim any of the surveyed factors make up a lot of their personal identity. From family to faith to ethnicity, Millennials see themselves as separated. The one exception is career, which Elders are less likely to identify with, undoubtedly a result of being primarily retired from the workforce.

In a similar survey in 2013, the only factor a majority of Millennials claimed to be central to their identity was family (62%). Less than half of Millennials pointed to any other factor as a central part of who they are: career (31%), friends (37%), faith (37%), personal interests (48%). It is perhaps significant that such a high number did indicate personal interests as a defining part of their identity—again, revealing a stronger attraction toward individual pursuits than collective ones.

Younger generations historically have a tendency to want to break away from traditional cultural narratives and to resist being "boxed in" by what they perceive as limiting expectations. It will be interesting to see if Millennials, like generations before them, begin to gravitate toward their own institutions and grounding narratives as they age.

The present opportunity for those who hope to reach the Millennial generation is to ask where they are finding their sense of identity. If traditional institutions and relationships are not as defining for them, what most impacts their identity? Their friendships? Their lifestyle? Technology or entertainment? The media they consume?

While Gen-Xers and Millennials might resist being defined by anything, their identities are certainly affected and shaped by external forces. Recognizing those forces and the impact they have—for better and worse—on their identity will help young adults make intentional decisions about where and how they give their allegiance.

Black Lives Matter and Racial Tension in America

Public outrage over the deaths of Trayvon Martin, Eric Garner, Freddie Gray, Tamir Rice, Alton Sterling, Philando Castile, and others has shed light on the often unheeded reality of racial tension in the United States. The nation witnessed the pain, grief, and indignation among black Americans as protests began in cities like Ferguson and Baltimore and spread across the country, sparking the Black Lives Matter movement.

But this movement has been met with a mixed response, reflecting deep division in how Americans view the problem of race in this country. What are the shades of this divide? And what do Americans really believe about the Black Lives Matter movement?

To explore the issue in more detail, Barna asked American adults about their experience with race. Is there anger and hostility between different ethnic and racial groups? Is racism a problem of the past, or the present? Do people feel disadvantaged because of their race or ethnicity? And perhaps most important to people of faith, can the Church play a role in racial reconciliation—or is the Church part of the problem?

Racial Tension Today
Even more than 50 years after Martin Luther King, Jr.'s March on Washington, the wounds of hundreds of years of racial injustice are still unhealed. When American adults are asked whether they believe racial tension exists, the answer to that question is a resounding "yes." The vast majority of adults agree there is a lot of anger and hostility between ethnic and racial groups in America (84%). This was true—and remarkably so—across the board. No matter the age group, region, ethnicity, socio-economic status, or faith segment, the vast majority among each group believe there is tension among racial and ethnic groups in this country.

But when asked more specifically about racism, that is, "prejudice, discrimination, or antagonism directed against someone of a different race based on the belief that one's own race is superior," the results were slightly different. There were two big standouts here, the first being evangelicals, who were almost twice as likely than the general population to agree strongly that "racism is mostly a problem of the past, not the present" (13% compared to all adults at 7%, or "no faith" at 3%). A high proportion of conservative respondents (12%) also see racism as mostly a problem of the past (compared to liberals at 4%).

Looking at this question from a different angle—for those who strongly disagree that "racism is mostly a problem of the past, not the present"—Barna identifies some differences between black and white Americans. Forty-two percent of the general population strongly disagree that racism is a problem of the past, and although both black and white Americans share that sentiment, black Americans (59%) are 20 percentage points more likely than white Americans (39%) to disagree that racism is history.

Differing Opinions About the Impact of Racism
When it comes to the lived experience of people of color in this country, seven in 10 Americans agree they "are often put at a social disadvantage because of their race" (67%). However, once again, evangelicals and Republicans are less likely than the general population to believe this is true. Evangelicals are 11 percentage points less likely than the adult average to believe people of color are at a social disadvantage (56% compared to 67%).

Evangelicals are more than twice as likely as the general population to "strongly disagree" that people of color are socially disadvantaged because of race (28% compared to 12%). This is also the case for Republicans, who are 10 percentage points less likely than the adult average (57% compared to 67%) and 21 percentage points less likely than Democrats (57% compared to 78%) to believe people of color are at a social disadvantage, and more than twice as likely as Democrats to "strongly disagree" that people of color are socially disadvantaged because of race (17% compared to 8%).

Racial Tension Today

n=1,026 | February 20–24, 2014;
n=1,000 | August 24–26, 2015

"There is a lot of anger and hostility between the different ethnic and racial groups in America today."

(% who strongly or somewhat agreed)

84%   87%   82%

All Adults   White   Black

This question also splits black Americans and white Americans. Eighty-four percent of black Americans agree that people of color are often put at a social disadvantage because of their race, while only 62 percent of white Americans agree—lower than the national average, though still higher than either evangelicals or Republicans.

These groups are similarly opposed when it comes to how they feel about "reverse racism." Seven in 10 white people strongly and somewhat agree that prejudicial treatment of them is a problem in our society today (71%). But, the black population isn't as convinced—less than half agree that prejudicial treatment of white people is a problem (46%). There is an equally deep divide between Republicans and Democrats, the former being one third more likely than the latter to believe reverse racism is a problem (77% of Republicans compared to 53% of Democrats). This makes sense in light of the fact that white people make up 85 percent of the Republican Party, while making up only half in the Democratic Party (54%).

Black Lives Matter

Following the death of Trayvon Martin and the acquittal of George Zimmerman, the Black Lives Matter movement emerged with the use of the social media hashtag #BlackLivesMatter. The cause continued to gain notoriety online, particularly following street demonstrations across the country in response to the death of Michael Brown.

Yet not all Americans embrace its message.

Millennials (45%) are most likely to support Black Lives Matter, but this support decreases with age (24% among Gen-Xers, 20% among Boomers, and 15% among Elders). Again, the outliers here are evangelicals and Republicans (especially compared to Democrats), both of whom are significantly less likely than the general population to support the movement (13% of evangelicals and 7% of Republicans compared to 27% of all adults).

The answer that consistently receives the largest response among all groups when asked how they feel about the Black Lives Matter movement is "I believe all lives matter." This is the response of about half the general population (52%), and the most common response across the board. This reflects a disconnect between the movement's broader goals and the message as interpreted by the general population.

The phrase emerged in direct response to the Black Lives Matter movement, but as President Obama observed in a press conference last year, "saying 'black lives matter' is not about reducing the importance of other groups, or suggesting nobody else's lives matter, but that there is a specific problem happening in the African-American community that's not happening in other communities. And that is a legitimate issue that we've got to address."

Despite this, the majority of American adults respond using the reactive phrase "all lives matter." Yet again, the standouts here are evangelicals, Republicans, and, this time, born again Christians. Evangelicals were by far the group most likely to say "I believe all lives matter" (76%), followed by Republicans (66%), and those who say they are born again (61%). As in previous responses, there are stark differences between Republicans (who were among the highest at 66%) and Democrats (who were among the lowest at 41%).

Race and Faith

Martin Luther King, Jr. once said, "It is appalling that the most segregated hour of Christian America is eleven o'clock on Sunday morning." He, like many others, believed the Christian Church could lead the charge when it came to racial reconciliation, but that it still had a long way to go. When asked whether Christian churches are part of the problem when it comes to racism, over six in 10 adults somewhat or strongly disagreed (62%). This is good news, although twice as many black people than white people strongly agreed it was a problem (17% black compared to 9% white).

Despite these differences, three-quarters of Americans agree "Christian churches play an important role in racial reconciliation" (73%). This is extraordinarily hopeful news for the Christian Church at large. When broken down by generation, the older you are, the more hopeful you are likely to be about the Christian Church's role in reconciliation. There is a gradual increase with age beginning with Millennials at 66 percent, Gen-Xers at 69 percent, Boomers at 79 percent, and Elders at 84 percent. Not surprisingly, evangelicals are the most

Social Disadvantages for People of Color

"People of color are often put at a social disadvantage because of their race." (% who strongly and somewhat agreed)

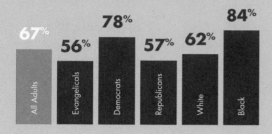

- All Adults: 67%
- Evangelicals: 56%
- Democrats: 78%
- Republicans: 57%
- White: 62%
- Black: 84%

Do you support the message of the "Black Lives Matter" movement?

(% who support their message)

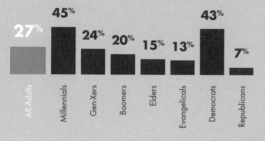

- All Adults: 27%
- Millennials: 45%
- Gen-Xers: 24%
- Boomers: 20%
- Elders: 15%
- Evangelicals: 13%
- Democrats: 43%
- Republicans: 7%

n=1,026 | February 20–24, 2014; n=1,000 | August 24–26, 2015

Can personal spiritual lives have an impact on broader society? Black Christians are pretty likely to say yes (46%), much more so than white Christians (27%).

n=1,026 | February 20–24, 2014; n=1,000 | August 24–26, 2015

hopeful with a staggering 94 percent who believe Christian churches play an important role in racial reconciliation in America.

Those who do not identify with any faith tradition (53%) are less likely to believe churches play any role in racial reconciliation; still, more than half of this group actually agrees the Church is a vital part of reconciliation, indicating a significant amount of hope for the Church, even among those outside it.

The Dilemma of the Church

"This research confirms the fear that the Church (or the people in it) may be part of the problem in the hard work of racial reconciliation," Brooke Hempell, vice president of research for Barna, says.

"If you're a white evangelical Republican, you are less likely to think race is a problem, but more likely to think you are a victim of reverse racism. You are also less convinced that people of color are socially disadvantaged.

Yet, these same groups believe the Church plays an important role in reconciliation. This dilemma demonstrates that those supposedly most equipped for reconciliation do not see the need for it.

"More than any other segment of the population, white evangelical Christians demonstrate a blindness to the struggle of their African American brothers and sisters," Hempell adds. "This is a dangerous reality for the modern church. Jesus and his disciples actively sought to affirm and restore the marginalized and obliterate divisions between groups of people. Yet, our churches and ministries are still some of the most ethnically segregated institutions in the country.

"By failing to recognize the disadvantages that people of color face and the inherent privileges that come from growing up in a 'majority culture,' white Christians perpetuate the divisions, inequalities, and injustices that prevent African American communities from thriving. Research has shown that being cognizant of our biases leads to change in biased behavior. If white evangelical Christians genuinely care for the well-being of their African American brothers and sisters, they must first be honest about their own biases.

"History, and Jesus' example, have shown that reconciliation comes from stepping out of our place of comfort and actively pursuing healing for those in need. We must do the same if we really believe *all* lives matter."

Immigration: The Ideal vs. the Reality

n=1,097 | April 7–14, 2016

3 out of 4 adults

 believe people from different cultures enrich America

Yet a plurality favor stricter immigration policies

In favor of stricter immigration policies  **VS**  Not in favor of stricter immigration policies

Agree that immigrants and/or refugees take jobs away from Americans **51%** VS **43%** Disagree that immigrants and/or refugees take jobs away from Americans

Disagree that amnesty and/or citizenship should be granted to illegal immigrants under 18 **52%** VS **39%** Agree that amnesty and/or citizenship should be granted to illegal immigrants under 18

Agree that we allow too many immigrants into the country **55%** VS **38%** Disagree that we allow too many immigrants into the country

Disagree that America should welcome refugees in a crisis **41%** VS **51%** Agree that America should welcome refugees in a crisis

Groups with strong views in favor of stricter immigration policies include Elders, conservatives, and evangelicals. Millennials, liberals, and those of no faith are found among those who feel strongly against stricter immigration policies.

The Religious Factor
Christians, especially evangelicals, support immigration less than the general population

● Evangelicals ● Practicing Christians ● No faith

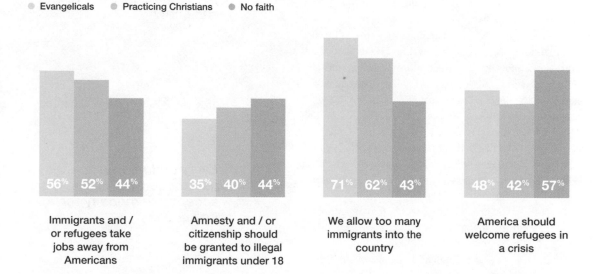

56% 52% 44%	35% 40% 44%	71% 62% 43%	48% 42% 57%

| Immigrants and / or refugees take jobs away from Americans | Amnesty and / or citizenship should be granted to illegal immigrants under 18 | We allow too many immigrants into the country | America should welcome refugees in a crisis |

Who Should We Let In?
According to Americans, these are the characteristics of an immigrant who should be given the greatest consideration when establishing immigration policies:

39%	36%	36%	21%	20%	16%	13%	11%	11%	10%
Personal Need	Education	Technical Skills	Age	Not Sure	Nationality	None	Religion	Other	Personal Wealth

The New Moral Code 💬

Christian morality is being ushered out of our social structures and off the cultural main stage, leaving a vacuum in its place—and broader culture is trying to fill the void. There is growing concern about the moral condition of the nation, even as many U.S. adults admit they are uncertain about how to determine right from wrong.

A majority of U.S. adults among every age group, ethnicity, gender, socioeconomic level, and political ideology expresses concern about the nation's moral condition—eight in 10 overall (80%). Among Elders (89%) and Boomers (87%) the proportion is closer to nine out of 10, while about three-quarters of Gen-Xers (75%) and Millennials (74%) report concern. Similarly, practicing Christians (90%) are more likely than adults of no faith (67%) or who identify with a religious faith other than Christianity (72%) to say they are concerned about the moral condition of the nation.

There are measurable differences between population segments, but moral concern is spread across the demographic board.

Much less widespread, however, is consensus on morality itself. What is it based on? Where does it come from? How can someone know what to do when making moral decisions?

According to a majority of U.S. adults (57%), knowing what is right or wrong is a matter of personal experience. This view is much more prevalent among younger generations than among older adults. Three-quarters of Millennials (74%) agree strongly or somewhat with the statement, "Whatever is right for your life or works best for you is the only truth you can know," compared to only 39 percent of Elders. And Millennials (31%) are three times more likely than Elders (10%) and twice as likely as Boomers (16%) and Gen-Xers (16%) to *strongly* agree with the statement.

When it comes to religion's impact on this question, active Christian faith is associated with greater

Morality and Truth

n=1,237 | July 3–9, 2015

Whatever is right for your life or works best for you is the only truth you can know

Every culture must determine what is acceptable morality for its people

The Bible provides us with moral truths that are the same for all people in all situations, without exception

% among U.S. adults, by generation and faith segment   ● agree strongly   ● agree somewhat

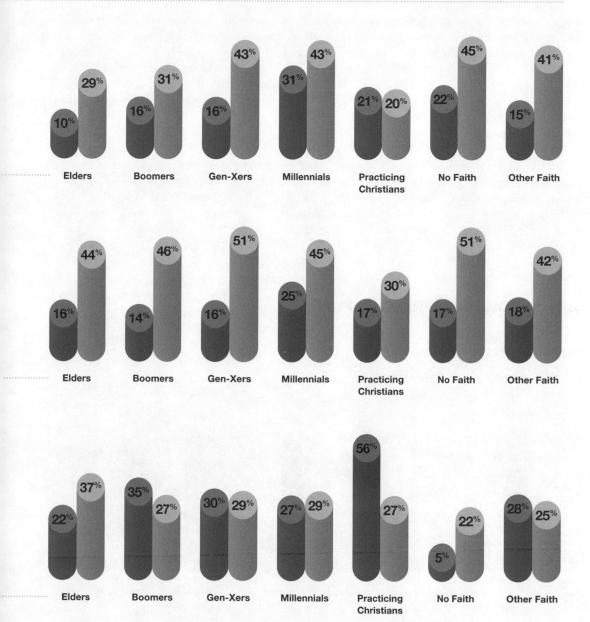

Elders 10% 29% Boomers 16% 31% Gen-Xers 16% 43% Millennials 31% 43% Practicing Christians 21% 20% No Faith 22% 45% Other Faith 15% 41%

Elders 16% 44% Boomers 14% 46% Gen-Xers 16% 51% Millennials 25% 45% Practicing Christians 17% 30% No Faith 17% 51% Other Faith 18% 42%

Elders 22% 37% Boomers 35% 27% Gen-Xers 30% 29% Millennials 27% 29% Practicing Christians 56% 27% No Faith 5% 22% Other Faith 28% 25%

disagreement: The proportions of practicing Christians who disagree (59%) and agree (41%) are the inverse of the general population (44% disagree, 57% agree). The difference is even more pronounced when practicing Christians are compared with adults with no faith, two-thirds of whom agree (67%) that the only truth one can know is whatever is right for one's own life.

A sizable number of Americans see morality as a matter of cultural norms. About two-thirds of all U.S. adults agree strongly (18%) or somewhat (47%) that "every culture must determine what is acceptable morality for its people." Again, Millennials (25%) are more likely than Elders (16%), Boomers (14%), or Gen-Xers (16%) to *strongly* agree with this view.

While most U.S. adults agree that culture plays some role in establishing moral norms, a majority also agrees "the Bible provides us with absolute moral truths which are the same for all people in all situations, without exception" (59%). There is broad agreement across age groups, which is surprising when one considers the notable generational differences on other morality questions. When it comes to faith groups, practicing Christians (83%), as one might expect, are more likely to agree with the statement than

others, especially those with no faith (27%). In fact, more than half of practicing Christians strongly agree (56%).

Two-thirds of U.S. adults either believe moral truth is relative to circumstances (44%) or have not given it much thought (21%). About one-third, on the other hand, believes moral truth is absolute (35%). Millennials are more likely than other age cohorts to say moral truth is relative—in fact, half of them say so (51%), compared to 44 percent of Gen-Xers, 41 percent of Boomers, and 39 percent of Elders. Among the generations, Boomers are most likely to say moral truth is absolute (42%), while Elders are more likely than other age groups to admit they have never thought about it (28%).

Practicing Christians (59%) are nearly four times more likely than adults with

Moral Truth: Absolute or Relative?

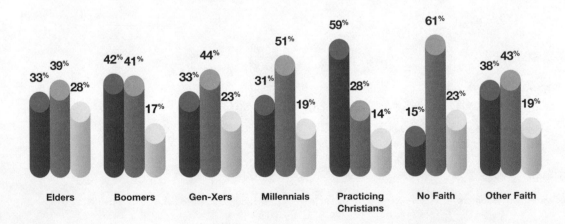

% among U.S. adults, by generation and faith segment

● absolute   ● relative   ○ never thought about it

	Elders	Boomers	Gen-Xers	Millennials	Practicing Christians	No Faith	Other Faith
absolute	33%	42%	33%	31%	59%	15%	38%
relative	39%	41%	44%	51%	28%	61%	43%
never thought about it	28%	17%	23%	19%	14%	23%	19%

no faith (15%) to believe moral truth is absolute. Those with no faith (61%), meanwhile, are twice as likely as practicing Christians (28%) to say it is relative to circumstances. Americans who adhere to a faith other than Christianity are roughly on par with the national average on this question.

The New Moral Code

Americans are both concerned about the nation's moral condition *and* uncertain about morality itself. As nominally Christian moral norms are discarded, what, if anything, is taking their place?

A nationally representative study reveals the degree to which Americans pledge allegiance to the "morality of self-fulfillment," a new moral code that, as Barna president David Kinnaman argues, has all but replaced Christianity as the culture's moral norm. The morality of self-fulfillment can be summed up in six guiding principles (see table). The highest good, according to our society, is "finding yourself" and then living by "what's right for you."

As Kinnaman and Q founder Gabe Lyons write in *Good Faith*:

> There is a tremendous amount of individualism in today's society, and that's reflected in the church too. Millions of Christians have grafted New Age dogma onto their spiritual person. When we peel back the layers, we find that many Christians are using the way of Jesus to pursue the way of self. . . . While we wring our hands about secularism spreading through culture, a majority of churchgoing Christians have embraced corrupt, me-centered theology.

Kinnaman adds, "There appears to be a dichotomy at work among practicing Christians in America. Most believe that the Bible is the source of moral norms that transcend a person's culture, and that those moral truths are absolute rather than relative to circumstances. Yet at the same time, solid majorities ascribe to five of the six tenets of the new moral code. Such widespread cognitive dissonance—among both practicing Christians and Americans more generally—is another indicator of the cultural flux Barna researchers have identified through the past two decades. But it also represents an opportunity for leaders and mentors who are prepared to coach people—especially young people—toward deeper wisdom and greater discernment."

Adapted from Good Faith by David Kinnaman and Gabe Lyons. Used by permission.

(Baker Books, a division of Baker Publishing Group, 2016)

n=1,237 | July 3–9, 2015; n=1,000 | August 2015

The Morality of Self-Fulfillment

% "completely" + "somewhat" agree

● % all U.S. adults
○ % practicing Christians

The best way to find yourself is by looking within yourself

People should not criticize someone else's life choices

To be fulfilled in life, you should pursue the things you desire most

The highest goal of life is to enjoy it as much as possible

People can believe whatever they want, as long as those beliefs don't affect society

Any kind of sexual expression between two consenting adults is acceptable

Generational Culture

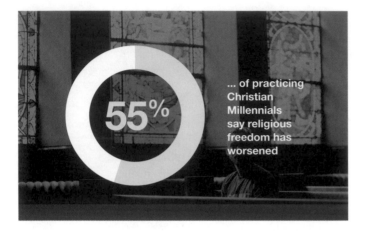

55% ... of practicing Christian Millennials say religious freedom has worsened

Younger Generations Show Concern About Religious Freedom

Barna research on religious freedom, conducted in partnership with the Alliance Defending Freedom, shows a growth of concern among younger generations. Millennial and Gen-X practicing Christians are the generational segments with the largest increase since 2012. Four years ago, one-third of Millennial practicing Christians (32%) and four in 10 Gen-X (40%) practicing Christians said religious freedom had worsened. Today, 55 percent of practicing Christian Millennials—a jump of more than 20 percentage points from 2012—and six in 10 practicing Christian Gen-Xers (59%) say so.

Millennial practicing Christians also express the highest level of concern about the future of religious freedom. More than half are concerned (56%), compared to just one in five in 2012 (19%). This is a significant increase in just a few years, particularly considering that, in 2012, the youngest generation of practicing Christians was far less concerned than older generations about religious liberty. Among practicing Christian Boomers, the percentage concerned about the future of religious freedom (48%) has remained the same since 2012.   *n=1,200 | August 7-September 6, 2015*

Old and Young Differ on Linking Biblical with Political

Young adults are not convinced that regular Bible reading is the solution to uncivil, ineffective politics, Barna research on behalf of American Bible Society indicates. About one-third of Millennials (31%) and half of Gen-Xers (47%) say Bible-reading would make politics more civil, compared to two-thirds of Boomers (66%) and seven in 10 Elders (71%). Likewise, one-third of Millennials (33%) and half of Gen-Xers (49%) say politicians would be more effective if they read the Bible more often. By comparison, two-thirds of Boomers (66%) and three-quarters of Elders (76%) say so. "As Gen-Xers and Millennials—and the generation following them—grow skeptical of the Bible's value, they also question its role in society," Barna editor-in-chief Roxanne Stone says. "In a world where the blending of religion and politics is seen as increasingly dangerous and extreme, it's not a surprise to see young people hesitant about granting political influence to a religious document of any kind."

The Institution and Me

Almost every generation is most likely to name church as the institution that "has their best interests at heart" (Gen-Xers, 34%; Boomers, 41%; Elders, 41%)—except Millennials. Thirty percent of them still trust church, but Millennials are just as likely (32%) to have faith in universities, an institution other generations seem wary of (Gen-Xers, 15%; Boomers, 8%; Elders, 9%). Millennials are also more willing to believe for-profit companies (20%) are looking out for them, while older respondents place little trust in this group (Gen-Xers, 10%; Boomers, 3%; Elders, 3%). The president and congressional representatives see low trust from every generation, perhaps because few believe in the government in general; Elders (2%), Boomers (4%), Gen-Xers (7%), and Millennials (10%) alike place this institution at the bottom of their list.

Which Generation Is Most Likely to Legalize Drugs?

The push to legalize marijuana has gained strength in recent years—and Barna wanted to know how Americans feel about it.

Nearly one-third of Americans (32%) believe that all drugs should be illegal. Broken down by generation, that percentage holds closely among Millennials (29%), Gen-Xers (28%) and Boomers (34%). Almost half of Elders (46%) feel that all drugs should be illegal.

Gen-Xers have the highest percentage of those who are pro-pot; 43 percent of them say recreational drugs like weed should be legalized. Millennials track alongside Gen-Xers, with 42 percent in favor of legal recreational drug use. Though this movement doesn't have quite as much support among older generations, one-quarter (24%) of Elders say drugs like marijuana should be legal—no small number. Move to Boomers, the generation immediately following, and the percentage of those in favor of legal pot climbs to 39 percent.

Fourteen percent of Gen-Xers think all drugs, even hard ones, should be legal, as long as they are regulated; 5 percent of them believe all drugs should be legal and unregulated. Millennials and Boomers express similar levels of support for legal, regulated drug use (12% each) and legal, unregulated drug use (2% and 1%, respectively). Among Elders, just 2 percent would support completely unregulated drug use, though the percentage of Elders who think all drugs should be legal with some regulation is on par with other generations (16%).

BARNA
TAKES

Technology in Its Proper Place

Andy Crouch,
Christianity Today
Executive Editor, Author
of *The Tech-Wise Family*

Technology is literally everywhere in our homes—in the form of invisible electromagnetic waves, not to mention the devices in our pockets. This change has come about overnight, in the blink of an eye in terms of human history and culture. None of us really knows what we are doing, and because the technological revolution has happened so fast, we are all equally flummoxed by it. When previous generations confronted the perplexing challenges of parenting and family life, they could fall back on wisdom, or at least old wives' tales, that had been handed down for generations. But the pace of technological change has surpassed anyone's capacity to develop enough wisdom to handle it. We are stuffing our lives with technology's new promises, with no clear sense of whether it will help us keep the promises we already made.

The pace of change and the lack of accumulated wisdom applies to me and my own family. I can't possibly tell you how to handle the new app, which I've never heard of as I write, that your 15-year-old will want to install on her phone next week. I don't even know, honestly, how to handle all the technology my family and I already have (and I'm a certified geek who has loved technology ever since my dad brought home a "computer terminal" and "modem" in the 1970s—kids, ask your grandparents what those were).

But I do know this: If we don't learn to put technology, in all its forms, in its proper place, we will miss out on many of the best parts of life in a family.

I want to make this clear: The "proper place" for technology won't be exactly the same for every family—and it is not the same at every season of our lives. One of my happy memories from my early twenties is watching *Star Trek: The Next Generation* every Tuesday night with my roommate Steve, cracking jokes at the plot twists and fighting over the chunks of cookie dough in the quart of Ben & Jerry's ice cream we consumed during the show each week. Twenty-five years later, given my other priorities, cotton-candy entertainment like *Star Trek* doesn't have a proper place in my weekly schedule—and a weekly half-quart of premium ice cream definitely doesn't have a place in my waistline!

So figuring out the proper place for technology involves the very things we need to develop as families: wisdom and virtue. We can let technology overwhelm us with its default settings, taking over our lives and stunting our growth in the ways that really matter. Or we can do the careful work of figuring out where technology fits—and where it doesn't belong—at each season of our lives.

It isn't easy to have the wisdom to see when and where to make technology part of family life—and it's definitely not easy to swim against the current and keep it limited to those times and places—but there are some general rules of thumb that make sense for almost every situation.

Technology is in its proper place when it helps us bond with the real people we have been given to love, and it's out of its proper place when we end up bonding with people at a distance, like celebrities, that we will never meet.

It's in its proper place when it starts great conversations—and it's out of its proper place when it prevents us from talking with and listening to one another.

It's in its proper place when it helps us take care of the fragile bodies we inhabit—and it's out of its proper place when it promises to help us escape the limits and vulnerabilities of those bodies altogether.

It's in its proper place when it helps us acquire skill and mastery of domains that are the glory of human culture (sports, music, the arts, cooking, writing, accounting—the list could go on and on). But when we let technology replace the development of skill with passive consumption, something has gone wrong.

It's in its proper place when it helps us cultivate awe for the created world we are part of and responsible for stewarding (our family spent some joyful and awe-filled hours when our children were in middle school watching the beautifully produced BBC series *Planet Earth*). And it's out of its proper place when it keeps us from engaging the wild and wonderful natural world with all our senses.

And if there's one thing I've discovered about technology, it's that it doesn't stay in its proper place on its own. Much like my children's toys and stuffed creatures and minor treasures, it finds its way underfoot all over the house and all over our lives. If we aren't intentional and careful, it becomes a quite extraordinary mess.

This is about much more than just social media, or even screens. It's about how to live as full, flourishing human beings, with technology helping all of us become everything we can be.

Read more Barna research on this subject in The Tech-Wise Family *by Andy Crouch. This adaptation is used by permission. (Baker Books, a division of Baker Publishing Group, 2017)*

Trending in ...
Life

It's about to get personal.

This section of *Barna Trends* is all about your daily life. Even as you drink your morning coffee, or take a Twitter break at your desk or debrief with loved ones at the dinner table, you're an active participant in broader societal shifts.

Working, reading, watching, dating, learning, parenting . . . These everyday,

even sometimes mundane, routines position you as a contributor and consumer. The way you embody these roles helps shape your home, your neighborhood, and our society.

In LIFE, Barna looks at trends such as:

- the evolution and proliferation of pornography
- America's favorite books, films, and TV shows
- what Millennials expect from and bring to the workplace
- the growing acceptance of cohabiting before marriage
- why people choose where they live and how it defines them
- what young people want from higher education

 Vocation & Education

 Habits

 Relationships

 Community

 Generational Life

Featuring:

Nicole Baker Fulgham, David Kinnaman, Megan Pritchett, Jefferson Bethke, Audrey Assad, Roxanne Stone, Bryan Loritts, Brooke Hempell, Mark Matlock

At a Glance: Life

The Porn Phenomenon: Behind the Research

Barna recently conducted a one-of-a-kind study on public perceptions and usage of pornography. The resulting report, *The Porn Phenomenon* (produced in partnership with Josh McDowell Ministry), sheds new light on just how much today's culture has embraced porn practices. Many of these findings are presented throughout *Barna Trends*.

A major component of the study was qualitative research in the form of open-ended online surveys with 32 adults and 20 pastors. These helped develop subsequent surveys for broader quantitative studies of 2,771 participants. The researchers felt that an online methodology was essential in the qualitative research to ensure confidentiality, anonymity and candid responses. Many related personal stories of their own or a family member's struggle, revealing the emotional factors surrounding pornography use.

This willingness to engage with an often personal topic was reflected in the quantitative studies as well. At the beginning of each survey, participants were warned about the nature of the questions and asked to confirm their interest in continuing. Again, at the beginning of the section about pornography use, respondents were asked if they wished to continue due to the sensitive nature of the topic. Only 3 percent of respondents dropped out of the survey at this point.

Page-to-Screen Stories Are Popular

When Barna asked adults which bestsellers they had read in their entirety, novels-turned-films like *The Martian* (read by 5%) and *The Girl on the Train* (read by 4%) topped the list. *Jesus Calling* had been read by 3 percent, and *The Shack* was still popular (read by 5%) a decade after its release.

I don't think meaningful work needs to have a global impact at all. I think living and working intentionally, being true to your values and doing everything you do with excellence can take on so many forms."
—*Scott Harrison, founder of charity: water, in the Barna FRAME* Multi-Careering

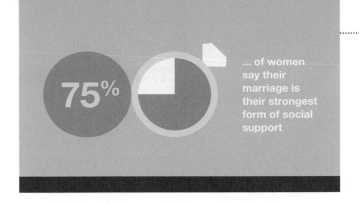

75% ... of women say their marriage is their strongest form of social support

For Better, for Worse (But Mostly for Better)

Research for the Barna FRAME *Wonder Women* shows that 75 percent of women say their marriage is their strongest form of social support.

"My marriage helps me ..."
Be satisfied with my life - 57%
Understand my priorities - 56%
Be the best person I can be - 53%
Set good boundaries - 51%
Live out my purpose - 49%
Connect to a community - 33%

n=1,404 (732 women) |
June 25-July 1, 2013

"I'll Believe It When I Link It"

What criteria do you use to know that the information you find online is true? Barna recently posed this question to people and found that among non-Christians over 40, the most common answer (59%) is "It fits with other things I already know." For non-Christians under 40, 68 percent say, "I verify it with another source." Practicing Christians of these ages have similar criteria; 64 percent of those over 40 believe information that fits with what they know, and 61 percent of those under 40 look to another source first. Respondents in all of these groups indicate they are less likely to accept online information as true simply because "it comes from a trusted friend."

America by the #s: Rush Hour

The average American spends about 38 hours a year stuck in traffic, according to Texas A&M Transportation Institute. That's the equivalent of honking your horn for a whole week of work. Barna found that for most adults it's important that their commute be reasonable, with three-quarters saying they live within 20 miles of their workplace (73%). Within that larger group, 41 percent live within one to five miles away, another three in 10 (30%) live six to 20 miles away. One in 10 commuters (9%) lives less than one mile from work, and an additional 9 percent of adults work from home.

This corresponds with other Barna data showing that most Americans (45%) describe where they live as "suburban." Because jobs tend to be concentrated within business districts in city centers—not in the suburbs—it appears that Americans are fine with building a bit of a commute into their daily routine, particularly if it means living outside of the urban hustle and bustle.

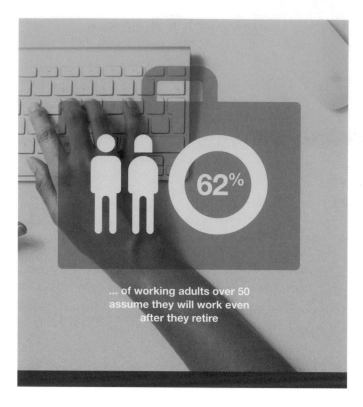

62%

... of working adults over 50 assume they will work even after they retire

Regarding Retirement

Nearly half of today's working adults over the age of 50 (46%) believe they will not be able to retire as early as their parents, and nearly two-thirds (62%) assume they will work even after they retire from their current career, research for the Barna FRAME *Multi-Careering* says. Of those who expect to do at least some work after they retire, nearly three-quarters (73%) say they'll work because they *want* to. Many imagine doing a new type of work—nearly three in ten (29%) expect to venture outside their industry after reaching retirement.

Among unretired adults, here are common hopes for retirement:

"When I retire, I want to ..."
Spend time with family - 76%
Pursue personal hobbies - 57%
Adventure - 42%
Volunteer - 23%
Use my skills in a new line of work - 19%
Own my own business - 15%

n=405 employed adults ages 50+ | July 29– August 1, 2013

What Gives?

When people set aside money for religious or charitable purposes, where is it going (and how much do they contribute)? Barna numbers for 2016 show that 73 percent of all adults give to nonprofits (organizations including churches), and 54 percent give specifically to places of worship. It's nice to know more than half of the population contributes in these ways, though these percentages are significantly lower than they were 15 years ago; in 2000, 89 percent reported giving to nonprofits, and 76 percent to places of worship. Fewer Millennials give to either nonprofits (61%) or places of worship (45%), and they also give in lower dollar amounts (however, those in this age group may not have the financial resources of older generations). Giving percentages for churched adults (those who have attended church at least once in the past month) have also declined with time, but they are more likely than the general population to give in each category, as well as to give higher amounts on average.

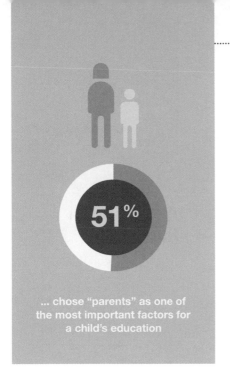

51%

... chose "parents" as one of the most important factors for a child's education

America by the #s: Parents and Educators

Americans generally feel the responsibility for education should be shared between parents and schools, though they tend to believe parents play the larger role. Eighty percent say the primary responsibility rests with parents; 56 percent also point toward the school system. Fifty-one percent feel that parents are the most important factor for a child's education; 47 percent say the same of teachers. When identifying factors that improve student achievement in low-performing schools, 76 percent mention parental support, and 70 percent say high-quality teachers. Christians are even more likely to look to parents; 85 percent of them see increased parental involvement as the top factor for improved student achievement.

n=1,062 | April 13-18, 2012

" Practicing Christians are more likely to turn off a movie because of sexual content, profanity, or nudity than they are because of violence, compared with all adults, who are more likely to turn it off because of violence. More than half of all adults say that there is a connection between watching violent movies and violent behaviors.

"In the New Testament, there's not a single instance where a follower of Jesus is encouraged to use violence. It's just not there. That's why for the first few centuries of the Church, Christians understood that they weren't to use violence in self-defense, and if they were part of the government, they couldn't be part of any government apparatus that ordered executions. They couldn't take part in that official violence. Is there any redemptive violence in entertainment? I think we have to say no. We can't ever watch a story and think violence is the right solution to the problem at hand. At the same time, we don't immediately turn off any forms of entertainment or turn away from all art that doesn't directly promote a Christian worldview. We can watch movies, we can play video games, we can watch television shows where violence is a part of it. The question is whether we're enjoying the violence, or we're recognizing this is a depiction of the reality that we live in that gives us an opportunity to think about how we can be a redemptive factor in that place."

—*Tyler Wigg-Stevenson, founder and director of the Two Futures Project, coauthor of the Barna FRAME* Fighting for Peace

It's Not All Bad

Much has been written about the ways that smartphones, social media, and a growing dependency on devices negatively affects people—spiritually, physically, socially, and mentally. Teachers, pastors, doctors, parents, and social researchers alike are quick to acknowledge the benefits of "turning off." But what about the benefits of our technologically advanced, highly resourced, digital lives? Being "connected" doesn't always have to be a bad thing, right?

Barna research for the FRAME *The Hyperlinked Life* shows many adults are willing to identify positive results from this new age of at-our-fingertips information. More than half (56%) think it's fun to learn new things. Forty-one percent feel greater confidence in their decisions. Almost one-third keep others informed on important issues (32%) or say they can avoid bad decisions (31%). Twenty-nine percent feel they have greater control over their lives.

Communications strategist Jun Young and Barna president David Kinnaman write in *The Hyperlinked Life*, "Many of us are somewhere in the middle: unsure if technology is good or bad for us, but caught up in it all the same. Ample research supports both extremes, and while the debate is heated, most agree on one thing: The knowledge revolution is happening, and this way of life is here to stay."

A Plan Worth Sticking to

How do you keep organized and stay on task? Three-quarters (78%) of people say making a list is their most effective way to plan. Almost one in four (23%) schedule specific tasks for productive times, 17 percent write down a plan, and 7 percent designate tasks for when they're feeling most creative.

The Porn 2.0 Generation

Barna research conducted with Josh McDowell Ministry found that teenagers are pioneers of "porn 2.0"—user-created sexual or nude content. Forty percent of teens and young adults say they have received a nude image, generally from a boyfriend or girlfriend. Twenty-six percent have sent one (again, usually to a boyfriend or girlfriend).

68%

... of Americans listen to non-religious music on the radio in a typical week

America by the #s: Radio Presets

When asked which radio formats they listen to in a typical week, most Americans (68%) indicate turning on non-religious music. Christian programming successfully reaches evangelicals (36%, Christian talk radio; 70%, Christian music stations), as well as audiences in the South, where 26 percent listen to Christian music and 15 percent tune in to Christian talk radio. People in the West really love standard talk radio (listened to weekly by 48%).

n=812 adults who listen to radio at least monthly | January 25–February 4, 2016

How Does Hollywood Treat Christianity?

People have mixed views on how well Hollywood portrays Christianity. Just over one-quarter of all adults (28%) feels Hollywood's general representation of Christianity is sometimes positive, sometimes negative; another 21 percent say it is neutral, neither positive nor negative. Twenty percent of all adults "don't know" when asked for their opinion. Practicing Christians hold a wide range of feelings about onscreen treatments of Christianity, most commonly that Hollywood portrays their faith negatively (25%) or depicts it sometimes positively, sometimes negatively (27%). Only one in nine practicing Christians (11%) believes that Hollywood describes Christianity positively.

> If we're considering opening our lives, our hearts, our home to an orphan, we need to know this first: That every orphan's journey as an orphan began with a tragedy. They have tasted the world at its most broken, and if we open our lives and hearts and welcome them, we will certainly taste some of that pain as well. That is why it's vital that anyone who is considering adopting or fostering go through the preparation to understand trauma, to understand the healing process, to understand what children need. It's why families shouldn't walk through this alone. It's a journey for the church to take together. Not every Christian is called to the lifelong commitment of adoption, and not every Christian is called to foster or mentor. But every one of us is called to somehow reflect God's great love for the orphan."

—Jedd Medefind, president of the Christian Alliance for Orphans, author of the Barna FRAME Becoming Home

Vocation & Education

The ways we learn, work, and pursue purpose

Homeschooling in America

The subject of much debate, homeschooling is a common form of K-12 education among American families. The national average of families who homeschool their children is around 8 percent, though this varies by state and city. The states with the highest rates of homeschooling include North and South Dakota (16%), Indiana (12%), Maryland (12%), South Carolina (12%), and Alabama (12%). The states with the lowest rates of homeschooling are Maine (<1%), Idaho (1%), Utah (1%), Kentucky (3%), and Wisconsin (3%). The areas with the highest rates of homeschooling include Charleston-Huntington, West Virginia (19%); Greenville / Spartanburg / Anderson, South Carolina-Asheville, North Carolina (18%); Miami-Ft. Lauderdale, Florida (16%); Indianapolis, Indiana (16%); and Tampa-St. Petersburg-Sarasota, Florida (15%). The cities with the lowest rates of homeschooling include Portland-Auburn, Maine (<1%), Lexington, Kentucky (<1%), Milwaukee, Wisconsin (1%), Salt Lake City, Utah (1%), and Syracuse, New York (3%).

The motivations behind providing education at home instead of at a public or private school are varied but tend to focus on concern about the environment, a desire for religious or moral instruction, and a general dissatisfaction with the academic instruction available at other schools. The moral factor becomes readily apparent when we look closely at several faith segments and religious behaviors like church attendance. For instance, evangelical parents homeschool at a rate twice the national average (17%). Practicing Christians are also three percentage points above average at 11 percent. These figures are even more telling considering how few atheists or agnostics homeschool (5%). Looking at church attendance, parents who attend church the most are more likely to homeschool their children. Active churchgoers (11%) are above the national average and it trends down from there, with somewhat (9%) and minimally active (7%) churchgoers, and those who are either dechurched (6%) or never churched (6%).

Finally, another key indicator for likelihood of homeschooling is ideology. Those who are mostly conservative (10%) are almost twice as likely as those who are mostly liberal (6%) to homeschool their children.

Most & Least Homeschooled

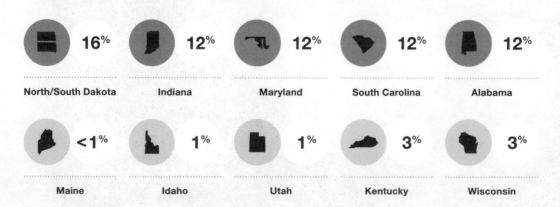

North/South Dakota	Indiana	Maryland	South Carolina	Alabama
16%	12%	12%	12%	12%

Maine	Idaho	Utah	Kentucky	Wisconsin
<1%	1%	1%	3%	3%

n=2,871 | July 2011—Jan 2015

A Q&A on Education Inequality

with Nicole Baker Fulgham

Nicole Baker Fulgham is an education expert and the founder of The Expectations Project, an organization that mobilizes faith communities to partner with public schools and to advocate for closing the academic achievement gap. She is the author of Educating All God's Children *and the Barna FRAME* Schools in Crisis.

Describe the academic achievement gap in America.

We essentially have two very distinct public education systems: a group of schools that are educating their kids at incredibly high levels, and a whole different school system where kids, particularly in poorer communities, are not getting a quality education. The academic achievement gap is just one of our nation's biggest disgraces. Graduation rates for kids growing up in poverty are 50 percent, and only one out of every 14 of those kids is going to go to college. Education inequality manifests across the divide of rich and poor, but also along the lines of race. Students of color and low-income students, who have the same God-given potential as their peers, are not seeing the levels of academic success that other students are obtaining. Educational inequity does not have to exist in our nation. This is a problem we can solve.

Do you see a link between your work and recent national conversations about the Black Lives Matter movement or violence against young black men?

Conversations about race in our nation have definitely impacted our work. For many people in the education space, and certainly for those just dipping their toes in, it's been more comfortable to talk about education inequality in the context of income, rather than explicitly talking about race. But I think the Black Lives Matter movement has provided another moment to discuss the connections of race to all types of inequality—including the inequality found in our nation's public schools. We've also been able to form alliances across organizations focusing on criminal justice

and black youth. These organizations are making connections to the school-to-prison pipeline and see quality schools as preventative. It's made our work more relevant to groups who may not have focused on it as much previously. Education inequality wields its biggest impact on African American, Latino, and Native American populations. The issues are inextricably linked. The legacy of racism in our nation's school system—segregation, boarding schools that pulled Native American students from their communities, school funding formulas that reinforce the racial segregations of neighborhoods—runs deep and wide. Beyond history, the same unconscious bias that many believe impacts the criminal justice system also impacts the education system. Black girls are suspended at six times the rates of all other girls, often for the same infractions. Perceptions play into how we discipline and educate students on multiple levels. This conversation can be very uncomfortable—but it has to be a part of the systemic change necessary for all of God's children.

An Academic Calling 💬👤

Higher education is an institution that overlaps with economic, spiritual, and cultural trends. Study of today's classrooms requires study of the broader forces—internal and external—shaping the modern academic experience. In 2015, Barna conducted a study in partnership with the Association for Biblical Higher Education (ABHE) to explore perceptions of biblical higher education, identify key priorities of prospective students, and determine key influences that shape enrollment decisions. While the research was tailored to specifically address the issues faced by Bible colleges and Christian colleges and universities, these insights hold relevance for the whole higher education landscape and anyone considering a college degree.

Most See College as Career Prep

One major trend in biblical higher education today (as well as higher education generally) is in the perception of what college is for.

Among the U.S. general population, almost seven out of 10 people agree that the purpose of college is to prepare for a specific job or career, 55 percent say that the purpose is to increase financial opportunities, and just under half believe college is for staying competitive in today's job market. No matter which way you look at it, people believe college is about jobs.

Just 14 percent say college is about developing moral character, and a mere

7 percent identify it as a time to encourage spiritual growth. It's worth noting here that respondents were allowed in this question to select as many phrases as they wished. Such low percentages for these moral and spiritual values suggests just how much Americans focus on college as a career preparatory experience.

While you might expect Christians in this sample to hold different priorities from the general population, this is not the case. Among Christian prospective students, their top three goals for getting a college degree are to increase their earning potential (48%), gain practical job skills (48%), and determine career path (43%).

These findings have profound implications for biblical higher education, and they raise several important questions. To what extent should Bible and Christian colleges develop their programs to prepare students for their careers? Should the primary focus be on preparing students for careers in ministry or those in the marketplace? Regardless of how individual institutions decide to answer these questions, the reality is that prospective students of every demographic view college through the lens of career.

After asking what the purpose of college is, Barna asked respondents what the purpose of having a job or career is. Eight in 10 people respond that the purpose of having a job or career is to make money or earn income, and less than half say it's for using your unique talents and skills (45%), part of being an adult (43%), or to help make your life meaningful (40%). Serving other people and society (28%), making yourself happy (27%), and pursuing God's purpose for your life (18%) are less-selected options.

This is the axis on which today's approach to higher education turns: You get a degree so that you can get a job, and you get a job so that you can earn income. Whether educational institutions agree or disagree with this logic, they must address the mindset of prospective students.

Spiritual Development Is a (Professed) Priority

Although career development is the main aim of Christian prospective students, they have not completely written off spiritual growth as a goal for their college career.

Among prospective students, 46 percent say that it is very important to them to grow spiritually while completing their degree, and another 33 percent say that it's somewhat important. Bible study also holds a fairly high degree of importance with this group of prospective students—37 percent say it's very important to them to study the Bible while completing their degree, and 30 percent say that it's somewhat important to them.

However, the research found fairly low percentages of Christian prospective students who are strongly considering biblical higher education (34% considering Christian colleges or universities, 17% considering Bible colleges). Even as students profess a desire for spiritual growth and learning about the Bible, many do not pursue an institution that formally integrates these priorities into their education. This disconnect suggests that other practical priorities drive them to make decisions about which higher education institution to attend, such as prospects for career and financial growth.

Overall these are encouraging statistics, but it should give Christian institutions pause to consider that almost one-quarter of Christian prospective students (22%) don't consider spiritual growth during college important (a combined percentage of those who consider it "not very important" and "not at all important"). For a substantial number of self-identified Christian students, the value of a biblical education is not apparent.

Churches Are Faltering Feeders

Another finding is that churches aren't always successful at feeding into biblical higher education institutions. Just 11 percent of Christian prospective students say that church pastors were one of the most influential people in their educational path, which suggests that church leaders aren't influential in this area of their congregants' lives. Barna uses the word *faltering* instead of *failing* to describe the pathway from the church to biblical higher education because some students are still being influenced by their church leadership to consider this type of education.

Pastors are likely to primarily recommend biblical education as a pathway to ministerial training. Based on the data from pastors, ministerial training is seen as the most applicable reason someone would pursue biblical higher education, followed by academic training, personal development, and professional development. While this is a great recommendation for prospective

Reasons to Pursue Biblical Education

In your opinion, which of the following are the main reasons someone might pursue biblical education?

● Most applicable ● Somewhat applicable ● Not as applicable ● Least applicable

Personal development
to dig deeper into their faith and earn an academic qualification in the process

Professional development
to improve their skills in a way that benefits a non-ministry career

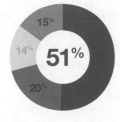

Ministerial training
for theological training and equipping with the necessary skills and understanding to enter paid Christian ministry

Academic training
to earn an academic qualification that will further their career as a biblical/theological scholar

n=980 senior and youth pastors | October 23–November 17, 2015 | ABHE

students who are interested in vocational church ministry, this assumption reflects a limited view of how a biblical education can be relevant to other paths and types of growth.

In light of students' emphasis on career development, it's notable that half (53%) of pastors surveyed say professional development would be the least applicable reason to pursue biblical education. This "silo strategy" of separating career and ministry might be one explanation for why churches have not been strong feeders into Bible and Christian colleges. As faith engagement has declined, churches have not adapted their assumptions about the benefits of a formal biblical education.

Awareness Is the Big Obstacle

One surprising finding from this study: The bigger issue for biblical higher education is a lack of awareness, not having a negative reputation.

Among people in the U.S. general population who knew at least a little about Bible colleges, Barna asked for general impressions of Bible colleges on a scale of very positive to very negative. More than two in five respondents (43%) say that their impression of Bible colleges is neither positive nor negative—which likely indicates that they lack enough information about Bible colleges to make an assessment about them. Just 12 percent of the general population say they have a negative impression of Bible colleges (6% "somewhat negative," 6% "very negative").

Support for the hypothesis that the general population does not know enough about Bible colleges to form an opinion about them appeared when Barna asked a sample of Christian prospective students how much they know about Bible colleges. A majority of them report knowing just a little bit or less about Bible colleges, and 6 percent say they have never even heard of Bible colleges. This poses a large problem for Christian higher education institutions—the prospective students they're relying on to consider their schools often don't know much about them, if anything at all.

Among general population respondents, when asked what words they felt described Bible colleges, the top responses are "Christian community" (56%), "spiritual learning" (56%), and "ministry preparation" (52%). What's notable about these words is that they are not necessarily negative but are primarily descriptive in nature; they describe what Bible colleges are, not nec-

According to 2013 Barna polling, 36 percent of American Millennials feel college prepared them for life. Twenty-nine percent wish they'd chosen a different college.

n=1,124 Christian prospective students | October 14-November 15, 2015; n=980 faith leaders | October 23-November 17, 2015 | n=1,011 U.S. adults | October 21-30, 2015 | ABHE

How Much Do You Know About Bible Colleges?

- ● I know a lot
- ● I know a good amount
- ● I know a little bit
- ● I know they exist
- ● I have never heard of them

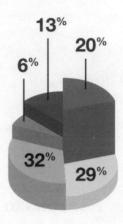

13%

20%

6%

32%

29%

n=1,124 Christian prospective students | October 14– November 15, 2015 | ABHE

essarily opinions about them. The last of these descriptors, "ministry preparation," highlights the generalizations that people make about biblical higher education and the kinds of learning that happen there.

These are critical trends in understanding the future of biblical higher education. Properly understood, they present opportunities for churches, pastors, and Christian educators to reengage in the cultural dialogue about the purpose of education.

The Future of Christian Higher Education

What's Next for
CHRISTIAN HIGHER EDUCATION

How the Career Goals
and Faith Priorities of
College-Bound Christians
Are Shaping the Future

A Barna Report Produced in Partnership with
the Association for Biblical Higher Education

You will find

- Statistics on prospective students, their parents, and their pastors
- An examination of student priorities at various stages of life
- Insights from stakeholders in Christian higher education
- Barna analysis of the Christian education ecosystem

Tens of thousands of Christian students make decisions about college each year. What priorities and preferences inform their choices? What do they expect from their education? What factors cause them to include or exclude Christian institutions from consideration? How do they perceive Bible colleges and Christian universities? Based on a yearlong, multiphase research study commissioned by the Association of Biblical Higher Education, *What's Next for Christian Higher Education* is Barna's answer to these and other questions. Like most faith-based institutions in North America, Bible colleges and Christian universities are facing the headwinds of gale-force cultural change. *What's Next for Christian Higher Education* is a tool to help leaders make prayerful, data-informed decisions for the future.

BARNA TAKES

The Learning Future

David Kinnaman,
Barna Group,
President

Six trends are reshaping the future of Christian higher education. Together they are creating a new climate of learning that impacts not only Bible colleges and Christian universities, but also parents, pastors, and mentors—or anyone, really, who teaches, trains, disciples, or coaches Christian learners.

1. Demographics: The Changing Face of Students

Delayed milestones of adulthood, such as graduating college, getting married, living on one's own, and becoming financially independent, as well as growing ethnic and cultural diversity in North America, mean the learning future must be *flexible*. In research for the Association of Biblical Higher Education (ABHE) on how students make their college decisions, Barna found that eight out of 10 prospective students 20 years and older say online learning is an important option for their education. Half of students over 25 say night or weekend classes are an important option. And significant minorities of adult learners say they want accelerated or decelerated degree programs. In short, they're looking for learning that fits their lives, not curricula into which they must fit. These findings have obvious—but not exclusive—implications for Christian educational institutions. Anyone involved in training Christian learners, at any age and stage, must consider the value of flexibility.

2. Technology: Digital Babylon

I've talked a lot in recent years about "digital Babylon," shorthand for the idea that pervasive internet connectivity, ubiquitous digital tools and hyper-social media are helping to create a new culture where Christians must learn to live as exiles—strangers in a strange land who are nonetheless called to be people of God under his rule and reign. This exilic calling means the learning future must be *kingdom-centered*: fluent, like the prophet Daniel, with the language, literature, and wisdom of "digital Babylon" (see Dan. 1), but also laser-focused—not distracted by Snapchat or

Twitter!—on God's mission of redemption and reconciliation. Everyone who teaches Christian learners has a role to play in equipping God's people to be kingdom-centered exiles who are "in but not of" digital Babylon.

3. Society: The Disintermediation of Institutions

Americans are increasingly disenchanted with the institutions that historically have been the glue holding society together. This is especially concentrated among Millennials, whose entire lifespans have been characterized by one institutional failure after another. They have little trust that the country's institutions "have my best interests at heart." Just one-third strongly agrees that universities can be trusted in this regard (32%); three in 10 say so about churches (30%); one in five trusts for-profit companies (20%) or the U.S. president (19%); and even fewer agree congressional representatives (13%) or the government (10%) have their best interests at heart.

This lack of trust has led to a *disintermediation* of institutions in our society—meaning that people no longer put their faith in institutions to be trustworthy mediators of our communal life. And it means the learning future must be relational. People may not trust institutions, but they do trust other people, especially those who love unconditionally and keep showing up—and these relationships make a measurable difference in Christian learners' lives. For example, Millennials who continue in their Christian faith into adulthood are twice as likely (59%) as those who don't (31%) to say that, as a young person, they had a close personal friendship with an adult in their church. Meaningful relationships matter if learning is to last.

4. Economy: Shifting Patterns of Work

The employment landscape is undergoing rapid reconstruction. According to *Forbes,* there are 53 million freelancers in America today, and one out of every two workers will be a freelancer by 2020.* Not all of these workers would choose to be on their own if they had other, more traditional, employment options. But many others intentionally choose nontraditional work arrangements. Whatever the case, Christian learners must be prepared for this reality—and that means the learning future must be *vocational.* Christian educators and others who are invested in discipleship and spiritual formation, such as parents and pastors, must work together to instill in Christian learners a commitment to faithfulness in life's complexity—a sense that, regardless of their employment circumstances, their work is an important arena of faithful discipleship.

5. Spirituality: The Rise of Post-Christian Skepticism

As we have examined at length elsewhere in *Barna Trends,* there's growing skepticism in North America about the authority of the Scriptures, the relevance of church and the significance of Christianity. For example, six in 10 Elders (61%) in America strongly agree "the Bible contains everything a person needs to know to live a meaningful life. Among Millennials, that number is halved (32%). And nearly one in eight young adults (13%) characterize the Bible as "a dangerous book of religious dogma used for centuries to oppress people." In response, the learning future must be *orthodox:* charitably, graciously, relentlessly faithful to the historic Christian faith. Imparting that orthodox faith to Christian learners is the high calling of parents, pastors, teachers, and mentors.

6. Morality: The New Moral Code

The morality of self-fulfillment says that each person's feelings are the measuring stick for his or her own life—and many Christians have adopted this self-centered morality. But the learning future must be *biblical.* In the Gospels, Jesus insists that radical selflessness—a willingness to lose one's very life for his sake—is the measure by which we will be judged (see Matt. 16:24–28). God's Word offers a counternarrative to the me-centered story of self—but only if we read, study, and let it shape our hearts. It's up to educators, pastors, parents, and mentors to teach Christian learners how.

---

*Brian Rashid, "The Rise of the Freelancer Economy,"
Forbes.com, Jan. 26, 2016.
http://www.forbes.com/sites/brianrashid/2016/01/26
/the-rise-of-the-freelancer-economy/#5102be63379a
(accessed June 2016).

When Millennials Go to Work 💬👤

Millennials live a life of paradox. Tech savvy and ambitious, yet perceived by many as lazy and self-centered. Passionate and serious about work, yet job-hopping as they experiment with and explore where to put that passion meaningfully to work.

Given these nuances, it's no wonder that much ink has been spilled dissecting why and how Millennials (those born in the early 1980s through the early 2000s) go to work. Barna's research digs deeper, unearthing the pillars that form the personal identity of Millennials and tracing the paradoxical relationship they have with their careers.

Millennial Identity: What's Most Central?

Although most Millennials would agree that their career is at least somewhat central to their identity, only a third would say their career is very central. In fact, Boomers are more likely than Millennials to believe their career is central to who they are.

So what do Millennials deem most central to their identity? "Family" and "personal interests" are the top two categories. "Career" is actually one of the least likely categories to be named—the only category it beats is "technology."

In order to make sense of these statistics, it's important to recognize that Millennials are struggling to find jobs. According to Pew Research Center, their employment rate in 2012 was only 63 percent, and 36 percent of them were living at their parents' home, the highest number in this age group in four decades. Even young adults with a bachelor's degree are struggling; their rate of

Shifting Priorities

What is most important to do in your 20s?

● Millennials
● Baby Boomers

Financial independence 59% / 72%

Finish education 52% / 64%

Start your career 51% / 64%

Find yourself 40% / 47%

Follow your dreams 31% / 33%

Become spiritually mature 29% / 39%

Get married 28% / 13%

Enjoy life 24% / 30%

Have kids 21% / 8%

Travel abroad 20% / 15%

Serve the poor 9% / 11%

Be in a serious relationship 9% / 3%

Become famous/ influential 5% / 1%

n=1,400 (404 Millennials, 513 Boomers) | June 25-July 1, 2013

unemployment jumped from 7.7 percent in 2007 to 13.3 percent in 2012.

Getting a job and starting a career is not a foregone conclusion—but it doesn't seem like Millennials care as much about that as their predecessors. Millennials see their twenties as a time to explore options beyond the traditional career ladder. This may be a little confounding to their parents. Two-thirds of Boomers (64%) say "starting your career" is crucial in your twenties, while only half of Millennials (51%) agree. Nearly three-quarters of Boomers (72%) believe "financial independence" is an important accomplishment in your twenties, compared to less than two-thirds of Millennials (59%). Surprisingly, though Millennials place high value on traveling abroad and self-discovery, they remain more likely than Boomers to say having kids and getting married is an important part of one's twenties.

Career Priorities, Projections, and Aspirations

Given that Millennials are more likely to select "personal interests" over "career" when identifying what is central to their identity, it makes sense that their top career priorities are "funding my personal interests" (29%) and "working for myself" (27%).

What these top two priorities have in common is that they enable one to pursue a life outside of work. The first priority provides the financial means to pursue personal interests, whereas the second priority provides, among other things, the autonomy to flexibly arrange one's work schedule around other personal priorities. Millennials approach their career priorities pragmatically.

The diminished importance of a career does not, despite the poor employment rates, come from a place of pessimism about Millennials' career prospects. They are optimistic—even if cautiously so. While a fair number of Millennials doubt they will land their dream job in the next five years, over half of them (52%) believe they will.

While many Millennials certainly do feel anxious about making the wrong career choice, 52 percent of them do not. This could be partly due to their belief in the transient nature of jobs. Nine in 10 Millennials expect to stay in a job for only three years.

Even if Millennials expect to float from job to job, they are not searching aimlessly. When asked what their "dream job" looks like, the most common answer, trumping financial security (34%) and having enough

Forty-two percent of American Millennials say they need their degree for their job, and 40 percent say their degree relates to their current job. Even so, 40 percent still wish they'd studied a different major.

n=1,400 (404 Millennials, 513 Boomers) | June 25-July 1, 2013; n=1,400 (297 Millennials) | June 2013

money to enjoy life (24%), was "I feel passionate about it" (42%).

This is one of the biggest paradoxes of the Millennial mindset. It's clear that starting and building a career isn't as important to them as it was to previous generations. Millennials have many other projects and priorities going on outside of their work, and they want the financial means and flexibility to pursue them.

Yet, when they are prompted to think aspirationally and not just pragmatically, they clearly desire a lot from their jobs. They want their work to be aligned with their passions. But what does this look like? For recent university graduates, at least, "making an impact" is certainly part of the picture. In 2012, a study done by NetImpact found that 59 percent of graduating university students—compared to 53 percent of working adults—believe that having a job where they can make an impact is essential or very important to their happiness.

This trend holds true among Christians. According to a 2012 study by Barna in partnership with Lead Well, those under 40 (including Millennials) are more likely than those over 40 to have thought about whether they feel "called" to their current work (31% compared to 36%). For Millennials, "calling" is more than just about being called toward religious or ministry professions—they are thinking about whether they are "called" by God to their secular jobs as

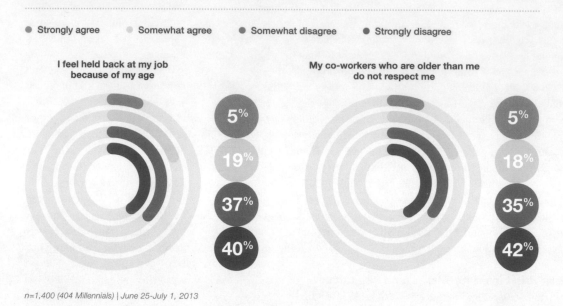

Working Age
Where do Millennials think they stand in the office?

● Strongly agree   ● Somewhat agree   ● Somewhat disagree   ● Strongly disagree

**I feel held back at my job
because of my age**

5%
19%
37%
40%

**My co-workers who are older than me
do not respect me**

5%
18%
35%
42%

n=1,400 (404 Millennials) | June 25-July 1, 2013

well. To be clear, most of them (69%) define "calling" not in a fixed, permanent way, but as something that can change over time as they age. This means they are likely thinking about whether they are called to their current work at this point in their lives, not for a lifetime.

Twenty-eight percent of Millennial Christians feel "called" to their current work. Thirty-seven percent feel called to do something different but haven't been willing to make a change because of their current situation.

Current Career Satisfaction

It is not too surprising to find that 19 percent of Millennials are not very satisfied with their current career. First, since they are younger than their colleagues, they are likely working in lower-rung jobs with little autonomy over their responsibilities. Second, the present economy means that they don't

have the luxury of picking and choosing jobs according to their interests, but simply have to take jobs that pay their bills. Lastly, Millennials clearly have wide-ranging expectations—funding for personal interests, autonomy, alignment with passion or calling—for their career, making it naturally difficult to find a job that meets all their criteria.

It's worth noting that their dissatisfaction does not stem from how they are treated because of their age at work. Most Millennials feel respected by older co-workers and do not feel held back at their job because of their age. In fact, they are more likely to agree than not that their age is an advantage in performing their current or most recent jobs.

Despite their poor career satisfaction, seven in 10 Millennials are satisfied with their lives overall. So while it is true that Millennials want a lot out of their jobs, it's also true that if they don't get what they want, they find other ways to be satisfied.

"We've seen [Millennials] demonstrate a consistent desire to make an impact in the world," observes Roxanne Stone, Barna's editor-in-chief. "Yet they are not limiting that desire to their occupations. While many would love to have that dream job through which they can change the world and express their personal gifts and talents, they also recognize the limitations of the workplace."

The Good, the Bad, and the Bossy

You've probably heard it said that people don't quit jobs, they quit bad bosses. A poor leader can ruin even the best of employees. In fact, Barna has found that one in five workers are actively looking to leave their job because of their supervisor. But is the opposite also true—can a good boss lead to less turnover?

In a study among Americans in the workplace, conducted in partnership with Leadercast, Barna uncovered the ways that both good and bad leadership styles shape the climate of a workplace.

"It's impossible to improve what you don't assess, so this research stresses the importance of self-awareness and feedback systems that allow leaders to face the truth about their leadership," says Barna president David Kinnaman, who directed the study. "Being a self-aware leader will help to improve your leadership culture. The people on your team will thank you for it—or they will be likely to leave your team."

Measuring the Impact of Good and Bad Leadership

Bad leadership costs employers and employees a lot. But good leaders have just as big of an impact. Good supervisors make for less turnover, a better work environment, and more inspired workers.

● Employees with good leaders
● Employees with bad leaders

They enjoy going to work each day
91%
62%

Their work makes a positive difference in the world
82%
63%

They feel empowered to be a leader at work
74%
61%

Some days at work don't get their maximum effort
47%
73%

They are often distracted at work
33%
58%

People often misrepresent truth at their workplace
19%
65%

They feel a lot of negative energy in their workplace
15%
66%

n=1,026 | February–March 2014 | Leadercast

BARNA
TAKES

5 Ways to Vocationally Disciple a Millennial

Megan Pritchett,
Barna Group,
Research Analyst

How does one begin to vocationally disciple Millennials? Many Christians don't have much experience either being discipled or discipling others. According to Barna research conducted in partnership with The Navigators, just 23 percent of Christian adults are being personally discipled by someone else, and 19 percent say they're personally active in discipling others. And that's just accounting for any kind of discipleship relationship: The pool of believers specifically being discipled vocationally is likely even smaller. Generational misunderstandings, personal insecurity, and schedule compatibility can be hindrances to developing a strong discipling relationship.

As a social researcher en route to becoming a career counselor, I think frequently about vocational formation. I have found that vocational growth is often deeply connected to other areas of our spiritual, emotional, and relational health.

With this in mind, and from my vantage point as a Millennial, I share the following advice in the hope that my unique orientation to this topic will be a tool for you as you seek to vocationally disciple young people in your life. While these pointers are contextually best suited for Millennials, they can be effective in facilitating vocational growth and understanding for anyone.

1. Ask Thoughtful, Discerning Questions

One way I've grown vocationally is by being asked specific questions that force me to examine my deepest motives and desires. I recently had lunch with a woman in my professional network who asked me this question 15 minutes after we introduced ourselves: "How do you see your current experiences preparing you for where God leads you in the next 10 years?" Although questions like this are inherently difficult to answer, they show deep care from the asker (*I want to know the unique work God is doing in you*) and help the responder articulate the vision he or she has for the next season of life (*Are my current choices leading me closer to fulfilling God's calling?*).

2. Help Millennials See Their Potentials (and Limitations)

A huge barrier to vocational development is lack of understanding about our unique abilities and gifts. This is a call to identify gifting, however, not give hollow praise. If anything, the (at times excessive) affirmation Millennials have received in their lives can actually make it harder for them to identify unique giftings; they may feel that they're "talented" or "special" but often can't exactly say how.

Discussions of weaknesses and limitations should also accompany discussion of strengths. In *Let Your Life Speak*, Parker Palmer writes, "We must honor our limitations in ways that do not distort our nature, and we must trust and use our gifts in ways that fulfill the potentials God gave us." Often, these potentials and limitations are embedded into the same gifting. My own gift of empathy is one example; naming this gift has allowed me to better understand why it's easy for me to relate and connect with others (strength) and difficult for me to separate my personal worth from my work (weakness). For a long time I assumed that my skills of empathy and strategic thinking were shared by everyone, until someone specifically told me that they appreciated my strength in those areas.

Identifying a gifting shouldn't be restrictive—for example, people with logical, scientific minds can also be creative artists—but they should illustrate which gifts a Millennial brings into the world and how they can carry those gifts to fruition.

3. Develop Trajectory Thinking

Like young adults of any generation, Millennials face a lot of life decisions: college graduation, new careers, dating, marriage, children, etc. However, the speed and order of these transitions has shifted significantly; in the survey "Multiple Generations @ Work," Future Workplace found that 91 percent of Millennials expect to stay in a single job less than 3 years. Barna research shows 70 percent want to be fully developed as a person before they get married. With no "life blueprint" to follow, the concept of trajectory thinking can be a grounding force in the midst of uncertainty and delayed adulthood. Although there are many different seasons in life, there are usually personal gifts, passions, and themes that remain consistent. These consistent elements can shape a vision of a personal trajectory. By helping Millennials to think of their decisions and transitions in light of God's trajectory for their lives, you give them a tool to understand themselves within the larger framework of God's story.

4. Remind Millennials to Slow Down

Millennials are results-driven and technologically overconnected. 2012 data from NetImpact reports that 37 percent of graduating university students expect their work to make an impact within 5 years. Barna has learned that more than half (56%) of Millennials check their phone first thing in the morning. The research also hints at the flip side of this tech saturation—71 percent of people feel overwhelmed by the amount of information they need to stay up to date. With so much access to information, it's tempting for Millennials to also believe that they can quickly discern their vocation.

However, trees don't mature in a day, and neither do our vocations. As you vocationally disciple Millennials, remind them to slow down—it takes time, intentional decisions and prayer to develop into the person God made us to be. The full unfolding of one's gifts and purpose is the endeavor of a lifetime, not the result of a single mentoring session.

5. Share Your Own Vocational Story

Don't underestimate how encouraging it can be to a Millennial to hear about your own journey with vocation! When did you first start thinking about the concept of vocation, not just "getting a job"? How did that change over time? What circumstances or events made your vocational call more clear? You don't have to have it all figured out (after all, Millennials highly value authenticity and honesty), but a thoughtful reflection of your experiences thus far can go a long way in building trust with Millennials and helping us better understand our own stories.

Ultimately, all of these suggestions about vocational discipleship are about developing authentic cross-generational relationships connected to the larger work of the church. Although finding a meaningful career is important work, any effort done outside of community is likely to bear little fruit.

Let's grow together.

Habits

The routines (and screens) that
make up our modern lifestyles

America's Reading Habits (or Lack Thereof)

Can paper and ink still compete in a digital age? A study from Barna examines the relationship between Americans and their bookshelves.

Although fears of America becoming a post-literate culture may be overstated, they are not completely unfounded. A majority of the general population reads five books or fewer every year (67%). One-quarter of all adults don't read any books at all (25%), while two out of five read anywhere between one and five books a year (42%). One-third of adults read five or more books a year (34%).

Almost half of adults of low socioeconomic status (those with a household income of $20,000 or less a year and no college experience) don't read any books at all (47%), compared to fewer than one in 10 (8%) for adults with an annual income of at least $70,000 and at least a four-year degree. Conversely, 51 percent of these adults of higher socioeconomic status read more than five books every year, compared to just 16 percent of adults with less income and education.

With novels consistently topping the bestseller charts, it may not come as a surprise that U.S. adults prefer fiction (53%) slightly more than nonfiction (45%) when choosing a book to read. When presented with a list of popular books, the greatest percentage of respondents (5%) had read *The Martian* by Andy Weir.

Among the practicing Christian audience, however—and within the genre of "Christian" books—the preference is toward nonfiction; twice as many practicing Christians prefer Christian nonfiction (35%) over Christian fiction (18%). This preference aligns with the reading motivations of practicing Christians, many of whom (34%) read to grow and develop spiritually. The overwhelming majority of Americans read principally for pleasure (64%). Despite the massive number of business-related titles on the market, fewer than one in ten adults say they read for work.

WHERE DO YOU MOST OFTEN GET YOUR BOOKS?

Most people are still reading physical books—either ones they bought in a store or borrowed from a library

Buy in a store

Order online

Borrow from a friend

Borrow from the library

Purchase an ebook for a tablet

Other

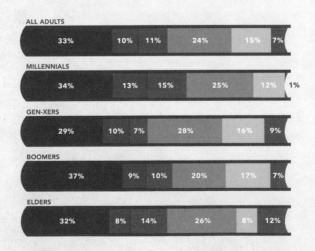

	Buy in a store	Order online	Borrow from a friend	Borrow from the library	Purchase an ebook	Other
ALL ADULTS	33%	10%	11%	24%	15%	7%
MILLENNIALS	34%	13%	15%	25%	12%	1%
GEN-XERS	29%	10%	7%	28%	16%	9%
BOOMERS	37%	9%	10%	20%	17%	7%
ELDERS	32%	8%	14%	26%	8%	12%

n=582 book readers (at least one book in the past year) | February 3–11, 2015

What's on Today's TVs?

The medium of television is undergoing massive disruption, from the surging number of cable stations to the rapid rise of subscription based internet streaming services.

Barna surveys show the effects of these seismic shifts on TV-watching habits, but when it comes to audiences' tastes and preferences, some things never change: People love comedy (and CBS is apparently very good at making them laugh).

Each generation reports a TV top-three list unique to their content and delivery desires. For example, most of the top shows watched by Elders (ages 70 and older) are dramas on CBS, and the rest indicate at least a preference for content on the "Big Four" television networks (CBS, ABC, NBC, and FOX). More than half (53%) of Elders report watching *NCIS* (CBS), 42 percent tune in to *Blue Bloods* (CBS), 37 percent regularly watch *Castle* (ABC), and about one-third (34%) keep up with *Madam Secretary* (CBS).

Millennials (ages 18 to 30) have broad tastes, watching a combination of comedies, dramas, and "dramedies" that air on network, cable, or internet streaming services. Nearly one in three say they view *The Big Bang Theory* (CBS, 32%), and one in five watch *The Walking Dead* (AMC, 28%), *Orange Is the New Black* (Netflix, 25%), or *Modern Family* (ABC, 22%).

Gen-Xers (ages 31 to 49) share with Millennials an affinity for *The Big Bang Theory* (32%) and *The Walking Dead* (24%), while Boomers (ages 50 to 68) split their loyalties between the younger generations' preference for *The Big Bang Theory* (31%) and the Elders' favorite, *NCIS* (38%).

Criminal Minds (CBS) is a consistent standout and the third most-watched program among all adults, with one in five (21%) saying they view the FBI drama. *The Blacklist* (NBC) also makes a strong showing, especially among Boomers (23%).

Despite its critical success, *Game of Thrones* (HBO) is watched by just 12 percent of adults.

n=1,011 | January 28-February 4, 2016

3 Trends in Movie-Watching

1. Viewers Aren't Watching Oscar Movies

Barna's annual movie-going survey asked Americans whether they had seen the Oscar-nominated shortlist, as well as what other movies they'd seen during the year. Interestingly, at the time of the survey (January 28 to February 4, 2016, in the thick of awards season), the Best Picture nominees were among the least watched of the 27 films surveyed, with the exception of *Mad Max* (21%) and *The Martian* (19%). A small 10 percent of respondents had seen *The Revenant*. The numbers begin to drop off after that, with only 6 percent seeing *Bridge of Spies*. *The Big Short* (5%), *Brooklyn* (4%), Best Picture victor *Spotlight* (3%) and *Room* (2%) all came in under 5 percent each.

If people aren't watching the most critically acclaimed films of the year, they are watching action films. Among the top five most-watched films of 2015, four were action flicks. *Jurassic World* was by far the most matched film of 2015, topping the list with almost 4 in 10 adults (38%) having seen the latest installment in the Jurassic franchise. Next up was *Star Wars: Episode VII—The Force Awakens*, with almost 3 in 10 (29%) adults having seen it, followed closely by *Minions* (27%), *Avengers: Age of Ultron* (27%), and *Furious 7* (25%).

n=1,011 | January 28–February 4, 2016

2. Viewers (of All Faiths) See Big-Screen Bible Adaptations

In recent years, the entertainment sector seems to have turned back to one of its favorite sources: the Bible. It's not surprising that practicing Christians are the group most likely to be aware of and interested in viewing films or shows with Christian content. But the market for faith-driven content is not exclusive to practicing Christians—as long as it's entertaining. Interestingly, Bible-driven movies like *Noah* and *Exodus* drew audiences in roughly equal proportions across all faith segments.

n=1,000 | February 3–11, 2015

3. Viewers Are Choosing Home Over the Theater

Groups most likely to have watched movies in the theater are Millennials, those with an annual income greater than $50,000, adults who have never been married, non-Christians, Hispanic Americans, and residents of the western U.S. On the other hand, while Elders are one of the groups least likely to have attended a movie in the theater, they are the group most likely to have watched a movie at home via cable, broadcast, or satellite television (on average, Elders watched 29 movies this way a year compared to only 21 among the general population). Adults watch, on average, 27 movies via DVD, Blu-Ray, or streaming at home (this is highest among Millennials, who say they watch 34 movies a year this way).

n=1,011 | January 28–February 4, 2016

Porn in the Digital Age: 10 Trends 💬👤

Pornography is not new, but the digital age has made it ubiquitous and more accessible than ever before. Smartphones and high-speed internet connections have fundamentally changed the landscape of pornography, and ushered it into the cultural mainstream where it enjoys increasingly widespread acceptance.

In Barna's landmark study *The Porn Phenomenon*, conducted in partnership with Josh McDowell Ministry, thousands of American teens, young adults and older adults were interviewed about their views on and use of pornography. Here are 10 of the most compelling findings:

1. There Is Growing Acceptance of Porn, Particularly Among Young Americans

Perhaps the most sobering finding from the study is the reality of how accepted viewing porn has become in our culture, particularly among teens and young adults. Around half of adults 25 and older say viewing porn is wrong (54%); and among teens and young adults 13-24, only a third say viewing porn is wrong (32%). This attitude toward porn among younger Americans is confirmed by how they talk about porn with their friends: The vast majority reports that conversations with their friends about porn are neutral, accepting, or even encouraging. They generally assume most people look at porn at least on occasion, and the morality of porn is rarely discussed or even considered. Just

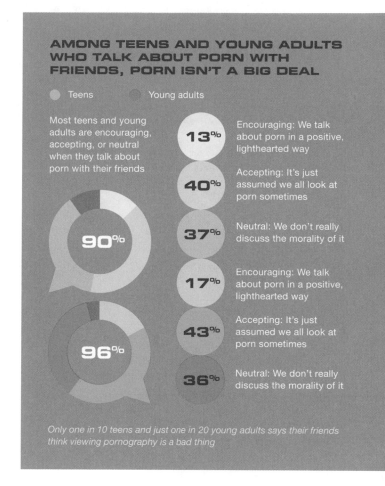

AMONG TEENS AND YOUNG ADULTS WHO TALK ABOUT PORN WITH FRIENDS, PORN ISN'T A BIG DEAL

● Teens   ● Young adults

Most teens and young adults are encouraging, accepting, or neutral when they talk about porn with their friends

13% Encouraging: We talk about porn in a positive, lighthearted way

40% Accepting: It's just assumed we all look at porn sometimes

37% Neutral: We don't really discuss the morality of it

90%

17% Encouraging: We talk about porn in a positive, lighthearted way

43% Accepting: It's just assumed we all look at porn sometimes

36% Neutral: We don't really discuss the morality of it

96%

Only one in 10 teens and just one in 20 young adults says their friends think viewing pornography is a bad thing

n=541 teens and young adults who talk to friends about porn | July 20-23, 2015 | © Josh McDowell Ministry

one in 10 teens and one in 20 young adults report talking with their friends about porn in a disapproving way.

2. Opinions About What Constitutes Porn Are Varied

"I know it when I see it," Supreme Court Justice Potter Stewart famously said when he was asked to define obscenity. His statement demonstrates a perennial problem: It is notoriously difficult to define pornography. What counts as sexually explicit material is both highly subjective and highly contested, and this was true in Barna's study.

When teens, young adults, and adults are asked an open-ended question about what makes something "cross the line" into porn, the responses are varied and cover *form* (content) and *function* (intention for use). The top four indicators are all within a 2 percent range, the most popular being something sexually explicit (17%). Just as common are when something displays a sexual act (16%) and sexual intercourse (16%), followed closely by whether something intends to arouse the viewer (15%) or contains full nudity (11%).

3. One in Three Americans Seek Out Porn at Least Once a Month

Measuring porn usage can be difficult, because living in a hyper-sexualized media culture means catching sight of explicit images with little or no effort. People often come across images they never intended to see through multiple inputs. That's why it was important to distinguish between those who "view" porn, and those who "seek it out." In other words, intention matters a lot. When looking at it this way, focusing exclusively on intentional viewing, Barna found that 6 percent of people aged 13 and older view porn daily, 14 percent view porn weekly, 13 percent view it once or twice a month, and 18 percent view it less often. By comparison, people report simply coming across porn daily (12%), weekly (21%), once or twice a month (19%), or less often (32%). Half (49%) say they never seek out porn, and 17 percent say they have never come across it.

4. Age, Gender, and Faith Practice Are the Three Biggest Factors in Frequent Porn Use

When looking closely at frequent porn users (those who seek out porn daily, weekly, and monthly), we begin to see patterns emerge according to age, gender, and faith practice. To begin with, men use porn more frequently than women by a wide margin. Twice as many male teens and young adults use porn than female teens and young adults (67% compared to 33%), and four times as many male adults 25+ use porn than female adults (47% compared to 12%). Practicing Christians are more than three times less likely to use porn than other teens and adults (13% compared to 42%), and young adults (57%) are much more likely than both teens (37%) or adults 25+ (29%) to be a frequent porn user.

5. Young Adults Use More Porn—and Are Less Likely to Say It's Bad for Society

Of the generational groups, young adults 18-24 are the most frequent porn users. Almost six in 10 young adults (57%) seek out porn either daily, weekly, or monthly. This

Teenage girls and young women are significantly more likely to actively seek out porn than women over age 25. More than half (57%) of American women ages 25 and under ever seek out porn and one-third (33%) seek it out at least monthly.

is compared to a little over one-third of teens (37%), and almost 3 in 10 adults 25+ (29%). They are also the least likely to say that porn is very bad for society (14%). The next closest are Gen-Xers at 24 percent, but the largest gap is a 23 percent differential between young adults and Boomers (37% compared to 14%). Like teens (16%), young adults (17%) are also the least likely to say porn is "somewhat bad" for society.

6. Teens and Young Adults View Not Recycling as More Immoral Than Viewing Porn

When asked to rank a series of action statements (lying, over-eating, stealing, etc.) according to a five-point scale: "always OK," "usually OK," "neither wrong nor OK," "usually wrong," and "always wrong," teens and young adults rank "not recycling" as more immoral than viewing pornographic images. Combining the percentages of those who chose always and usually wrong for each statement, theft (taking something that belongs to someone else) ranked first at almost nine in 10 (88%). Not recycling ranked #4 at 56 percent, and porn was all the way down at ninth with only a third (32%) of teens and young adults ranking it as morally wrong.

n=2,001 (1,188 age 25+, 813 age 13-24) | July–August 2015 | © Josh McDowell Ministry

7. Most Porn Users Say Using Porn Doesn't Bother Them

When asked their feelings about porn use, a majority of adults (52%) say it doesn't really bother them. Gen-Xers (54%) are the most unbothered by their porn

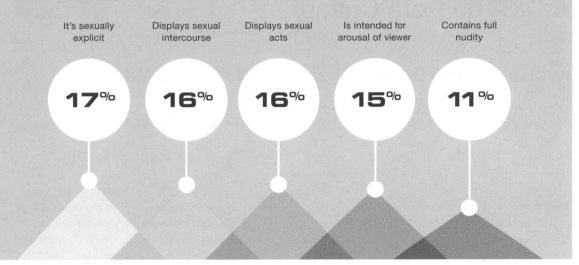

5 SIGNS IT'S PORN

The following are the top five indicators for people that something has "crossed the line" into porn

n=541 teens and young adults
who talk to friends about
pornography | July 20-23, 2015
© Josh McDowell Ministry

It's sexually explicit	Displays sexual intercourse	Displays sexual acts	Is intended for arousal of viewer	Contains full nudity
17%	16%	16%	15%	11%

usage. Young adults (51%) and teens (50%) follow closely, with Elders and Boomers appearing the most uncomfortable with their use (47% each).

8. Very Few Adults Feel a Sense of Guilt When They Use Porn

Sociopaths aside, human beings tend to feel a sense of guilt when they do something they believe is wrong. When asked about how comfortable they feel about their porn use, only 15 percent of adults overall report feeling much guilt. Generationally, teens are the most likely age segment to experience feelings of guilt (38%), along with young adults (21%), followed by Boomers (17%), and Gen-Xers (15%).

Interestingly, minorities (24% nonwhite compared to 11% white), practicing Christians (29% compared with 12% of non-practicing Christians), and conservatives (25% compared to 13% of liberals) are significantly more likely to experience a sense of guilt compared to others surveyed.

9. Most Porn Users Are OK With How Much Porn They Use—But Practicing Christians Are Divided

Predictably, practicing Christians who seek out porn at least on occasion are much less comfortable than the general population with their porn use. About two in five say they are comfortable (39%), compared to nearly seven in 10 among all teens and adults (68%). They are also about twice as likely to say they'd like to stop (40%) than to say they'd like to use less (21%). Among the general population of teens and adults, 14 percent say they want to use porn less, and 18 percent would rather not use it at all.

10. Few Adults Are Actively Trying to Stop Using Porn

There are a number of effective approaches to combating porn use (accountability groups, counseling, filtering software, etc.), but very few adults have either tried or are actively fighting to break their habit. When the general population are asked whether they have tried to stop using porn, but have been unable to (or started again), 9 percent say so. The rate doubles among practicing Christians (16%) but remains fairly low overall. When asked whether they are currently trying to stop using porn, 9 percent of the general population agree, while a much larger 19 percent of practicing Christians say they are working to kick their habit.

"For now, porn is everywhere and is likely to stay that way, particularly considering its widespread acceptance and demand," Barna editor-in-chief Roxanne Stone says. "This presents a significant challenge to the Church, and we must respond."

A Q&A on Porn Culture

with Jefferson Bethke

Bethke is a speaker and the author of the books Jesus > Religion *and* It's Not What You Think. *Jeff makes YouTube videos and hosts a podcast with his wife, Alyssa. They live in Maui with their daughter, Kinsley.*

You've talked about today's teens and young adults being the most "exploited and exploitive" generation ever. How do you see porn contributing to their exploitation? What results do you think we'll see if the trend continues?

For starters, we are being exploited by advertisers and people behind the websites who make billions off our addiction, which in my opinion is immoral in itself (similar to drug dealers making money by supplying people with something that ruins their lives). But our generation is also exploiting each other all the way down the ranks through sexting, exchanging nude photos, and perpetuating the culture and need that leads others to do things like human trafficking and illegal exploitation.

One of your videos connects porn and human trafficking, pointing out the irony that Millennials fight sex trafficking—and consume porn—more than any other generation. In conversations you've had with porn users, does considering the possibility of exploitation and abuse seem to make a difference?

It does seem to make a difference. One thing the Millennial generation hates is hypocrisy. And there isn't anything much more hypocritical than fighting trafficking while porn grows as one of the biggest consumer industries in the world. It's simple supply and demand. The demand that traffickers supply starts with pornography.

and Audrey Assad

Assad is an author, speaker, producer, and critically lauded songwriter and musician. She releases music she calls "soundtracks for prayer" on Fortunate Fall Records, a label she co-owns with her husband.

There is a persistent belief in the culture and in the Church that young women are not at risk of sexual addiction or even temptation in this area. What are your thoughts on this?

I think gender stereotypes run rampant inside Christianity. Femininity is traditionally associated with things like purity and modesty. Because of these stereotypes and how deeply they are ingrained in the Church, women do not feel free to confess or speak publicly about lust, sexual addictions, pornography, masturbation, or anything of the sort. This perpetuates a cycle of shame and bondage and silence for the women who are affected, and in turn reinforces the erroneous idea that women do not struggle with things like this—the idea that it's a "guy problem" remains the status quo because women do not feel safe to speak—they feel they will not be seen as feminine or womanly.

What changes would you like to see in how the Church talks about and handles sex addiction, generally and among women?

I would love to see pornography addiction destigmatized and stripped of any unnecessary stereotyping in terms of gender. I personally believe that pornography addiction is proof of humanity's search for God (just as, arguably, all sin is). If Christians stop treating it like a secret to be ashamed of and begin to confront and confess it honestly, dig down to the roots of it, and proactively address the heart issues underneath it, I think real progress could be made.

**BARNA
TAKES**

The Sexting Crisis

Roxanne Stone,
Barna Group,
Editor-in-Chief

Teens and young adults are living in an environment where porn is more acceptable—and more ubiquitous—than ever before. When they talk to their friends about pornography, the conversations are cavalier. Only 11 percent of teens and just 5 percent of young adults say their friends think viewing porn is bad. The vast majority say their conversations with friends around porn are either neutral, accepting, or even encouraging. A plurality say it's just assumed we all look at porn sometimes. When it comes to watching pornography, teens and young adults aren't getting accountability from their friends—they are getting peer pressure.

And it is into this context—a context in which viewing porn is, simply put, an acceptable reality—that a new and particularly insidious form of pornography has emerged. A pornography that is no longer distant and delivered. But, instead, is personal and created.

We are calling this "porn 2.0."

Porn 2.0 is user-created—often shared with a known person: a friend or significant other or a potential romantic interest. You know what I'm talking about: sexting, Snapchatting nude pictures, posting provocative Instagram photos.

In many ways, porn 2.0 has sneaked in under the radar, perhaps because many don't consider it porn at all. Teenagers, who are more likely to think everything is porn than other generations, make an exception when it comes to sexting.

When you look at teen sexting and the motivation behind it, it's important to see it as a sort of replication of broader social behavior. Teens and young adults have seen this behavior—this sort of "self-pornification"—rewarded when celebrity icons have done it. Look at Kim Kardashian, who basically broke the internet with her recent nude photos. Young people have come of age in an increasingly pornified culture that rewards the pornographic impulse and encourages seductive images meant to market oneself.

There is also the truth that teens and young adults are simply on their phones more. They have become used to viewing pornography via their phone or an app—more so than any other generation. So it is not a surprise that the blurring of lines between pornography and personal happens—it's all the same device, right? How easy it is to begin to view a nude image of a stranger with the same eyes as one views a nude image of a girlfriend!

But is porn 2.0 actually porn? Can we really consider sexting with a romantic interest on the same plane as watching unknown actors have sex? Or looking at nude pictures of strangers?

Why not? If our general definition of pornography is a sexual image used for personal arousal, then is our goal in getting a nude picture of a boyfriend or girlfriend any different?

Porn 2.0 offers much of the same promise as traditional pornography: a disembodied, visual experience without the attachments or intimacy of sex. And there is variety here as well, because the truth is sexting often happens well before a relationship begins. In those early "get to know you" stages, it's not at all unlikely that a person is sexting with multiple potential partners at any one time.

Even if we all agree together to call sexting and Snapchatting nude pictures a form of pornography, we must also acknowledge together that porn 2.0 is not just porn reimagined in a new format.

Porn 2.0 is a new step in pornography because it is personal. And it is a particularly dangerous step because it invites us to not only sexualize our relationships—which we've already been doing for a long time—it also invites us to disembody and therefore detach from our relationships. In short, to objectify them.

You have a crush on a girl? With a little bit of persuasion, you can convince her to send you a topless photo. You get to experience her body—and probably personal pleasure—without intimacy, without physical proximity, without any of the embodied risks of physical sex. You give nothing of yourself.

Of course, you have asked something of her. And this is another danger of porn 2.0. Those who are sending photos begin to feel their own sense of validation and self-worth coming from the objectification and the distribution of their bodies. "If I want him to like me, I have to do this. All the other girls would do this."

I know I'm beginning to gender this, to assume that the requester is a boy and the sender is a girl. But the stats bear this out: Barna found that girls are both more likely to send and to receive nude images. At first, this seemed odd. Almost as if someone wasn't telling the truth; if girls are saying they send more images than guys and they receive more images than guys, then who are they sending and receiving from?

The more I thought about this, though—and the more I reckoned it with my own experiences and those of my friends—the more I realized what's happening. Men are the initiators. They are the ones asking for the pictures. They are also the ones often sending the pictures.

However, not all guys are engaging in this. There are plenty of men who aren't asking for or sending nude photos. They are choosing not to do this and so they are, primarily, immune to the phenomenon.

Girls, on the other hand, are indiscriminately targeted. They may not initiate, but they will inevitably be forced to respond to a request for a photo or to a photo showing up in their text. Whether they want to engage or not, women will experience this reality.

Porn 2.0 may feel like a sideways conversation from the broader concerns of pornography. But porn 2.0 is destructive. It's destructive to our ideas of healthy sexuality, our body images and self-confidence, our fledgling relationships, and our call to live in intimate, embodied presence with one another.

The Porn Crisis Is Here

Barna

THE PORN PHENOMENON

THE IMPACT OF PORNOGRAPHY IN THE DIGITAL AGE

A Barna Report
Produced in Partnership with
Josh McDowell Ministry
(a Cru Ministry)

What's included

- Statistics on porn use among key age and faith segments
- An overview of scholarly research on porn's effects
- Barna analysis of the cultural factors at play
- Insights from experts and ministry leaders
- More resources at SetFreeSummit.org

Pornography is pervasive—permeating our culture from shop windows to smartphone apps. Once kept literally under wraps, porn is now a standard feature of everyday life. The ubiquity of porn today—and the unwillingness or inability of local Christian communities to have meaningful conversations about it—has precipitated a crisis the Church can no longer afford to ignore. Produced in partnership with Josh McDowell Ministry (Josh.org), *The Porn Phenomenon* is an assessment of the cultural place of pornography today, based on existing social science research and nearly 3,000 new interviews with American teens, adults, and Protestant youth and senior pastors. This is an important tool for pastors, ministry leaders, and parents, and an invaluable resource to help those in your congregation, organization, family, and friends.

After Hours

Thirty-six percent of Americans say they spend most of their time at work. What about the rest of their hours?

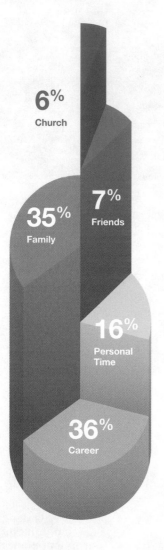

6%
Church

35%
Family

7%
Friends

16%
Personal Time

36%
Career

n=1,000 | June 25–July 1, 2013

Americans Say They Regularly...

● Engage in physical exercise ● Set aside time for relaxation
● Pray and/or meditate ● Set aside time for personal hobbies
● Spend leisure time with close friends

45%   **54%**   37%   44%   42%

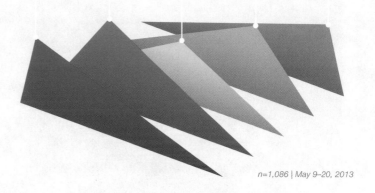

n=1,086 | May 9–20, 2013

They Make Sure to Set Aside Time Daily for...

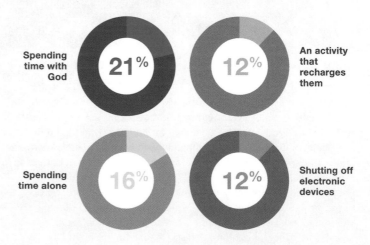

Spending time with God — **21%**

An activity that recharges them — **12%**

Spending time alone — **16%**

Shutting off electronic devices — **12%**

n=1,000 | June 25–July 1, 2013

How Do Americans Recharge?

n=1,000 | June 25–July 1, 2013

58%	21%	16%	46%	42%	48%	15%	49%	18%	20%
Watch TV / movies	Surf the web	Check social media	Read	Talk with friends	Nap	Meditate	Exercise	Have a special drink	Eat a special food

Technology Time
Americans are spending a good portion of their leisure time in front of a screen

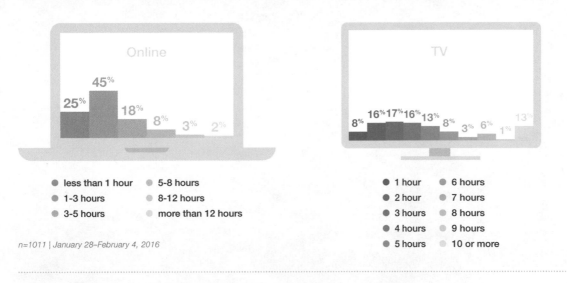

Online

45%
25%
18%
8%
3%
2%

- less than 1 hour
- 1-3 hours
- 3-5 hours
- 5-8 hours
- 8-12 hours
- more than 12 hours

TV

8% 16% 17% 16% 13% 8% 3% 6% 1% 13%

- 1 hour
- 2 hour
- 3 hours
- 4 hours
- 5 hours
- 6 hours
- 7 hours
- 8 hours
- 9 hours
- 10 or more

n=1011 | January 28–February 4, 2016

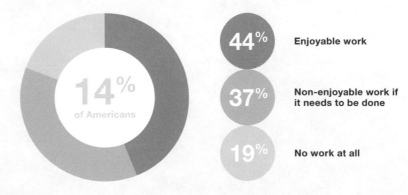

Fourteen percent of Americans set aside a day of rest. Yet most still find some work to do on these days.

14% of Americans

44% Enjoyable work

37% Non-enjoyable work if it needs to be done

19% No work at all

n=1,000 | June 25–July 1, 2013

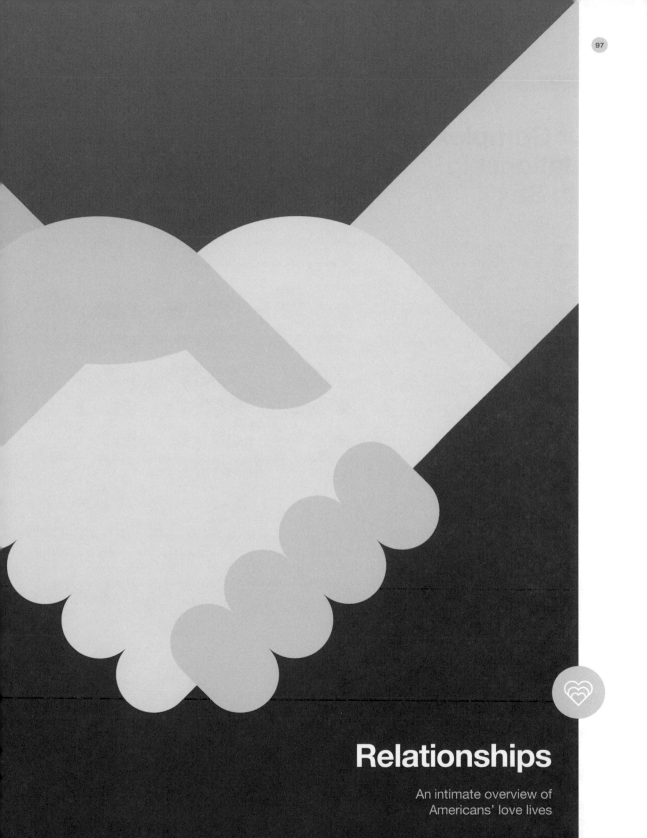

Relationships

An intimate overview of
Americans' love lives

Our Complex Relationship with Sex

What do Americans think about sex? Specifically, what kind of ethics inform their views about the purpose and practice of sex?

Half of American adults (50%) agree strongly that "choosing not to have sex outside of marriage is healthy." But generational differences are significant. Six in 10 Elders (59%) agree strongly with this statement, compared to 53 percent of Boomers, 49 percent of Gen-Xers, and 43 percent of Millennials.

Practicing Christians (72%) are almost twice as likely as adults of no faith (38%) to say that choosing not to have sex outside marriage is a healthy choice. Women (56%) are also more likely than men (43%) to hold this view. Compared to those who have never been married (41%), people who are married (53%) and, somewhat surprisingly, cohabiting adults (49%) are more likely to strongly agree with the statement.

It may be that these differences of opinion spring at least in part from confusion or ambivalence about the purpose of sex. When U.S. adults are asked to choose one or more phrases from a list of options that summarizes what sex is for, not everyone agrees.

Among all American adults, the most common answers given when asked about the purpose of sex were "to express intimacy between two people who love each other" (63%), "to reproduce/ to have children" (60%), and "to connect

Views of Traditional Christian Sexual Ethics *n=1,000 | August 24–26, 2015*

Traditional Christian sexual ethics teach that sex should only be within a marriage between a man and a woman. Which of the following words, if any, best describe your opinion of those ethics?
(Respondents could choose up to three options.)

% among U.S. adults, by faith segment

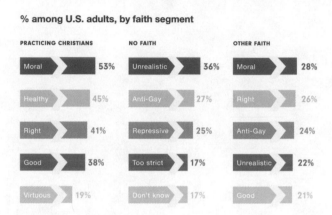

PRACTICING CHRISTIANS		NO FAITH		OTHER FAITH	
Moral	53%	Unrealistic	36%	Moral	28%
Healthy	45%	Anti-Gay	27%	Right	26%
Right	41%	Repressive	25%	Anti-Gay	24%
Good	38%	Too strict	17%	Unrealistic	22%
Virtuous	19%	Don't know	17%	Good	21%

with another person in an enjoyable way" (45%). There are disparities—for instance, between generational cohorts. Overall, Elders and Boomers tend to share a stronger consensus about the purpose of sex. Clear majorities among the older generations say sex is for procreation (79% Elders; 71% Boomers), expressing intimacy between two people who love each other (68% Elders; 73% Boomers), or uniting a man and woman in marriage (62% Elders; 50% Boomers).

The two younger adult generations are much less likely to embrace these traditional views of sex. Most Gen-Xers and Millennials continue to believe conventional ideas of sex: that it is to express intimacy between two people who love each other (57% Gen-Xers; 56% Millennials) or to procreate (52% Gen-Xers; 51% Millennials). However, the notion that intercourse should unite a man and woman in marriage is endorsed by just one-third of Gen-Xers and Millennials.

Nearly half of younger generations say that the purpose of sex is to connect with another person in an enjoyable way (44% Gen-Xers; 49% Millennials), though this sentiment is not much stronger than it is among older adults. Notably, Millennials are much more likely than older adults to say the purpose of sex is self-expression and personal fulfillment (41%).

Gender seems to play a role in one's view of sex. Seven out of 10 women (69%) say the purpose of sex is to express intimacy, but a smaller majority of men, 57 percent, believe the same. Conversely, men are more likely than women to indicate sex unites a man and woman in marriage (45% men; 39% women) or satisfies a biological need other than procreation (43% men; 36% women).

Practicing Christians (56%) are more than twice as likely as those with no faith (25%) to say the purpose of sex is to unite a man and woman in marriage. At the same time, those with no faith are much more prone than practicing Christians to say sex is for connecting with another person in an enjoyable way (60% no faith; 36% practicing Christians) or for self-expression or personal fulfillment (46% no faith; 26% practicing Christians). There are also notable differences between these groups and Americans who identify with a religious faith other than Christianity. For instance, those of other faiths are more likely to say the purpose of sex is to unite people of any gender in marriage (32%) than the other groups (23% no faith; 15% practicing Christians), or to satisfy a biological need (46% compared to 33% no faith; 32% practicing Christians).

Traditional Sexual Ethics: Moral, Good, and Unrealistic

Barna also asked American adults their opinion of traditional Christian sexual ethics, which teaches "that sex should only be within a marriage between a man and a woman." Among all adults, the top five descriptions of this phrase are "moral" (36%), "good" (28%), "healthy" (27%), "right" (27%), and "unrealistic" (22%). Other characterizations include "anti-gay" (16%), "too strict" (13%), "repressive" (13%), "virtuous" (12%), "unenlightened" (9%), "wrong" (7%), and "damaging" (6%).

Generationally, there is again greater consensus among older adults than among younger Americans on this matter. The top five descriptions among Gen-Xers and Millennials are similar to their older counterparts, but smaller proportions share the traditional point of view on traditional Christian sexual ethics. For example, "moral" is the number-one choice of both Millennials and Elders, but the younger cohort (26%) is half as likely as their elders (51%) to choose this option. Also, Millennials were the only generational segment that had "anti-gay" (19%)

Though it seems many Americans are hesitant to connect the purposes of sex explicitly to marriage, most adults age 25 and older (89%) still say it is usually always wrong to have a romantic relationship with someone other than a spouse.

in their top five, as well as the only one not listing "right" (16%) among their top five.

Unsurprisingly, Christians hold more positive opinions than non-Christians when it comes to traditional Christian beliefs about sexual ethics. On the other hand, adults who say they are not believers (atheists, agnostics, or unaffiliated) view Christian sexual ethics in a distinctly negative light: Just 11 percent believe traditional ethics are "moral," and that definition ranks ninth among their preferences—the highest of all positive descriptors. Otherwise, non-believers say that such sexual ethics are unrealistic (36%), anti-gay (27%), repressive (25%), too strict (17%), or that they aren't sure what to make of it (17%).

It is interesting to note that people who hold to faiths other than Christianity (such as Jews, Muslims, Buddhists, and so on) are likely to embrace a mix of favorable and unfavorable views of traditional sexual ethics. Their top five descriptors include "moral" (28%), "right" (26%), "anti-gay" (24%), "unrealistic" (22%), and "good" (21%).

"The big story here is how little everyone agrees on when it comes to the purpose of sex," Roxanne Stone, editor-in-chief of Barna, says.

"There's never been a shortage of conversations and cultural imagination around sex, but this current lack of consensus points to a growing ambiguity and tension over its place in society and in the individual's life."

n=1,000 | August 24–26, 2015

Home Life Is the New Dating Life

A recent Barna study asked Americans about their views on cohabitation—the pros and cons, motivations for and effects of living together prior to marriage. The majority of adults (65%) either strongly or somewhat agree it's a good idea to live with one's significant other before marriage, compared to one-third (35%) who either strongly or somewhat disagree.

Though it may seem that couples would live together primarily for convenience or cost-saving, almost all adults see it as a rite of passage in the path to marriage. The idea of living with one's significant other before getting married for the sake of convenience (9%) or to save rent (5%) isn't as persuasive as the value of testing compatibility (84%).

The most prominent cohabitation detractors are religious groups. Among those who believe living with one's significant other before getting married is not a good idea, the biggest factor is religious

(34%). The expectation of abstinence prior to marriage is a major driver here; 28 percent chose "I don't believe people should have sex before getting married" as their biggest reason for believing cohabitation is a bad idea. Of lesser importance were issues of practicality (16%), valuing family and tradition (12%), and other reasons (10%).

Almost six in 10 (57%) either currently live with their boyfriend/girlfriend or have previously done so—a number very close to the 65 percent who believe it is a good idea. Older, conservative, and more religious (Christian or otherwise) Americans are the least likely to have ever cohabited. Surprisingly, Millennials are one of the groups least likely to cohabit. Younger, less religious and more liberal Americans are more likely to have lived with a significant other before marriage. Interestingly, church attenders are among this group, a fact that demonstrates how pervasive this cultural shift has been.

Though the debate has raged over whether cohabitation reduces or increases the pressure of marriage, it appears that among those who have actually done it, there was no major effect either way. The majority (62%) believes that living together did not affect the pressure to get married at all, and those who say it reduced (19%) or increased (18%) the pressure to get married were evenly split.

While most Americans favor or participate in cohabitation, they are a little more divided when it comes to their own children choosing to move in with a significant other. More than four in 10 adults (44%) would be OK with their child cohabiting before marriage, and four in 10 would not be OK. When it comes to the strongest views, respondents were more likely to say "definitely not" (24%) than "absolutely" (16%).

n=1,011 | January 28–February 4, 2016

Living Together

n=1,097 | April 7–14, 2016

Most American adults agree that it is a good idea to live with one's significant other before getting married

65% **35**%
Agree   Disagree

... and most adults either currently or have previously lived with their boyfriend/girlfriend

57%

The major reason for cohabitation is to test compatibility:

 **84**%

Though most Americans say cohabitation neither reduced nor increased the pressure to get married:

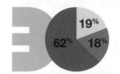 **19**% **18**% **62**%

Reduced pressure

Increased pressure

Did not affect the pressure

Religion plays a major role in determining views about cohabitation. The biggest reason for why living with one's significant other before getting married is not a good idea is related to religion:

- Religious reasons
- Family/tradition (e.g. my parents would kill me)
- I don't believe people should have sex before getting married
- It isn't practical/doesn't make sense
- Other

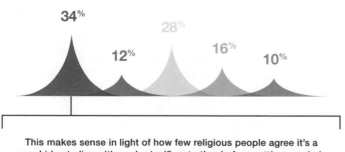

34%   12%   28%   16%   10%

This makes sense in light of how few religious people agree it's a good idea to live with one's significant other before getting married.
(% of those who strongly and somewhat agree)

6%	35%	41%	88%
Evangelicals	Born Again	Practicing Christian	No Faith

Age and ideology also play a key role in determining views, with older and more conservative adults less approving of cohabitation:
(% of those who strongly and somewhat agree)

72%   69%
Millennials (18-31)   Gen-Xers (32-50)

63%   36%
Boomers (51-69)   Elders (70+)

37%   86%
Conservative   Liberal

Let's Get Serious About Cohabitation

Roxanne Stone,
Barna Group,
Editor-in-Chief

America is well beyond the tipping point when it comes to cohabitation. Living together before marriage is no longer an exception, but instead has become an accepted and expected milestone of adulthood. A growing number of parents—nearly half of Gen-Xers and Boomers, and more than half of Millennials—want and expect their children to live with a significant other before getting married.

The institution of marriage has undergone significant shifts in the last century. What was once seen as primarily an economic and procreational partnership has become an exercise in finding your soulmate. Where once extended families lived within a handful of miles from each other, now the nuclear family often strikes out on its own. Such shifts placed a new emphasis on marriage as the core of family life and revealed fault lines in many marriages. These pressures, along with a number of other social phenomena, including women's growing economic independence, led to unprecedented divorce rates in the second half of the 20th century. As a result, many of today's young people who are currently contemplating marriage see it as a risky endeavor. Living together has become a *de facto* way of testing the relationship before making a final commitment.

Religious Americans have been slower to adopt this perspective. As in most aspects of family life, religious people tend toward a more conservative or traditional viewpoint. American Christians—as well as those of other faiths—celebrate marriage as a key religious ritual and see it as a lifelong commitment. Importantly, that commitment is consummated by sex. The assumption of premarital sex in a cohabiting relationship precludes most religious Americans from endorsing it.

However, religious leaders will be wise to notice that a growing number of their constituents—particularly in younger demographics—accept cohabitation as the norm. As with premarital sex, the arguments against cohabitation will seem increasingly antiquated as the general culture accepts and promotes it. Religious leaders will need to promote the countercultural trend by celebrating the reasons to wait—rather than trying to find evidence for why it's wrong (because such tangible, measurable evidence may not exist).

What are the spiritual reasons for waiting? How does waiting promote better discipleship? Better marriages? Better family life? These are questions that young people, in particular, will need answers for in order to resist the trend toward cohabitation.

Can Men and Women Just Be Friends?

Today's world demands that men and women interact at unprecedented levels. They are co-workers, friends, supervisors, partners, and more. The social narrative has often been that men and women cannot be in a relationship without sexual tension getting in the way. However, most Americans' lived experience does not bear that out. The majority of Americans say they have never felt unspoken romantic tension with someone of the opposite sex. Of course, there are understandable exceptions: Younger Americans and those who are single have experienced more sexual tension. The most likely relationship for anyone to feel such sexual tension: friendships, both with a close friend and a casual one.

Have you ever felt there was unspoken romantic tension with someone of the opposite sex in the following contexts?

● All adults ● Millennials ● Married ● Single

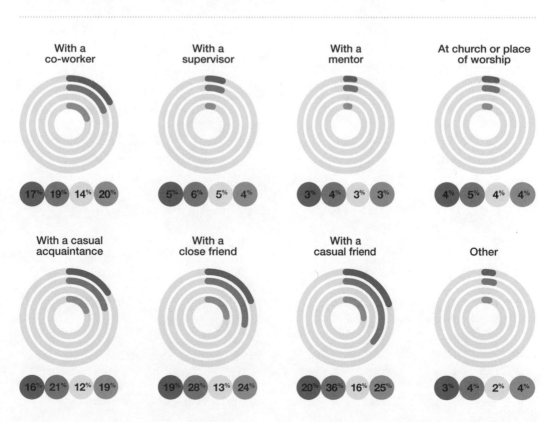

With a co-worker	With a supervisor	With a mentor	At church or place of worship
17% 19% 14% 20%	5% 6% 5% 4%	3% 4% 3% 3%	4% 5% 4% 4%

With a casual acquaintance	With a close friend	With a casual friend	Other
16% 21% 12% 19%	19% 28% 13% 24%	20% 36% 16% 25%	3% 4% 2% 4%

n=1,025 | April 29–May 1, 2015

Community

How do you connect with the
world next door?

Americans Are Putting Down Roots

Contrary to the oft-touted notion of the American "nomad," it appears that, in actuality, Americans tend to stay put. Mobility in the United States has declined over the long term, and most adults (59% according to a Barna survey) either never plan to move or aren't sure if they ever will move.

When asked how much longer they plan to live in their current city or town, Millennials are significantly more likely than older generations to say they plan to move in the short-term. They are at least twice as likely to say they plan to

stay for "less than a year" (14%, compared to 6% of the general population) or just "another 1 to 4 years" (28%, compared to 16% of the general population). Of course, younger people often move for college or early career shifts. They are also less likely to have children, own homes, or have established institutional or relational connections.

As Americans get older and settle down, they tend to stay put. Twelve percent of Boomers and 6 percent of Elders have no intentions to move for at least another decade. But many more Boomers and Elders are very likely to remain in their current city indefinitely; 39 percent of Boomers and 63 percent of Elders say they never plan to move. The reasons that drive Millennials to be mobile are no longer pertinent to those in life stages of career stability or retirement.

Among adults who were not born in their current city or town, the most influential factor in their decision to move was "family" (42%). Career is the second-most cited reason people move to a new city, with nearly three in 10 Americans saying they moved to their current location for "work" (28%). The next most common factors are "the city itself" (9%) and "education" (4%).

Among age groups, "education" is nearly four times as important for Millennials. "Work" is highest among Gen-Xers, and "family" is the greatest moving motivation among Boomers.

Most Americans Are Not Planning to Leave Their Current City

- All Adults
- Millennials
- Gen-Xers
- Boomers
- Elders

I don't ever plan to move

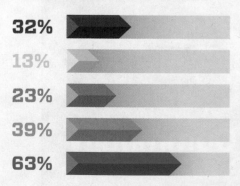

32%
13%
23%
39%
63%

I don't know

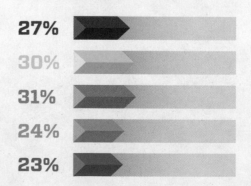

27%
30%
31%
24%
23%

n=1,000 | February 3–11, 2015

Home Is Where the Relationships Are

With new stages of life come changing priorities—including the people, places, and opportunities Americans want nearby. For Millennials, work is the most important thing to have in proximity. (Gen-Xers, Elders, and, to a lesser extent, Boomers want to live near a hospital.) The pressing concerns of life stages, from job hunting in younger years to failing health among senior citizens, are at work whenever people choose a home.

As people age, they want to be closer to family and church; the data shows a difference of 10 to 20 percentage points between Millennials and Elders in these categories.

Proximity to work is also less important with age. For example, three times as many Gen-Xers (31%) as Elders (8%) say it's important to live within five miles of work.

Interest in specific community activities and recreation also shifts with the generations. An emphasis on being near to restaurants and entertainment declines among Boomers (22%) compared to 28 percent for Millennials, Gen-Xers, and Elders. Thirteen percent of Elders are very concerned with being near parks and the outdoors, while a quarter of Millennials and Gen-Xers (24% each) see it as important.

Taking miles and maps out of the question, what do people *appreciate* about the places they call home? Millennials (3%) are the least likely generation to name their church or community of faith; one in 10 among Boomers and Gen-Xers (11% each) and 15 percent of Elders do. About one in seven Millennials (15%) and Gen-Xers (14%) most appreciate economic opportunities where they live, compared to 6 percent of Boomers and 4 percent of Elders. Friendship is a top factor among all adults (19%) and the most appreciated by Millennials (27%). Some evidence of this relational emphasis: More than four in 10 respondents report being within five miles of their friends and family (44%) and an additional one in five (22%) live six to 10 miles away from family and friends.

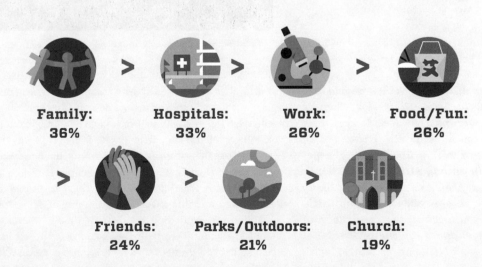

It's Very Important to Me That I Live Within 5 Miles of ...

Family: 36% > Hospitals: 33% > Work: 26% > Food/Fun: 26%

> Friends: 24% > Parks/Outdoors: 21% > Church: 19%

n=1,000 | February 3–11, 2015

A Q&A on Life and Faith in the City

with
Bryan Loritts

Bryan Loritts is the lead pastor of Abundant Life Christian Fellowship in Silicon Valley. Previously, he was cofounder and lead pastor of Fellowship Memphis in Memphis, Tenn, and pastor for preaching and mission at Trinity Grace Church in New York City. He is the president of the Kainos Movement, an organization aimed at establishing the multiethnic church in America as the new normal. Loritts has written several books, including: God on Paper, Letters to a Birmingham Jail, Right Color/Wrong Culture, A Cross-Shaped Gospel, *and* Saving the Saved.

Some of the top things people love about where they live include friendships (19%) and work and economic opportunities (10%). Church ranks lower (10%), especially among Millennials (3%). In cities, people are also more likely to be unchurched or of no faith. How can churches engage and offer support for the professional and social lives of residents?

I would exhort churches in major cities to find a way to offer people an incredible sense of community. Of course, every church should do that, but I think it's a heightened need in most cities. I moved to Los Angeles in December of 1995, fresh out of college. I was 3,000 miles away from home, and one of the first things I felt a driving need for was community. I ended up being a part of a church, and the glue for me was this awesome small group; in fact, we still get together annually. There was this shared commonality of being transplants, seeking more education, trying to figure out life in a new city. I think that church really thrived because it offered community.

Another disconnect I've felt is that city churches don't often know what to do with high-powered or highly educated individuals. Is having them hand out bulletins before service the best way to use them? The church has got to do a better job of saying, "We've got this incredible pool of people who have high capacity—how do we leverage that for the Kingdom? How do we train them to be able to leverage those gifts?" When I would stand to preach in New York City, I was mindful that I was going to be preaching to some of the brightest of the bright, people who graduated from Princeton, Harvard, and so on. There was much more of a cognitive gear from a preaching perspective, an air of, "Tell me something I haven't heard before." If a church doesn't do that in places like the Bay Area or Manhattan, those people are probably going to lose interest pretty quickly.

Barna data shows that young people are gravitating more toward urban areas and city centers. Why do you think that is? What does that mean for churches?

This is an interesting conversation. I look at it through my cultural lens of being African-American, and I see a disconnect. Black people and minorities are not as enamored with cities as the urban young white hipster is. Many of us grew up in the city, in impoverished neighborhoods. This mass migration of white young people moving into the city comes with a cost: displaced and, in many cases, embittered minorities. My life's work is multiethnic ministry, and I think it's important to say that this love affair with the city is really for those who can *afford* to live in the city—and typically, those who can afford to live in the city happen to be white.

Additionally, when we talk about Christians who are moving into an impoverished neighborhood to do incarnational ministry or live in missional community, we're usually talking about young white people. If you're planting or leading a church in the city, especially a city that is experiencing some form of gentrification, and your church is not addressing those issues, then your church is complicit in what I would call "spiritual colonization." You are becoming a part of the problem and not the solution. We have to deal with and address all of the complexities that come with the city. In most cities, that means asking, What does it look like to be multiethnic? What does it look like to be multiclass? What does it look like to do this holistic kind of ministry? Wrestle with the costs on the front end, before you actually plant and do ministry in the city.

Church planting in the city is the *en vogue* thing to do. Yet, I would also add that the gospel is for everybody, and America needs great vibrant churches in cities *and* in suburbs. If Jesus adopted this philosophy of ministry to the city as the be-all-end-all, he would have just stayed in Jerusalem. He didn't do that. Jesus set up shop, his main base, in Galilee, a regional area, a collection of towns. He was, essentially, in the suburbs. Biblical purists cannot adopt this notion that the city is varsity and suburbs are junior varsity.

What are some of the challenges of city life that churches can uniquely address?

Finances are a unique nuance of city living. A ton of people would love to stay in major cities longer, but the normal financial pressures start weighing on people. Living in places like San Francisco or Manhattan, one of the things leaders must figure out is how to help people steward resources in such a way that they're able to live and thrive in the city. That's a unique challenge. How do churches help people think it through and equip them? How can people make it work long-term so they are able to invest well in the city and build something together?

Defining the Self-Identity of Americans

While many factors make up human self-identity, most Americans agree the primary factor that makes up their identity is family. Nearly two-thirds of Americans say their family makes up "a lot" of their personal identity (62%). While it may not come as a surprise that "family" ranks first, it is perhaps unexpected how much more likely certain groups (Elders, practicing Christians, residents of the Midwest, Catholics) are to say so and how much less likely other groups (Millennials, people with no faith, residents of the West) are to point to family as a key part of their identity. What other factors do adults consider central to their identity? And how do faith, age, politics, and even area of the country affect people's self-perceptions?

Family, Country, God

"God, family, country" might be a common creed of country music, but most Americans scramble the order. As mentioned above, adults are most likely to point to their family as making up a significant part of their personal identity; "being an American" comes second, and "religious faith" is in third place. In a tie for a distant fourth are career and ethnic group. Significantly fewer adults would claim their state or city have much impact on their personal identity.

When asked how much each of the factors make up their personal identity—"a lot," "some," "not too much," or "not at

WHAT AMERICANS RANK AS CENTRAL TO THEIR PERSONAL IDENTITY *n=1,000 | February 3–11, 2015*

#1 MY FAMILY

#2 BEING AN AMERICAN   #3 MY RELIGIOUS FAITH   #4 MY ETHNIC GROUP

#5 MY CAREER   #6 MY STATE   #7 MY CITY/TOWN

all"—nearly two-thirds say their family makes up a lot of their personal identity (62%).

Patriotism still runs strong in most Americans: More than half of all adults say being an American makes up a lot of their personal identity (52%).

While religious faith squeaks into the top three, there is a sharp drop from the first two factors in the number of Americans who say their faith is a major part of their identity. A majority of Americans agree their family and their country are central aspects of who they are, but fewer than two out of five adults say their religious faith makes up a lot of their personal identity (38%). About the same proportion of adults give little or no credence to the idea that faith is part of their identity: 18 percent say faith doesn't make up much of their identity and an additional one in five say it doesn't affect their identity at all.

Most seem to agree with the familiar maxim that what you do is not who you are: Less than one-quarter of adults say their career makes up a lot of their personal identity (23%), though more than a third admit their career makes up some of their personal identity (36%). Similar percentages point to their ethnic group as an identity-shaper: just under a quarter (23%) say it makes up a lot of their identity.

Hometown and state pride might spike during football and basketball seasons, but in general Americans don't believe their state or their city significantly affects their personal identity. Only one in five Americans say their state makes up a lot of their personal identity (21%) and even fewer say their city or town does (16%). However, more than two out of five—more than for any of the other factors—admit their locale has at least some impact on their personal identity: 41% say their state makes up some of their identity and 43% say their city does. In other words, geography is not a predominant aspect of self-identity, but it plays a surprisingly important part in the background for most adults.

Differences of Identity

For each of the factors surveyed, there are significant gaps along religious, socioeconomic, political, generational, and even regional lines.

When it comes to identifying as an American, there is a nearly 50-point drop between the oldest generation and the youngest. Four out of five Elders say that being an American makes up a lot of their personal identity, but only one-third of Millennials (34%) say the same.

Gen-Xers and Millennials are significantly less likely than their older counterparts to claim *any* of the factors make up a lot of their personal identity. The exception is career: 23 percent of Millennials, 22 percent of Gen-Xers, and 25 percent of Boomers say their career makes up a lot of their personal identity. Only 17% of Elders, who are primarily retired from the workforce, say so.

The most dramatic differences, after patriotism, are in family and faith. While Millennials, like most adults, identify more with family than any other factor—53 percent say family makes up a lot of their personal identity—they are still well behind any other generation in feeling this way. Even Gen-Xers, typically much closer to Millennials in their answers, are more likely than Millennials to connect family to their identity (61%). This may be the result of more Gen-Xers than Millennials having started families of their own.

There are few surprises in terms of who highlights religious faith as essential to their identity. Practicing

Republicans are much more likely than average to say being an American is central to their identity (65% compared to 52% of the general population), while Democrats are less likely than average to do so (42%).

n=1,000 | February 3–11, 2015

Protestants of all denominations are significantly more likely than the general population to say faith is central to their identity; in fact, aside from practicing Catholics, these groups are all more likely to say their faith, more than any other factor surveyed, makes up a lot of their identity. Practicing Catholics are more likely to say family makes up a lot of their identity (86%) than to say their religious faith does (79%).

Of course, those with no faith are least likely to say religious faith makes up a lot of their personal identity (6%). Residents of the Northeast (where a larger proportion of non-religious people live) are also less likely (27%). Conversely, residents of the South (the "Bible Belt") are more likely than average to say faith makes up a lot of their identity (45%). Black Americans, Republicans, and women are also more likely than average, while Democrats and men are less likely. Non-practicing Christians are the second-least-likely group, behind those with no faith, to say faith makes up a lot of their personal identity (22%).

Black Americans are 30 percentage points more likely than the national average to say their ethnic group makes up a lot of their personal identity. Other segments that tend to have high numbers of ethnic minorities—Catholics, Democrats, practicing Christians, mainline Christians, the unemployed, or those of low socioeconomic status—are also more likely to say so.

Friendship Requests

Surveying our social circles

n=1,025 | April 29–May 1,2015

 1/5 adults regularly or often feel lonely

 On average, people have five close friends

Who are the lonely?

Men 22% > **Women** 15%

Millennials 25% > **Gen-Xers** 24% > **Boomers** 13% > **Elders** 6%

Single 24% > **Married** 13%

Downscale 27% > **Upscale** 13%

 **69%** In the event of a personal emergency or a difficult time, more than two-thirds of adults say they would have someone besides a family member who would help or support them

Most People Meet Their Closest Friends Through Work

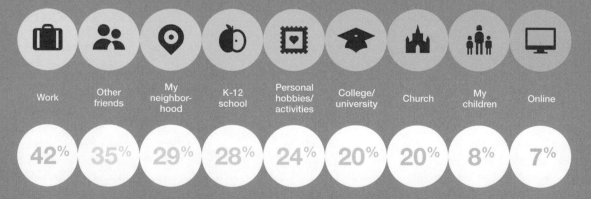

Work	Other friends	My neighbor-hood	K-12 school	Personal hobbies/ activities	College/ university	Church	My children	Online
42%	35%	29%	28%	24%	20%	20%	8%	7%

Adults of lower socioeconomic status are more likely to …

Be lonely: 27%
Say they have no one close by to call on in an emergency: 47%
Have fewer friends in general: (on average, 2.5 close friends)
Say they have no close friends at all: 20%

Opposites (Don't) Attract

In general, people make friends who are like them

● Mostly Different　● Mostly Similar

Would you say your current friends are mostly similar to yourself or mostly different from yourself in each of these areas?

Religious Beliefs
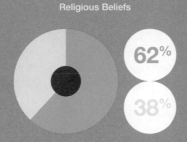
62%
38%

Racial or Ethnic Background
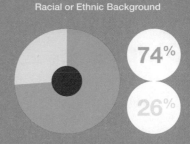
74%
26%

Level of Income

56%
44%

Level of Education

63%
37%

Social Status

70%
30%

Political Views

62%
38%

Life Stage
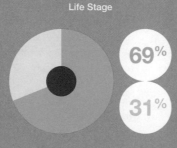
69%
31%

Evangelicals are less likely than most to have friends who are different than them, especially when it comes to religious beliefs, ethnicity, and political views

Religious Beliefs

9%

Racial or Ethnic Background

12%

Political Views

14%

Americans Struggle to Talk Across Divides 💬👤

The United States is in a cultural crisis. There are gaping fissures between rich and poor, growing tensions between races, disunity among faith groups, increasing resentment between genders, and a vast and expanding gap between liberals and conservatives. Generation, gender, socioeconomics, ethnicity, faith, and politics massively divide the American population.

This splintering of American culture has made it more difficult than ever to have a good conversation. In research for Barna president David Kinnaman's book *Good Faith,* coauthored with Gabe Lyons, Barna discovered just how difficult it is for people to reach across cultural divides. Most Americans think it would be difficult to have a natural and normal conversation with a person from a minority group who is different from them. As shown in the table, a majority of Americans would struggle to have a conversation with a Muslim (73%), a Mormon (60%), an atheist (56%), an evangelical (55%), or someone from the LGBT community (52%).

Evangelicals (as defined by Barna) seem to have a particularly difficult time talking to those outside their group. They report higher tensions than any other group when it comes to dialoguing with people different from them. For instance, almost nine in 10 evangelicals (87%) believe it would be difficult to have a natural and normal conversation with a member of the LBGT community, but only six in 10 adults who identify as LGBT (58%) say it would be difficult to have such a conversation with an evangelical.

This is consistent across the board. Evangelicals consistently report higher levels of difficulty with other groups than those groups report toward them. Nearly nine in 10 evangelicals (87%) think it would be difficult to have a conversation with a Muslim, but just seven in 10 of those from non-Christian faiths (69%) report difficulty conversing with evangelicals. Similarly, when it comes to speaking to atheists, 85 percent of evangelicals think it would be difficult, but two-thirds of atheists, agnostics, or those who don't profess any faith (66%) say they would have a hard time talking with evangelicals.

Not surprisingly, most groups tend to have more *internal* than *external* harmony. Yet almost three in 10 evangelicals (28%) think it would be difficult to have a conversation with another evangelical. That's a comparatively low percentage—especially when 87 percent of evangelicals think it would be difficult to have a conversation with a Muslim—but even three in 10 points to growing tensions even within like-minded groups. And this internal struggle goes beyond evangelicals. Four in 10 LGBT adults (39%) think it would be difficult to have a conversation with another member of the LGBT community.

Even when two people agree, honest interaction can seem elusive, as Kinnaman and Lyons point out in *Good Faith*. Try to talk about things like gay marriage—or anything else remotely controversial—with someone you disagree with and the temperature rises a few degrees. Being friends across differences is hard, and cultivating good conversations is the rocky, uphill climb that leads to peace in a conflict-ridden culture.

In order to have meaningful conversations, we must first realize that it's not enough to be nice. Though important, being winsome often means leaving some of the inevitable conflict at the door, which limits meaningful dialogue. A desire to be nice also causes an uncomfortably large segment of Christians to agree with people around them rather than experience even the mildest conflict. We must embrace the hard edges of dialogue, extending kindness and hospitality, but doing so in the face of *inevitable*, but healthy and constructive, conflict.

Unfortunately, Barna's research also reveals that social media has changed Americans' capacity for healthy, effective, good conversations about our differences. According to the data, most people believe these digital tools have made meaningful dialogue and deep connection more difficult. In fact, 56 percent of adults say they believe social media has made people less social, less capable of deep friendships and strong connections. Furthermore, Americans are

Difficult Conversations

Which groups do you think it would be difficult for you to have a natural and normal conversation with? Mark all that apply. % "very" + "somewhat" difficult

● Muslims ● Mormons ○ Atheists ● Evangelicals ● LGBT Community

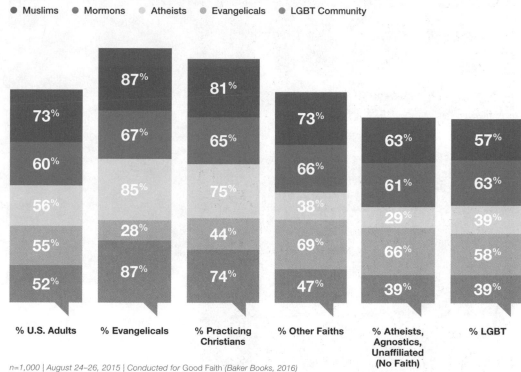

	% U.S. Adults	% Evangelicals	% Practicing Christians	% Other Faiths	% Atheists, Agnostics, Unaffiliated (No Faith)	% LGBT
Muslims	73%	87%	81%	73%	63%	57%
Mormons	60%	67%	65%	66%	61%	63%
Atheists	56%	85%	75%	38%	29%	39%
Evangelicals	55%	28%	44%	69%	66%	58%
LGBT Community	52%	87%	74%	47%	39%	39%

n=1,000 | August 24–26, 2015 | Conducted for Good Faith (Baker Books, 2016)

twice as likely today to say they are lonely compared to 10 years ago. It would appear that social media doesn't always make us more social.

Social media, for all the remarkable benefits of digital tools like Facebook, Twitter, Snapchat, and Instagram, can make connecting across these gaps more difficult, not less. In spite of the truly wonderful gifts of the digital revolution, social media at its worst can magnify our differences, making it even harder to have conversations that matter. For one thing, it can make it more difficult to see other people for who they really are. For another, it helps us find the tiny cliques of people who are already convinced of the crazy things we believe. Social media makes it far too easy to self-select voices that always affirm and never challenge our assumptions and sacred cows. Plus, many of our sanest thinkers and leaders are choosing to stay out of the fray altogether. They've clued in that the most strident and extreme voices are liked, shared, and retweeted—not the most reasonable ones.

The conversational health of our society is in bad shape, but Christians can be part of the solution. If Christians are to be agents of good faith, they also have to overcome the real or perceived barriers to talking with people who don't already agree with them.

They need to become experts at engaging in difficult conversations.

n=1,000 | August 24–26, 2015 |

Conducted for Good Faith (Baker Books, 2016)

Society Is Changing—How Should Christians Respond?

GOOD

BEING A CHRISTIAN WHEN SOCIETY THINKS YOU'RE IRRELEVANT AND EXTREME

DAVID KINNAMAN & GABE LYONS

Leaders of Barna and Q & Bestselling Authors of *unChristian*

FAITH

You will learn

- How to respond with compassion and confidence to the most challenging issues of our day

- The cultural trends that are creating both obstacles and opportunities for Christians

- The heart behind opposing views and how to stay friends despite differences.

- How to empower a new generation to hold to their beliefs while loving their friends

Society is changing its mind about the Christian way of thinking and living. *Good Faith* includes vast amounts of new research documenting the increasing cultural tensions and fault lines between faithful Christians and the wider public. Christians are increasingly viewed as irrelevant and extremist and must figure out how to respond.

Good Faith is for everyone—from students to retirees, parents to grandparents, and Millennials to Boomers—who wants to be informed and equipped to live as a Christian in a complex, changing culture. You will come away with new ideas and inspiration to live and lead with love that is grounded in belief.

BakerBooks

a division of Baker Publishing Group
Grand Rapids, Michigan

Purchase wherever books and ebooks are sold

BARNA TAKES

We Need Media with Depth—But Do We Want It?

Brooke Hempell,
Barna Group,
Vice President of Research

In early 2016, Barna conducted in-depth interviews with "born again" people (41% of U.S. adults, and about half of those who consider themselves Christian) who also would be considered moderately or highly "culturally engaged." The latter identifies people who are forward-thinking, entrepreneurial, interested in what is happening in the world, information seekers, and early adopters. While social researchers are aware of American culture's increasingly short attention span, the segment's lack of initiative to grow in knowledge

was surprising. Though theoretically engaged, the audience interviewed was remarkably unintentional in their media habits and not "hungry" for depth.

Almost all of those interviewed regularly use social media, with Facebook cited as a routine provider of news and articles. Some cited the importance of news being quickly consumable and catchy. By contrast, very few indicated a desire for professional or trustworthy sources or for clarity or accuracy in content.

More concerning than this is the implication that obtaining and sharing news in a social network exposes one primarily to ideas that reinforce, rather than challenge, existing beliefs. This inherently leads to further polarized and entrenched perspectives.

Beyond social media, most of what these audiences read on the web is found organically (and unintentionally) through internet searches, one click leading to the next. A self-proclaimed "Google queen" says she follows wherever the internet leads.

Emphasizing the desire for brevity, this audience widely acknowledges having given up books. "My concentration is not as good as it used to be, so I don't read whole books anymore," says one middle-aged respondent. Another, younger interviewee proclaims, "It's a commitment to buy a book, you have to pay money for it, read the whole thing. I would go to Google or chat about it instead of buying a book."

Among those who are reading books, quite a few do not remember the titles or authors they are currently reading.

It's disappointing that a significant proportion of educated adults in our country is content to consume a steady diet of media "junk food." The challenge for thought leaders, producers, and publishers is to find new, creative ways to deliver quality content; the challenge for consumers is to get on the same page.

A Mobile Family Plan

The explosive growth and widespread dissemination of new communication technologies during the past two decades—particularly the proliferation of high-speed internet and internet-enabled devices—has fundamentally altered the way we communicate and interact. Technology has made our lives simultaneously easier and more complicated. It has allowed us to connect with more people than we could ever imagine, but it has also caused us to feel more isolated than ever.

These are the tensions of the new digital age, and there is no institution more acutely impacted by these shifts than the family. In order to better understand the impact of devices on the family dynamic, Barna conducted a study for Andy Crouch's book *The Tech-Wise Family* with more than 1,000 parents of school-age children to uncover the reality of parenting in this new context.

Parenting Today
Raising kids today is vastly different than it was a few decades ago. In just a single generation, smartphone ownership has exploded and young people have access to a whole world of new information—good and bad. Eight in 10 parents (79%) agree that raising kids is more complicated than it was when they were a kid. And the number one factor cited that contributes to making parenting more difficult was technology/social media (65%). Monitoring technology and social media use (33%) was rated with time management

(34%), helping their child develop good moral character (34%), and discipline (34%) as one of the most difficult things about family life and raising children.

Technology: Pros and Cons
Technology, for the most part, has made life easier. We can order whatever we want and expect it to arrive in two days (or sooner); we can video chat with family and friends from around the globe with one click; and we can access more information and resources than generations before us could ever imagine. However, it's not without its downsides.

Among the parents in the study, technology has made their lives easier by providing access to large amounts of information (67%) and making them feel better informed about the world (49%). They also feel more connected to friends and family (54%). But technology also makes life more complicated and demanding. Wasting time (42%) and being more distracted (40%) are the main ways in which parents say technology has made their lives more difficult.

Tech Usage
Walk along any busy street these days and you'll find a startling amount of humans glued to their screens. This is especially true among the younger generations. According to parents, their children spend an average of 4.65 hours in a typical weekday using an electronic device (tablet, phone, computer). The ubiquity of smartphones and other devices has made this easier. Almost nine in 10 teens (88%) and about half of pre-teens (48%) have a phone. Among those who have a phone, almost all of them are attached at the hip, and sleep with their phone in their bedroom (82% for teens, 72% for pre-teens).

Parental Control
When parents were asked about the biggest challenges they face when it comes to technology and their family, the top answers range from the need to limit (30%), filter (30%), or monitor (30%) use, to finding a balance between time spent using technology and time spent with family (25%) and other non-wired activities (31%). When it comes to limiting use, six in 10 parents (60%) actually set a limit to the amount of time their children can spend on electronic devices.

Most of that time is spent playing video games (64%), chatting with friends or family (34%), using social media (30%), or some other type of entertainment (35%). Beyond recreation time, young people are also using electronic devices for homework (41%) and reading (28%).

Key Challenges of Tech in the Family ...

- **31%** Balancing physical activity with online activity
- **30%** Limiting my children's time with/use of technology
- **30%** Filtering what kinds of content my child watches, reads or plays
- **30%** What my child is exposed to by their friends
- **25%** Finding time for our family to be together without technology

Kids Rely on Electronic Devices for ...

- **64%** Playing video games
- **41%** Doing homework
- **35%** Using other types of entertainment
- **34%** Chatting with friends or family
- **30%** Using social media
- **28%** Reading

n=1,021 parents of school-aged children | January 26–February 4, 2016 | Conducted for The Tech-Wise Family (Baker Books, 2017)

Meal Time

Among the parents surveyed, their families eat an average of 6.3 meals per week together intentionally, either in their home or at a restaurant. At those meals, their family members are evenly split when it comes to bringing phones or other devices to meals with them. Forty-six percent either always or sometimes bring a phone or other device to the table, but 54 percent either rarely or never do.

The culprit is most likely a parent, with 45 percent admitting they or their spouse at least sometimes use their phone at the table during a family meal. By comparison, only about three in 10 of their children (27%) use devices during dinnertime. Overall, parents are divided about whether electronic devices are a significant disruption to their family meals. Forty-two percent believe they are, compared to 44 percent who believe they aren't, with another 14 percent undecided.

n=1,021 parents of school-aged children | January 26–February 4, 2016 | Conducted for The Tech-Wise Family (Baker Books, 2017)

Generational Life

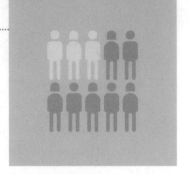

Every Generation Gets Porn Primarily Online

Much of Barna's research for *The Porn Phenomenon* focused on somewhat alarming findings about the prevalence of porn among young people, especially teens. However, the report also speaks to how this cultural crisis reaches all generations.

Barna asked adults 25 and older when they started viewing porn and found the likelihood of starting porn use before puberty doubles in each successively younger age cohort. That is, Gen-Xers (13%) are twice as likely as Boomers (6%) to say they began viewing porn before puberty, and older Millennials (27%) are twice as likely as Gen-Xers to say so.

The ways people access and view porn also depends on their age. Compared to other generations, there's a spike among young adults ages 18–24 in viewing images sent via text (17%) or in an app (15%). More outdated media and technology are still sought out by older viewers; for example, 16 percent of Gen-Xers say they view porn through rented / purchased DVDs, compared to just 7 percent of young adults ages 18–24. Even so, online videos and pictures are the primary source of pornography for everyone surveyed. Even among Boomers who view pornography, 56 percent do so through online videos and 42 percent through online pictures.

n=1,188 | July 22–29, 2015 | © Josh McDowell Ministry

"What Have I Done Wrong?"

Three in 10 adults worry they've disappointed someone close to them with their life choices. Looking at each generation, this concern applies to 33 percent of Millennials, 35 percent of Gen-Xers, 29 percent of Boomers, and 20 percent of Elders.

n=1,404 | June 25-July 1, 2013

Old and Young Not Together on Living Together

Millennials (72%) are twice as likely as Elders (36%) to believe cohabitation is a good idea—which is no surprise, considering that Millennials have come of age in a more secular culture when gender norms, career trajectories, and marriage expectations are rapidly changing.

n=1,097 | April 7-14, 2016

> " A lifetime career trajectory is not an expectation for most Millennials; they anticipate changing jobs often and will likely do so in pursuit of work that better aligns with their passions. As Millennials become a larger and larger segment of the employee market, companies will need to shift policies and incentives to appeal to these desires. Training, mentorship, opportunities for independence, and fluidity within roles will become important factors in employee retention."
>
> —*Roxanne Stone, editor-in-chief of Barna Group*

On the Coffee Table

A daily read takes on different forms for people of different ages. Elders are most likely to read a newspaper at least daily for new information (37%), while Boomers (25%), Gen-Xers (14%), and Millennials (8%) are significantly less likely to pick up this kind of periodical. Magazines also have decent daily readership numbers among Elders (14%) but drop off with younger generations (4% Boomers, 6% Gen-Xers, 6% Millennials). When it comes to books, things even out; no age group is cracking a spine that frequently. For all generations, only about one in 10 report getting new information from a book at least daily (10% Elders, 9% for all others).

Most Women Agree on Their #1 Priority

n=1,404 (732 women) | June 25-July 1, 2013

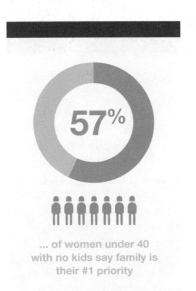

57%

... of women under 40 with no kids say family is their #1 priority

As decades pass, society has changing ideas of what it means to be a wife, a mom, and a woman in business. It's tempting to let these expectations be a source of frustration or division, but research for the Barna FRAME *Wonder Women* reveals how women of varying ages—both mothers and those without children—have some important things in common.

Most women say that family is their number one priority (57% women under 40 with no kids, 71% moms with no kids at home, 83% moms with kids at home). For women under 40 with no kids, however, work remains the top time commitment (45%). Though most moms put the bulk of their hours toward their families (whether or not their kids are at home), work still competes for their schedule. One-quarter (23%) of moms with kids at home and 30 percent of moms with no kids at home say work is their number one time commitment.

A Q&A on Cross-Generational Community

with Mark Matlock

Mark Matlock has been working with youth pastors, students, and parents for more than two decades. He is the president of WisdomWorks, former executive director for Youth Specialties, and creator of the PlanetWisdom student conferences. He has written several books for teens (Living a Life That Matters, Smart Faith, and Don't Buy the Lie) and for parents (Real World Parents, Raising Wise Children, and Ideas for Parents). Matlock and his family live in Texas and attend Irving Bible Church, where he was ordained and serves as a teaching pastor.

There is a tendency between generations to focus on our differences or divisions. How can old and young understand one another better?

There are some generalizations—both fair and unfair—that can be made about each generation.

One of the greatest examples of this is the concept of "extended adolescence" that we see placed on Millennials—the "boomerang generation." There is a stereotype that if you throw them off to

college, they come back to live in their parents' basements. They can't seem to get a job. They're getting married later. While the statistics confirm some of these trends, there are different filters you can use to try to understand Millennials. One is the extended adolescence filter: "Well, these people just don't want to grow up." But there's also the "emerging adulthood" filter that younger sociologists have developed. Emerging adulthood examines three different phases that a young person goes through between the ages of 18 and 30, and how they are uniquely experienced by each generation. Because of recent major disruptions in our world—the internet, the rise of the middle class, globalization, financial crises—some believe that the Millennial generation is actually experiencing a whole new cycle of development. These are not just stylistic changes on the surface; they are deep, structural changes.

People can have a positive or negative explanation of the same events, and that can greatly affect their willingness to engage a generation. But I've noticed that proximity changes things.

What do you think we can expect of Generation Z (those born after 2002)?

If you look at those born even a few years before Gen-Z, their parents didn't really know how to raise them around technology. There were no rhythms or best practices. I was a parent of two children during that time. It was fascinating; none of us knew what to do with all the technology that was exploding around us. We made some good choices, and we made some bad choices. But now, parents with school-aged children firmly rooted in Gen-Z have a lot more awareness and wisdom from past experience in navigating this digital era. Gen-Z has grown up in a world where literally everything's interactive. You might have to tell them, "That's a window, not a touch screen!"

Gen-Z is also being raised by parents who are likely more mature because they waited later in life to have children. Both parents are probably educated and have career experience, so they are more likely to have financial stability. They are also more likely, at this point, to be parenting an only child. How will that affect Gen-Z as they grow up? That will be an interesting thing to see play out.

I also think there will be a lot of independent consultant types when Gen-Z enters the workforce. They'll work through communities and collectives rather than in stable, linear careers. They're probably going to be selling their skill sets instead of choosing one particular occupation. Millennials will have established a modular, free-flowing workplace. Gen-Z will have really different goals, values, and aspirations as a result.

What are some practical ways people can strengthen intergenerational relationships—between parent and child, teacher and student, boss and employee, or mentor and mentee?

Everyone needs to recognize that we have generational bias based on the era when we were born or our current stage of life.

For Millennials and Gen-Z, it's important to have a concept of wisdom—principles and patterns that repeat themselves over and over again. The longer you live, the more patterns you're able to recognize. Millennials and Gen-Z need the wisdom of older generations to find and apply solutions moving forward. Methods and tactics go out of style; wisdom doesn't. It's a powerful combination when younger people are willing to say, "I want to leverage the wisdom of Gen-Xers, Boomers, and Elders." That creates an unstoppable business, an unstoppable church, an unstoppable school.

In turn, older generations don't often harness the imaginative power of younger generations. We give them tasks to do or say, "Look, this is what is required." But we should realize the value that they bring; they're thinking in a completely different way. Younger people should be invited into the imagination (or re-imagination) of what work, a company, a church, or a community could be. In church, we shouldn't just say, "We've always let our students serve in this capacity." These are the roles that other generations have defined. Do these roles even need to exist today? What new roles need to be created? What are the opportunities around us? Invite them to imagine answers with you. That will help build a bridge between generations.

In my own experience, there were times when we were trying to roll out new programs, and out of curiosity, I brought in some of my younger employees who weren't even at an executive level. They felt really honored and significant for being invited into the conversation, but we also learned some things from them that we wouldn't have learned otherwise.

We have to rethink hierarchy in our organizations; it shouldn't be about what level someone has attained or the time they've been around, but about an individual's contribution to a team. Think about people in terms of skills and strengths, rather than their age or "level."

Trending in ...
Faith

In recent years, the big religion headline has been the surge of "nones" (those who do not affiliate with any particular religion). But there are many sidebars and storylines to this broader trend that haven't received as much attention. *Why* do people abandon church? What about those who have stayed? What unique challenges face church leaders today? Where are signs of growth and promise in the Church?

This concluding section of *Barna Trends* probes the ever-evolving expressions of our most ancient and precious tradition: faith.

In FAITH, Barna looks at trends such as:
- the modern woman's relationship to church
- the faith leader's place in a post-Christian culture
- how the Church can play a role in racial reconciliation
- the state of Christianity in secular Europe (and what it reveals about America)
- why most Christians view their faith as a force for good
- which spiritual practices are actually being practiced

 Practices

 Church

 Beliefs

 Leadership

 Global Religion

 Generational Faith

Featuring:

Bonnie Camarda, Christine Caine, Kara Powell, Jake Mulder, Brad Griffin, Joyce Chiu, Cory Maxwell-Coghlan, Jon Tyson, Roxanne Stone, Brooke Hempell, David Kinnaman, Gareth Russell

At a Glance: Faith

How Far Does the Bible Reach?

In a recent survey conducted on behalf of American Bible Society, Barna discovered that, while most Americans support and advocate for global access to the Bible, they are largely unaware of how much work remains to be done in order to give every person access to the Bible in his or her own language.

Nearly all Americans—98 percent—believe people should have access to the Bible. And indeed, most people in America not only have access to but personally own a Bible. Nine in 10 American households report having at least one Bible, with the average household owning four copies. Of course, ownership does not equal readership; three out of five Americans say they want to read the Bible more (60%).

Much of the globe, however, does not enjoy such free access. More than half of the world's languages still do not have a completed Bible translation (57%). Three in 10 active first languages do not even have a translation begun in that language (31%). An additional one-quarter have only segments of Scripture completed, with more portions in the translation process (26%).

A Rural Faith

If you live in a rural area, it's likely that you're religious. Only 15 percent of rural Americans identify as having no faith, while 83 percent self-identify as Christian. Ten percent qualify as evangelical, compared to 7 percent of all Americans.

The Planter Profile

A Barna study done in partnership with Thrivent Financial shows the median age of a church planter is 38—much younger than the average of pastors overall (55). Most are married (96%) and have children living at home (79%). Before they began their current ministry, seven in 10 church planters had a non-ministry career (70%).

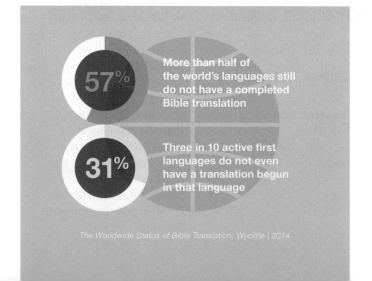

57%
More than half of the world's languages still do not have a completed Bible translation

31%
Three in 10 active first languages do not even have a translation begun in that language

The Worldwide Status of Bible Translation, Wycliffe | 2014

America by the #s: Unchurched Cities

Currently, about four in 10 U.S. adults (43%) qualify as "unchurched" under Barna's definition (have not attended a church service, except for a holiday or special occasion, at any time within the past six months). Many cities outpace the overall U.S. population when it comes to church avoidance. The top five unchurched metropolitan areas are:

1. San Francisco/Oakland/San Jose, CA - 61%
2. Burlington/Plattsburgh, VT - 55%
3. Boston, MA/Manchester, NH - 53%
4. Portland/Auburn, ME - 52%
5. Chico/Redding, CA - 52%

Are You Extremist?

A strong majority of adults believe "being religiously extreme is a threat to society." Research for the book *Good Faith* shows three-quarters of all Americans—and nine out of ten Americans with no faith affiliation—agree with this statement. The perception that Christianity is extreme is now firmly entrenched among the nation's non-Christians; 45 percent of atheists, agnostics and religiously unaffiliated in America agree with the statement "Christianity is extremist." Almost as troubling, only 14 percent of atheists and agnostics strongly disagree that Christianity is extremist. Another four in ten (41%) disagree somewhat with this description. So even non-Christians who hesitate to label Christianity as extremist still harbor some negative perceptions toward the religion.

"I think more attention needs to be given to articulating what it means to 'be like Christ.' It sometimes feels like we've created a 21st-century American suburban Jesus who is most concerned with personal morality. The Middle Eastern peasant who was crucified for political and religious treason is who we're seeking to be like. Jesus hung out with people most Christians try to avoid. He lived so close to unholy people that he developed a reputation for being a drunk and a glutton. He loved his enemies and challenged the religious status quo every chance he got. All that to say, we need to de-cliché our language; we need to unpack what it means to actually become like the Jesus who is revealed in the Gospels."
—*Preston Sprinkle, vice president of Eternity Bible College's Boise extension, host of* What Does the Bible Really Say?, *and author of* Go: Returning Discipleship to the Front Lines of Faith, *in Barna's* The State of Discipleship

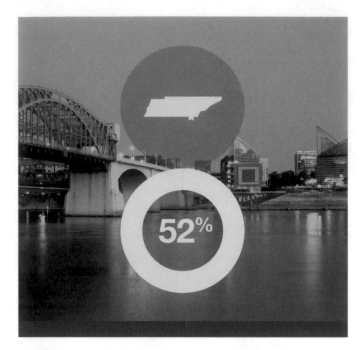

America by the #s:
Bible-Minded Cities

Each year, on behalf of American Bible Society, Barna ranks the nation's top media markets based on their level of Bible engagement. Individuals who report reading the Bible in a typical week and who strongly assert the Bible is accurate in the principles it teaches are considered to be Bible-minded. This definition captures action and attitude—those who both engage and esteem the Christian Scriptures. In 2016, the South remains the most Bible-minded region of the country, with all of the top 10 metropolitan areas located below the Mason-Dixon line.

1. Chattanooga, TN - 52%
2. Birmingham/Anniston/Tuscaloosa, AL - 51%
3. Roanoke/Lynchburg, VA - 48%
4. Shreveport, LA - 47%
5. Tri-Cities, TN - 47%
6. Charlotte, NC - 46%
7. Little Rock/Pine Bluff, AR - 45%
8. Knoxville, TN - 45%
9. Greenville/Spartanburg/Anderson, SC/Asheville, NC - 44%
10. Lexington, KY - 44%

n=65,064 | 2006–2016 | American Bible Society

Churches were situated in the center of town, historically, and their ornate architecture signified a transcendent or 'otherness' function. While a church building was not a place of everydayness, its physical embeddedness within the larger built environment made it a visible and integrated part of the community. Modern churches that choose to build on large lots at the edge of town are demonstrably isolating themselves from the community and are often less accessible to community members because of the distance they have to travel. This type of 'commuter' church building does not invite its members to invest in one geographic place together (ideally around the church building). Consistent communal interaction among attendees throughout the week is weakened. I believe these realities hinder a church community from putting down roots in a particular place, and work against our call to steward the built environment for the common good."

—*Sara Joy Proppe, urban planner and real estate developer, in Barna's* Making Space for Millennials

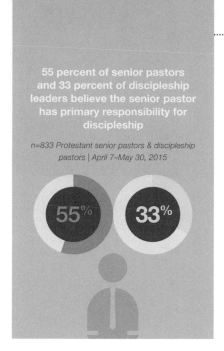

55 percent of senior pastors and 33 percent of discipleship leaders believe the senior pastor has primary responsibility for discipleship

n=833 Protestant senior pastors & discipleship pastors | April 7–May 30, 2015

55%

33%

Discipleship Is a Priority— But Whose Responsibility?

Most church leaders (61%) feel their church places discipleship among its top three priorities, according to a study produced in partnership with The Navigators. Looking specifically at senior pastors and discipleship leaders, the percentage is similar (62% and 58%, respectively). Twenty-six percent of all church leaders believe discipleship is the top priority. But who is primarily responsible for discipling? Fifty-five percent of senior pastors believe it falls on their own shoulders. "Senior pastor" is still the top answer among discipleship leaders, though for just 33 percent. Many are inclined to say Sunday school/life groups (21%) or discipleship pastors (20%) play the main role in a church's discipleship approach.

Why Pastors Use the Internet

In 2000, just over eight in 10 pastors said they used a computer at church (83%). Today, more than a decade into the new millenium and in the midst of a rapidly changing digital era, nearly all pastors are plugged in (96%).

While the primary way pastors use a computer has stayed essentially the same—in both years, more than half say they use it for word processing or writing (59% today and 51% in 2000)—the percentage who use it for accessing the internet (39% today compared to only 24% in 2000) and for email (46% compared to 24%) has increased dramatically. Additionally, more pastors today are using their computers for study or research (56% compared to 29%) and for creating slides/presentations (44% compared to 10%). One might conclude that pastors

are working hard to keep pace in the screen-driven era of communication. While two of the primary ways pastors used the internet in 2000—to find information (97% today compared to 78% in 2000) and to keep up on existing relationships (80% compared to 64%)—have increased dramatically since then, pastors are also now using the internet for an increasing array of activities that they only marginally participated in 15 years ago. Significantly more pastors use the internet to buy products (88% compared to 46%), check out new music or videos (71% compared to 19%), have a spiritual or religious experience (39% compared to 15%), and make new friends (26% compared to 9%).

The Value of Youth Ministry and Missions

Barna research done in partnership with Youth Specialties and YouthWorks shows that six in 10 (61%) senior pastors say youth ministry is "one of the top priorities" of their church's ministry, and 7 percent say it is the single highest priority. However, despite this clear majority, one-third of pastors (32%) say it is either somewhat, not too much, or not at all a priority.

The research also looked into the value of immersive programs outside of weekly youth activities—specifically camps, retreats, and missions. Youth leaders say the most important of these is youth mission trips (74%), which are in a class by themselves in terms of importance. This is followed by overnight retreats (45%), weeklong camps (43%), family mission trips (35%), and large youth conferences (23%). Overall, 88 percent of the youth ministry leaders interviewed say they offer mission trips as part of their youth programs. These are most commonly inside the U.S., but 57 percent of the leaders who have taken such trips have done so outside the U.S. Also among those who offer mission trips, 42 percent say they offer trips specifically designed for an entire family to participate.

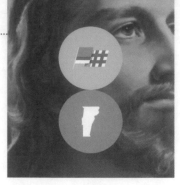

America by the #s: A Sinless Savior?

When Jesus walked the earth, did he commit sins like other people? The people of Vermont are more likely than residents of any other state to say yes. Fifty-six percent of its population agree at least somewhat that Jesus sinned, with 33 percent strongly agreeing.

n=65,064 | 2006-2016

Busyness Could Block Your Growth

Facing obstacles in your spiritual growth? Slow down. A majority of all church leaders (85%) believe busyness is a major obstacle to discipleship, and one-quarter (23%) of practicing Christians call it a significant barrier. Two-thirds of church leaders (65%) also feel busy schedules keep mature believers from discipling younger ones.

n=2,013 Christians | March 6–April 15, 2015;
n=833 church leaders | April 7-May 30, 2015

Millennials Positive About Bibles in Public

In separate nationwide studies including teens and Millennials (conducted with InterVarsity and American Bible Society), Barna asked what young people think when they see someone reading the Scriptures in public. Thirty-seven percent of teens and 29 percent of Millennials say they are "happy to see other Christians around," the most common response. Practicing Christian teens (76%) and practicing Christian Millennials (57%) are even more likely to express this sentiment.

Transforming Scotland: Behind the Research

Barna's yearlong research effort in Scotland, in partnership with Barna Global and the Maclellan Foundation, was the organization's first major public study outside the U.S. The extensive methodology included 29 in-depth interviews with key Christian leaders, national surveys of 1,019 Scottish adults and 200 Protestant ministers, two studies of a selection of baseline and growing Protestant churches, and interviews with a cohort of faith-engaged Millennial Scots. Barna president David Kinnaman calls the project "a strategic decision, not only because we aspire to serve leaders in many countries and contexts, but also because we believe the challenges facing Christians in America cannot be addressed effectively without a broader, more global set of insights."

"America's diversity offers the church opportunities for growth. There are countless nonwhite Millennials who are more likely than their white counterparts to stay connected to the church and to put down deep roots in their faith and neighborhood communities. But if we rely on mostly white (and male) leadership to develop and implement strategies for outreach, evangelism, and discipleship to this diverse generation, these initiatives are more likely to fail.

White leaders, including pastors and lay leaders, should put themselves under the mentoring of leaders of color who are living out the generational transition in their congregations and families."

—*Kathy Khang, multiethnic director for InterVarsity Christian Fellowship Great Lakes West region and coauthor of* More than Serving Tea, *in Barna's* Making Space for Millennials

Practices

How Christians today publicly express
and privately cultivate their faith

Are People Growing?

36%

SAY THEY ARE ALMOST TO WHERE THEY WANT TO BE IN THEIR SPIRITUAL LIFE

38%

OF CHRISTIANS SAY THEY ARE HAPPY WITH WHERE THEY ARE IN THEIR SPIRITUAL LIFE

HAVE YOU MADE PROGRESS IN YOUR SPIRITUAL GROWTH IN THE PAST YEAR?

● PRACTICING CHRISTIANS   ● NON-PRACTICING CHRISTIANS

40%	51%	20%	43%
A LOT	SOME	A LOT	SOME

TOP 3 REASONS CHRISTIANS WANT TO GROW SPIRITUALLY

43% — I DESIRE TO KNOW JESUS, OR GOD, MORE

39% — IT'S IMPORTANT TO BE IMPROVING OR GROWING IN ALL THINGS

35% — I DESIRE TO BE MORE LIKE JESUS

What Is Working?

HOW DO CHRISTIANS WANT TO BE DISCIPLED?

(AMONG THE 9 IN 10 CHRISTIANS WHO SAY SPIRITUAL GROWTH IS IMPORTANT)

- ON MY OWN
- WITH A GROUP
- ONE-ON-ONE
- MIX OF GROUP + ONE-ON-ONE

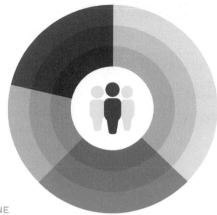

37%
25%
16%
21%

1 IN 3 CHRISTIANS IS LOOKING FOR ONE-ON-ONE DISCIPLESHIP

1 IN 4 CHRISTIANS IS CURRENTLY BEING DISCIPLED BY SOMEONE

1 IN 5 IS DISCIPLING SOMEONE ELSE

I BELIEVE MY SPIRITUAL LIFE HAS AN IMPACT ON ...

37% 36%

RELATIVES   FRIENDS

33% 29%

COMMUNITY   SOCIETY

I BELIEVE MY SPIRITUAL LIFE IS ENTIRELY PRIVATE

41%

WHO HAS THE MOST IMPACT ON YOUR SPIRITUAL JOURNEY?

1. FAMILY MEMBERS
2. PEOPLE AT CHURCH
3. BIBLE STUDY OR SMALL GROUP
4. FRIENDS
5. A MENTOR
6. CHRISTIAN COMMUNITY OTHER THAN CHURCH
7. ONLINE SOCIAL NETWORKS

WHAT HAS BEEN MOST HELPFUL FOR YOUR SPIRITUAL JOURNEY?

1. REGULAR PRAYER
2. ATTENDING CHURCH
3. QUIET TIME
4. PERSONAL BIBLE STUDY
5. GROUP BIBLE STUDY
6. MEDITATING ON SCRIPTURE
7. A SPIRITUAL MENTOR

n=2,013 | March 6–April 15, 2015; n=833 church leaders | April 7–May 30, 2015 | The Navigators

Social Justice: Christian Concern

A Barna study on global poverty, in partnership with Compassion International, confirms that practicing Christians are more concerned about and engaged with global poverty than the broader American public, by a substantial margin. Only 16 percent of the general population say they are "extremely concerned" about global poverty, compared to 28 percent of practicing Protestants and 26 percent of practicing Catholics. When it comes to taking specific actions to address global poverty—such as donating to a

nonprofit or volunteering for a church or nonprofit—the trend is similar: higher participation among Christians. Young Christians are twice as likely as the national average to have volunteered for a church (31% compared to 15%) or for a nonprofit (19% versus 11%). Nearly two-thirds of practicing Protestants (62% compared to 39%) have made a donation in the past year to a nonprofit to address poverty; two out of five (40%) have volunteered for a church; and one-quarter (25%) have volunteered for a nonprofit.

Christians also donate more than non-Christians to poverty-related causes, but overall giving is quite low among all adults, regardless of faith. Just 7 percent of Americans give more than $50 per month to alleviate global poverty, and nearly 40 percent give nothing at all.

The median donation to poverty alleviation among U.S. adults is $5 per month. This means half of Americans give $5 or less and half give $5 or more. Practicing Protestants, by contrast, have a median annual giving amount of $15—three times the national norm and three times more than their Catholic brethren. Christians over 40 have the highest mean donation ($35) but a lower median donation ($10), which means there are big givers in this demographic whose large donations skew the averages. Younger Christians, on the other hand, have closer mean ($22) and median ($15) donations.

Would You Say You Are Concerned About Global Poverty?

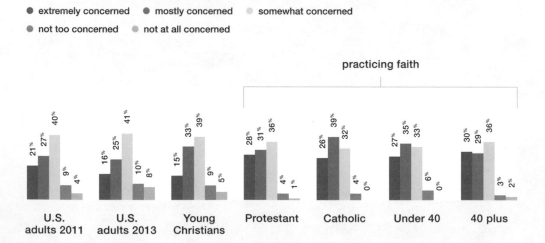

- extremely concerned
- mostly concerned
- somewhat concerned
- not too concerned
- not at all concerned

practicing faith

U.S. adults 2011: 21%, 27%, 40%, 9%, 4%
U.S. adults 2013: 16%, 25%, 41%, 10%, 8%
Young Christians: 15%, 33%, 39%, 9%, 5%
Protestant: 28%, 31%, 36%, 4%, 1%
Catholic: 26%, 39%, 32%, 4%, 0%
Under 40: 27%, 35%, 33%, 6%, 0%
40 plus: 30%, 29%, 36%, 3%, 2%

n=819 adults 35+; 644 adults 18–34 | December 11–28, 2013; n=1,429 | September 8–15, 2011 | Compassion International

Social Justice: Christian Action

Volunteering is an essential part of a healthy civil society. Whether it's to gain experience, acquire new skills, or meet new people, volunteering serves as an objective good to local communities across America. But how much volunteering do Americans participate in, and where do they focus their efforts?

When asked whether they volunteered some of their free time to help a church during the past week, 18 percent of the general population answers "yes." Volunteerism is high among practicing Christians (46%) and evangelicals (51%) and lower among those with no faith (4%).

It may come as no surprise that Christians focus their volunteer work toward their local church. In research for the FRAMES series, Barna asked American adults why they think it's important to attend church, and although most said "to be closer to God," 16 percent said they go because "the church is God's hands and feet in the world."

If you take church out of the equation and ask whether people have volunteered some of their free time to help a nonprofit organization (not including a church), the amount of the general population who take part remains basically the same (19%). Christians are more involved in general volunteer activities, and this is true across the board of each faith segment. Whether it's practicing Christians (27%), evangelicals (25%), or very active church attenders (34%), all are more likely than the general population to have volunteered some of their free time to help a nonprofit organization beyond church. Again, those with no faith (13%) were among the least likely to volunteer.

It appears, within and beyond the walls of their churches, Christians of all stripes are leading the charge and actively seeking the welfare and flourishing of their communities through volunteering and service.

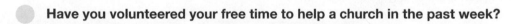 Have you volunteered your free time to help a church in the past week?

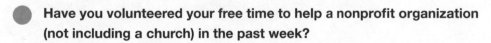 Have you volunteered your free time to help a nonprofit organization (not including a church) in the past week?

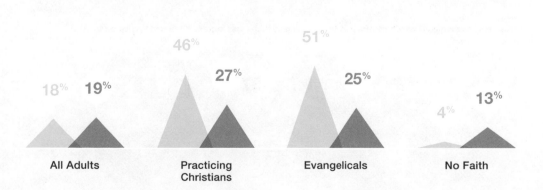

18% 19%   46% 27%   51% 25%   4% 13%

All Adults   Practicing Christians   Evangelicals   No Faith

n=1,086 | May 9-20, 2013; n=1,011 | January 28-February 4, 2016

Which Spiritual Disciplines Are Millennials Practicing?

Bible reading is one among a host of spiritual disciplines that facilitate connection with God and promote spiritual growth. However, practicing Christian Millennials (PCMs) say Bible reading is more important than other spiritual disciplines. The plurality of PCMs say Bible reading is more important than silence/solitude (50% say Bible reading is more important), prayer (49%), worship (51%), acts of service (48%), communion or Eucharist (44%), and evangelism (42%). This is true of both practicing Protestant and Catholic Millennials. In contrast, non-practicing Christian Millennials and non-Christian Millennials (who have read the Bible) say in each instance that reading the Bible is of equal importance to the other spiritual disciplines.

Such a distinct preference for Bible reading among PCMs indicates a church-wide emphasis on Bible reading as the primary means of connecting to God and growing in faith. Four in ten say it is the greatest source for absolute moral truth (39% of PCMs) and believe it is the actual word of God that should be taken literally (46%). Yet, while PCMs say reading Scripture is more important than prayer or worship, they are more likely to do both of the latter than to read Scripture. More PCMs say they prayed in the last month (81%) and participated in worship (59%) than read the Bible (50%).

But PCMs aren't necessarily happy with this discrepancy: Most (92%) desire to read the Bible more often than they do. However, life seems to get in the way. Most point to busyness and lack of time as the reasons they don't read Scripture more often. Despite a deeply held belief in its importance, PCMs appear to idealize the Bible more than they read it.

A plurality of practicing Christian Millennials say that personal Bible reading is more important than any of the other polled spiritual disciplines

However, when asked which disciplines they practiced in the last month, Bible reading came in third

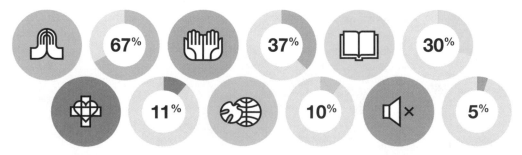

n=1,000 young adults 18–30 | August 18–22, 2014

Church Attendance & Faith Practice

One of the most interesting cultural shifts in recent decades has been the gradual move away from institutions as a binding force and marker of identity in America. Stemming from a growing distrust of institutions like the government, universities, and the church, Americans—and particularly Millennials—are increasingly breaking away from traditional cultural narratives. Coupled with a broader secularizing trend, this anti-institutional sentiment has caused an overall decline in church attendance among the general population. In 2000, almost six in 10 adults (58%) had attended church in the past month. In 2015, that number had decreased to 46 percent, a difference of 12 percentage points.

But although church attendance has declined significantly, the drop in those who continue to call themselves Christian has not been as pronounced. This has created an interesting group of "spiritual but not religious" Christians who self-identify as Christian and say "faith is very important in my life"—but do not regularly attend church. Their mantra might resemble something like: "Forget the Church, Follow Jesus." But how much of a contributor to active faith is the practice of attending church? To answer this question, Barna compares "spiritual but not religious" Christians with practicing Christians, a group who self-identify as a Christian and also say "faith is very important in my life" but do regularly attend church.

Looking at a number of faith practices like prayer, Bible reading, and volunteering, the data clearly shows that, comparing these two Christians groups, engagement in other faith practices significantly declines among those who do not attend church regularly. For example, 68 percent of practicing Christians read the Bible in the past week, compared to just one-third of "spiritual but not religious" Christians (32%). Forty-one percent of practicing Christians volunteer at church, compared to only 4 percent of "spiritual but not religious" Christians. Three in 10 practicing Christians (29%) volunteer with a nonprofit, also compared to just 4 percent of "spiritual but not religious" Christians. Prayer is the only practice where these two groups see similar numbers, with 98 percent of practicing Christians and 91 percent of "spiritual but not religious" Christians praying to God in a given week.

Some Christians may believe they can hold to their faith even as they attend church less, but, as Barna research shows, those who are disconnected from church—even those who continue to self-identify as Christian—are less likely to engage in other faith activities. This correlation does not necessarily equal causation, but it tells an interesting story about the impact of being rooted and active in a church when it comes to living out one's faith.

n=1,000 |1995; n=10,471 | 2000-2002; n=15,710 | 2003-2006;
n=16,265 | 2007-2010; n=24,722 | 2011-2015

Bible Reading in America 💬👤

Americans hold the Bible in high esteem. A Barna study conducted on behalf of American Bible Society (ABS) reveals that although there are increasing doubts about the origins, reliability, and veracity of the Christian Scriptures—especially among younger generations—more than half of U.S. adults believe it is either the actual, literal word of God or the inspired word of God without error. Nearly half read the Bible at least once a month and three out of five say they wish they spent more time reading it.

The Word of God

The best definition of the Bible, according to most Americans, is either the actual word of God (24%) or the inspired word of God with no errors (30%). Some Americans are more convinced than others, however. For example, 31 percent of Elders 70 years and older subscribe to "the actual word of God" as the best definition of the Bible—making them twice as likely as Millennials (14%) to do so. Similarly, black Americans (40%) are twice as likely as whites (20%), and residents of the South (30%) nearly twice as likely as Northeasterners (17%), to believe the Bible is the literal word of God.

David Kinnaman and the Barna team have written at length in the past decade about the major cultural and generational shifts underway in our society. To some extent, skepticism among Millennials (and Gen-Xers, to a lesser degree)

with regard to the Bible's authority is emblematic of their skepticism toward all authority. U.S. Millennials are twice as likely as Elders to say the Bible is "just another book of teachings written by men that contains stories and advice" (23% vs. 11%) and half as likely to believe it is the actual word of God (14% vs. 31%).

The beliefs of practicing Christians differ dramatically from those who do not practice the faith. Nine out of 10 practicing Christians believe the Bible is the actual or inspired word of God (91%), compared to 68 percent of other adults. When it comes to beliefs about the Bible, young practicing Christians are much more like their older sisters and brothers in the faith than like their generational counterparts outside the Church. Among practicing Christians, there is remarkable consistency across generations. The share of practicing Christians among Millennials (19%) is a smaller proportion than among older generations (29% Gen-Xers, 36% Boomers, 45% Elders), but their beliefs about the Bible are quite similar to older practicing Christians.

A majority of Americans may hold a "high" view of the Scriptures, but that doesn't mean a majority reads it—at least, not very often. Slightly more than one-third reads the Bible once a week or more frequently (36%) and about the same proportion reads the Bible less than once a year or never (35%). The remaining three in 10 fall somewhere between once a month and once a year.

As with beliefs about the Bible, women, older adults, and black Americans are leaders when it comes to Bible reading. And practicing Christians stand out from others, with seven in 10 reading the Scriptures at least once a week. Millennial practicing Christians read the Bible less than older Christians, but they are more similar to older adults in the faith than they are to their age cohort more generally; they read the Bible somewhat less frequently than older practicing Christians but far more often than their age group in the general population.

Readership among U.S. adults may be lower than one might hope, but a healthy majority expresses a desire to read the Bible more (62%), and nearly one-quarter says they actually did increase their reading over the last year (23%).

Bible Engagement

When Barna and ABS launched the first "State of the Bible" study in 2011, one of the goals was to create a metric that could be used to track Americans' level of engagement with the Scriptures—involving both views of the Bible and habits of Bible reading.

- **Bible engaged:** These U.S. adults believe either that the Bible is the actual word of God or the inspired word of God with no errors and read it at least four times a week; or they

The Best Definition of the Bible

n=12,062 | 2011–2016 |
American Bible Society

- The actual Word of God and should be taken literally, word for word
- The inspired Word of God and has no errors, although some verses are meant to be symbolic rather than literal
- The inspired Word of God but has some factual or historical errors
- Not inspired by God but tells how the writers of the Bible understood the ways and principles of God
- Just another book of teachings written by men that contains stories and advice
- Other/don't know

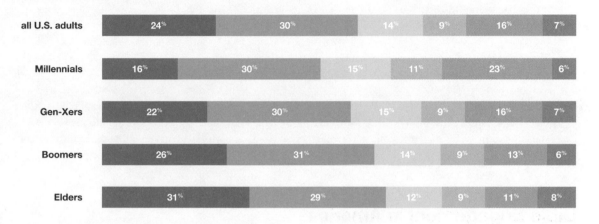

all U.S. adults	24%	30%	14%	9%	16%	7%
Millennials	16%	30%	15%	11%	23%	6%
Gen-Xers	22%	30%	15%	9%	16%	7%
Boomers	26%	31%	14%	9%	13%	6%
Elders	31%	29%	12%	9%	11%	8%

How Frequently Americans Read the Bible

n=12,062 | 2011–2016 |
American Bible Society

- every day
- 4+ times/several times a week
- once/week
- once/month
- 3-4 times/year
- 1-2 times/year
- less than once a year
- never

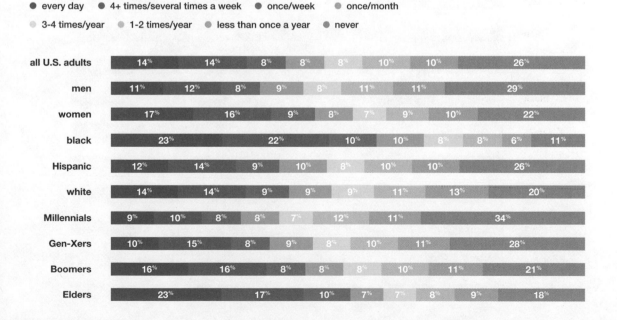

	every day	4+ times/week	once/week	once/month	3-4 times/year	1-2 times/year	less than once a year	never
all U.S. adults	14%	14%	8%	8%	8%	10%	10%	26%
men	11%	12%	8%	9%	8%	11%	11%	29%
women	17%	16%	9%	8%	7%	9%	10%	22%
black	23%	22%	10%	10%	8%	8%	6%	11%
Hispanic	12%	14%	9%	10%	8%	10%	10%	26%
white	14%	14%	9%	9%	9%	11%	13%	20%
Millennials	9%	10%	8%	8%	7%	12%	11%	34%
Gen-Xers	10%	15%	8%	9%	8%	10%	11%	28%
Boomers	16%	16%	8%	8%	8%	10%	11%	21%
Elders	23%	17%	10%	7%	7%	8%	9%	18%

believe the Bible is the inspired word of God with some errors and read it every day.

- **Bible friendly:** These folks believe the Bible is the actual or inspired word of God with no errors but read it less than four times a week.

- **Bible neutral:** Those who are neutral believe the Bible is not inspired but tells how the writers understood God's ways; or they believe it is the inspired word of God with some errors and read it less than every day.

- **Bible skeptic:** These Americans say the Bible is just another book of teachings written by men that contains stories and advice.

Different age, ethnic, and faith cohorts have varying tendencies when it comes to Bible perceptions and reading habits—so these groups also tend to have higher or lower levels of Bible engagement, based on those views and habits. For example, Elders and Boomers are generally more highly engaged than Millennials and Gen-Xers, and black adults are more highly engaged than Hispanics and whites. And, in keeping with their stark differences in belief and practice regarding the Bible, practicing Christians of every age are far more engaged with the Scriptures than other adults.

Reading Preferences

As digital devices have proliferated in recent years, so has the availability of the Bible in formats other than print. And while a print version of the Bible remains

Bible Engagement in America

n=12,062 | 2011–2016 | American Bible Society

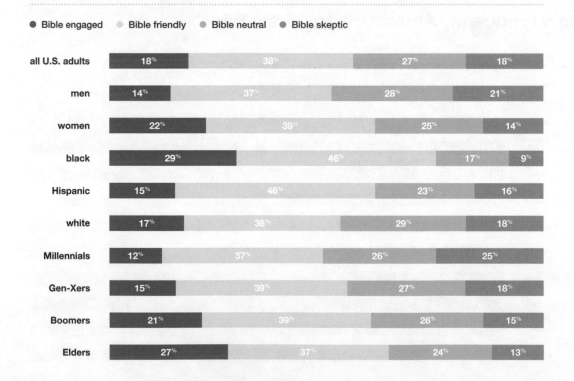

● Bible engaged   ● Bible friendly   ● Bible neutral   ● Bible skeptic

	Bible engaged	Bible friendly	Bible neutral	Bible skeptic
all U.S. adults	18%	38%	27%	18%
men	14%	37%	28%	21%
women	22%	39%	25%	14%
black	29%	46%	17%	9%
Hispanic	15%	46%	23%	16%
white	17%	36%	29%	18%
Millennials	12%	37%	26%	25%
Gen-Xers	15%	39%	27%	18%
Boomers	21%	39%	26%	15%
Elders	27%	37%	24%	13%

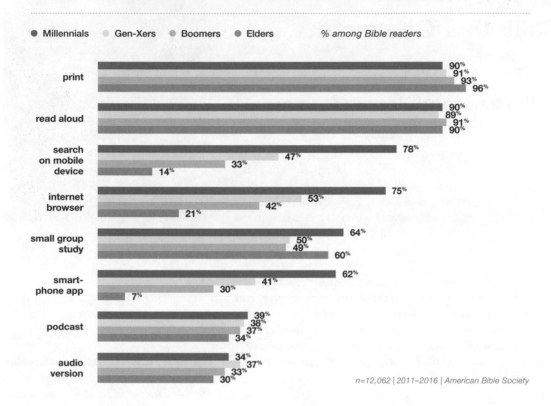

Bible Formats Used Within the Past 12 Months

● Millennials   ● Gen-Xers   ● Boomers   ● Elders   *% among Bible readers*

print
90%
91%
93%
96%

read aloud
90%
89%
91%
90%

search on mobile device
78%
47%
33%
14%

internet browser
75%
53%
42%
21%

small group study
64%
50%
49%
60%

smart-phone app
62%
41%
30%
7%

podcast
39%
38%
37%
34%

audio version
34%
37%
33%
30%

n=12,062 | 2011–2016 | American Bible Society

the preference of most U.S. adults, other formats are gaining in popularity.

Nine out of 10 Bible readers—those who report reading the Bible at least three or four times a year—say they have read from a print version or heard the Bible read aloud in a worship service or Catholic Mass. About half (a fairly consistent percentage since 2011) say they studied the Bible in a small group.

The most significant changes are among Bible readers who have used alternate technologies to access the Bible. Using the internet to read the Bible has increased by 12 percentage points since 2011; listening to a Bible podcast has increased 13 points; and searches for Bible content on mobile devices has increased by an incredible 25 points. One-third of Bible readers have accessed the Bible through a Bible app.

The growing popularity of these technologies represents an enormous opportunity for those who seek to increase Bible engagement—especially among Millennial Bible readers, who are most likely to report using digital versions of the Bible. And while they're just as likely as Gen-Xers and Boomers to express a preference for print (about eight in 10), 18 percent say they prefer a smartphone or tablet app—making them twice as likely as Boomers (9%) and six times more likely than Elders (3%) to say so.

A Q&A on Faith that Connects

with Reverend Bonnie Camarda

Camarda is divisional director of partnerships for The Salvation Army of Eastern Pennsylvania and Delaware, forming relationships with business and government leaders, donors, social service organizations, and individuals. She has business administration and administrative science degrees and a Masters of Divinity. She is highly involved in her community, Hispanic Christian groups, and other faith organizations.

Barna research conducted on behalf of American Bible Society shows that 15 percent of Hispanic Americans read the Bible four or more times a week, slightly below the national average of 18 percent. They are, however, more likely to have a high view of Scripture; 72 percent believe it is the actual word of God, and 59 percent believe it is true in all it teaches.

As a bilingual leader, have you observed differences in how Spanish-speaking Christians and English-speaking Christians engage with the Bible personally or corporately, or both?

I have observed that Spanish-speaking Christians tend to display their faith in a more vibrant and open manner than English-speaking Christians. This was very evident during the Pope's visit to Philadelphia—I witnessed thousands of Hispanic Christians marching through the streets holding signs, playing instruments, and singing and dancing on their way to Mass. Spanish-speaking Christians, particularly the impoverished, seem to turn naturally to their spirituality to guide them through life's challenges. They tend to be very verbal about their beliefs. That being said, I know Christians of all ethnicities who know the gospel, who are fervent and devoted to the Bible's teachings, whether or not they display it publicly. Regardless of language, engaging with the Bible is so important in urban ministry, especially how its lessons help us address the root challenges of violence and poverty.

You earned a graduate seminary degree in an era when women were still just a tiny minority of divinity students.

In what ways has your education in theology and biblical studies informed your leadership both inside and outside the church?

I was one of the few women in that particular seminary to obtain a graduate degree at the time. I was blessed that the president of the seminary, an 80-year-old man, recognized the need for women in leadership in the next generation. Having him as a mentor helped set me up for success as a leader throughout my life.

In my leadership roles inside and outside the church, I have come to believe that biblical teaching has to go beyond the church walls. We must go out into the community. Christianity should not be centralized within a physical church; rather our faith is about connecting with people in the community and sharing the gospel.

Mapping Bible Engagement across a Changing Culture

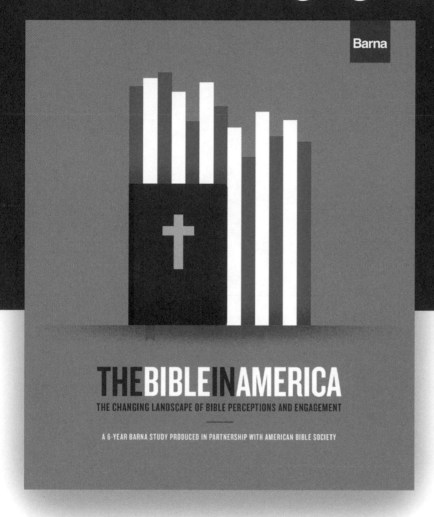

Barna

THE**BIBLEINAMERICA**

THE CHANGING LANDSCAPE OF BIBLE PERCEPTIONS AND ENGAGEMENT

A 6-YEAR BARNA STUDY PRODUCED IN PARTNERSHIP WITH AMERICAN BIBLE SOCIETY

You will learn

- Whether Americans believe the Bible is authoritative for their lives

- How often people read, hear, and study the Scriptures

- What the data suggests about the future of Bible engagement

- How technology is changing the ways people relate to the Bible

This is a crucial season in American public life. Rising skepticism is creating an atmosphere of hostility and antagonism toward claims of faith. But despite a rapidly changing culture, the Bible remains one of God's most important instruments in the redemption and transformation of his creation. *The Bible in America* is a multiyear survey of attitudes toward and perceptions of the Bible. On behalf of American Bible Society, Barna researchers conducted more than 14,000 interviews with American teens and adults since 2011. The study offers analysis, insights, and encouragement to leaders eager to understand how Americans engage with the Scriptures today and how to cultivate a deep-rooted biblical faith that holds steady in an ever-changing world.

Order at
**barna.com
/bibleinamerica**

Church

Getting to know the people
who are in the pews

Who's (Still) in Church?

From technology to politics, a lot has changed in 30 years. Spiritual routines are no exception. Church attendance, though still a vital part of many Americans' lives, has been inconsistent since Barna began tracking it in 1986. Back then, nearly half (48%) reported going to a church service in the past week. That number has declined and climbed over the years but has recently trended downward to its lowest point yet (35%).

In 1993, Barna also began recording how many Americans have not gone to church in at least six months, a group described as "unchurched." At the time, 22 percent matched this definition; in 2016, twice as many meet this criteria (44%).

There are a number of factors that influence church attendance habits, such as geography, ethnicity, and age. For example, Millennials are the least likely generation to regularly go to church; less than three in ten (28%) of them have attended in the last week. Among Gen-Xers, the number climbs slightly to 33 percent. Meanwhile, Elders are the most churched generation; 48 percent say they have been to a service in the past week, a full 12 percent more than Boomers (36%).

Barna founder George Barna and Barna president David Kinnaman collaborated on the 2014 book *Churchless* to further examine the nation's unchurched community. "More Americans than ever are not attending church. Most of them did at some point and, for one reason or another, decided not to continue," Kinnaman says. "This fact should motivate church leaders and attenders to examine how to make appropriate changes—not for the sake of enhancing attendance numbers but to address the lack of life transformation that would attract more people to remain an active part."

Church Attendance: A 30-Year Review

Americans who report attending church in the past week

n=1,205 | February 1993; n=1,200 | December 1986; n=2,005 | January 20-February 16, 2016

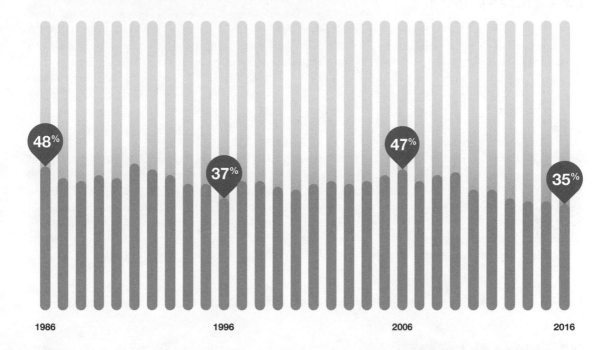

48%   37%   47%   35%

1986   1996   2006   2016

America by the #s

 61%

 62%   59%

1 Chattanooga, Tennessee, ranks first for active church attendance; 63 percent of its population went in the past week. Sixty-one percent of those in San Francisco, California, have not been to church in the past six months, making it the most unchurched city.

2 You're most likely to find churchgoers in Utah; 62 percent of its residents report weekly attendance, more than in any other state. Nearly the same percentage (59 percent) in Vermont qualify as unchurched.

n=65,064 | 2006-2016

What People Think of Church 💬👤

The church has been a cornerstone of American life for centuries. But although most American adults still value the church's presence and service in their community, their views of its role in other areas of life have shifted. Barna found that 80 percent of adults believe the presence of a church was *very* or *somewhat* favorable for a community. A small minority (3%) believe a church was a very unfavorable thing for a community.

When it comes to serving various needs in their community, half of adults (50%) believe the church can feed the needy (e.g., via food banks/food pantry), and more than four in 10 adults believe the church can provide shelter for the homeless (43%) and clothing for the needy (47%). These numbers seem high, yet at least half of all adults believe the church is unable to perform these duties.

When it comes to instilling morals or teaching people about the Bible and Jesus, the numbers are even lower (38% for both). Unsurprisingly, those who have never attended church have little confidence that the church fulfills these tasks (17% and 13% respectively). Does this loss of faith in the church also apply within its walls? Even among weekly churchgoers, just over four in 10 (42%) believe the church can instill values, and almost half (48%) believe it can provide teaching on the Bible or about Jesus.

More than two out of five Americans believe that, when it comes to what happens in the country today, "people of faith" (42%) and "religion" (46%) are part of the problem. Further, perceptions of clergy have changed. Clergy members were once commonly viewed as important leaders of society, trusted on a spectrum of issues. Today only one-fifth of U.S. adults strongly believe that clergy are a credible source of insight on the most important issues of our day.

What Needs Does Church Serve in Your Community?

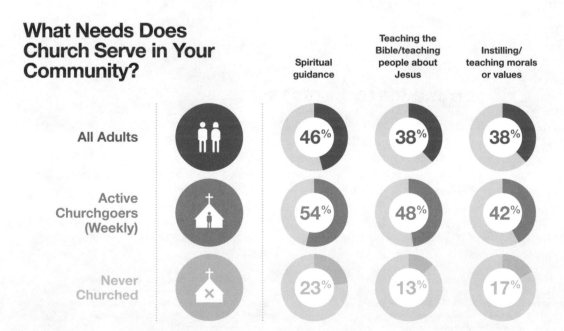

	Spiritual guidance	Teaching the Bible/teaching people about Jesus	Instilling/teaching morals or values
All Adults	46%	38%	38%
Active Churchgoers (Weekly)	54%	48%	42%
Never Churched	23%	13%	17%

n=1,000 adults | August 2015

Counting the Cost for Church Planters

Barna

CHURCH STARTUPS *and* MONEY

A Barna Report
Produced in Partnership
with Thrivent Financial

THE MYTHS & REALITIES OF CHURCH PLANTERS & FINANCES

You will learn

- How church planters perceive their financial situation

- The primary sources of income for planters

- The sources of income that correlate to greater financial stability

- What kind of training and support planters need in order to be effective startup leaders

Church planters are risk-takers who dive headfirst into God's calling to multiply his church. But the financial and administrative challenges of starting a church can take their toll on even the most energetic kingdom entrepreneur.

Produced in partnership with Thrivent Financial, *Church Startups and Money* is a study of the financial realities faced by church planters across the country. Barna interviewed more than 700 leaders whose ministries are in "startup mode" to find out how money—or lack thereof—impacts their ministry, family, and overall well-being. This research provides planters, planting networks, and other stakeholders support to speak honestly about the resources startup leaders need to thrive and plant thriving churches.

Order at
**barna.com
/churchplanting**

Why Many Women Are Leaving Church

Historically, men have been less likely to regularly attend church than women. Just over a decade ago, the gender gap was three unchurched men for every two unchurched women; fully 60 percent of unchurched people were men. Today, only 52 percent of the unchurched are men. The gender gap has narrowed from 20 points to just 6 points in the last 10 years.

While just over half of all adult women have gone to church in the past week or past month (36% and 14%, respectively), four in 10 (42%) have not been to church in the past six months.

The majority (87%) of unchurched women are dechurched. Fewer than one in 10 American women (8%) have never been to church at all. Meaning it's not that most of these unchurched women are unfamiliar with or inexperienced in church, but rather that at one point they decided church was no longer for them.

Below are five trends Barna sees as contributing factors to this shift away from church among women.

1. Competing Priorities

When asked, "How important is it for you, personally, to attend a local church?" only one-third of women said that local church attendance is very important to them. At the other end of the scale, just over a quarter of these women (27%) say

that attending a local church is not at all important to them, and similarly, 24 percent say it's not too important.

If more than half of women say attending church is not particularly important to them, where are they placing their priorities? When asked to rank several priorities in their life, women far and away ranked family relationships as their top priority (68%). Church or religious activities did come in second—but a very distant second (11%) and were ranked equally important as personal time/development (10%).

Interestingly, the top priority least selected by women is work or career (5%), but it is also the second most common top time commitment for women (31%). Although women may not feel comfortable identifying their job as their top priority, their actual time commitment reflects a high value for that part of their lives. Family relationships are the top time commitment for 44 percent of women.

2. Busyness

Many women today are just busy. And they are experiencing

a tension between things they might want to do and things they actually have time for. Research conducted for the Barna FRAME *Wonder Women* found 72 percent of women feel stressed out, 58 percent are tired, and 48 percent say they are overcommitted. The percentages are even higher among moms with kids at home.

Nearly nine in 10 women (88%) say they want to improve in at least one area of life—and what is the area they cite the most, over work, family, and friends? Church. Although only 5 percent of women selected church or religious activities as their top time commitment, this is an area of life that two in 10 (22%) women want to improve in, indicating that many women find their desires for church or religious engagement to be at odds with the constraints of their everyday realities.

There is still a desire among many women to be spiritually active in a church community, but there are barriers preventing that desire from becoming behavior. Many women—and especially moms—feel like they just don't have time for church in today's busy, fast-paced life.

3. Lack of Emotional Engagement or Support
Fewer than half of women indicate receiving any emotional support from people at their church or synagogue. Only 17 percent of women say they feel very supported at church and fewer than a quarter (23%) say they feel somewhat supported. Nearly half of women (43%) say they do not feel any emotional support at all from church. This relational disconnect may provide a key for understanding how women are able to disengage from churches. Without strong relational bonds within a church community, women's absence from church can largely go unnoticed. This poses the question of where women are finding such support—and indicates a large opportunity for those churches that are seeking to engage women in their community.

4. Changing Family Structures
Many churches are built around the traditional nuclear family structure: husband, wife, children. However, young women are increasingly less likely to fit into this mold. The average age of first marriage has risen dramatically over the last decades. Most women do not get married until they are in their mid-to-late twenties now. And while young women still want to get married at some point in their life, they have a lot of personal things they want to do

Women's departure from church corresponds to a broader trend in the United States. Church attendance decreases with every generation, and six in 10 20somethings who grew up in church have dropped out at some point.

n=1,026 | February 20–24, 2014; n=1,000 | August 24–26, 2015

first, including developing more fully as a person and becoming financially stable. Such delays in marriage and parenting have significant effects on churches that prioritize family ministry and have little to offer in terms of connecting faith and work.

5. Changes in Belief
The majority of unchurched women still say they are Christians—56 percent self-identify as Christian, even though they haven't attended a church service in at least six months. However, particularly among younger Christians, the number of those who have not only left the church but have also left the faith is growing. Just 48 percent of unchurched Millennial women self-identify as Christian. The number of women who identify as atheist or agnostic has risen from 8 percent in 2000 to 15 percent today. Among Millennial women that number is even higher; more than a quarter now identify as atheists (26%), up from 18 percent in 2005.

An Untethered Faith
Barna editor-in-chief Roxanne Stone recently analyzed this data on women leaving the church in an article for *Today's Christian Woman.*

She writes, "Aside from delaying marriage and children, young adults are eschewing other forms of 'settling down' as well. They are more prone to regularly switching jobs (and, with that, often where they live). In other words, there are very few

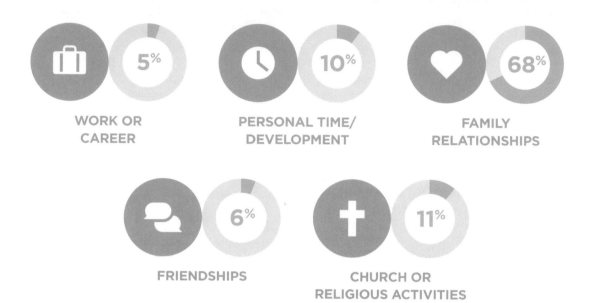

TOP PRIORITIES FOR WOMEN

5%
WORK OR CAREER

10%
PERSONAL TIME/ DEVELOPMENT

68%
FAMILY RELATIONSHIPS

6%
FRIENDSHIPS

11%
CHURCH OR RELIGIOUS ACTIVITIES

n=1,404 (732 women) | June 25-July 1, 2013

institutions—either social or economic— binding Millennials.

"In a recent Barna Group study on identity, Millennials were significantly less likely than other generations to claim any of the surveyed factors (family, faith, country, city, state, ethnicity, career) as central to their identity. This generational sense of disenfranchisement has not helped draw young adults in general to a church—let alone young women, among whom such societal untetheredness is unprecedented. These massive changes—the delaying of family, an increase in institutional skepticism, and the separation of individuals from traditional social structures—are sufficient to affect church attendance," Stone continues. "Unfortunately, they also correspond with the great cultural lament of our time: Everyone is really, really busy.

"Many women—particularly those still identifying as Christian—may want to believe that they can hold to their faith even as they find less and less time in their life for church. However, Barna's research over the years has shown that people who are disconnected from church—even those who self-identify as Christian—are less likely to engage in other faith activities: including Bible reading, prayer, volunteering, and charitable giving. While correlation never equals causation, these are important indicators to pay attention to," concludes Stone. "Whether we want to admit it or not, church attendance roots believers in regular faith rhythms and increases many other related faith practices."

A Q&A on a Changing Church Landscape

with Christine Caine

Christine Caine is an evangelist, activist, and international speaker. She is the founder of A21, an anti–human trafficking organization that fights slavery around the globe, and Propel, an initiative that seeks to serve women who lead. She has authored several books, including her most recent, Unashamed*.*

Even as other denominations face decline, the charismatic church has seen continued growth in recent years, especially among Millennials. Why do you think this is?
Primarily, the charismatic movement connects the truth of the Word of God with the reality of the Spirit of God. This generation wants to experience God, as well as get to know him through his Word. They want the gifts of the Spirit and the fruit of the Spirit to work alongside each other. They want a gospel that is full of power that will help them to navigate the complexities of living in this world. This is not an either/or generation, but a both/and generation. They do not fear the supernatural power of God, but in fact long for it to be a reality in their everyday lives. They want a living, active, dynamic, personal faith that can transform the world around them. Millennials love to experience everything for themselves, and this is evident in their faith practice. Faith for them must be dynamic, growing, moving, felt, tasted, touched, seen, and heard. It must invade all of their life.

Barna research shows 42 percent of women today are considered "unchurched" (have not been to church in the past six months). How do you think the Church can better understand and reach today's women?
One of the greatest challenges for the Church today is to make the gospel relevant to women. We are hemorrhaging a generation of women who have often been made to feel that they have a limited role to play in the Church. The landscape has changed dramatically for many women in the western world when it comes to their inclusion in and contribution to all sectors of society and decision making—but there has not necessarily been a corresponding shift in church. Women often feel more esteemed, valued, celebrated, and included outside of the church than within the Church. We need to be willing to admit this disparity exists and be committed to helping to forge a new pathway forward. Women have been thrust into a new landscape in our world where they can have and do it all, but lack the road maps to navigate this new reality. I believe the Church can be a huge answer to the angst many women feel, if we choose to acknowledge who today's woman is, what her struggles really are, and commit to helping her find her place in the body of Christ. Church leaders must welcome the voices of women at our tables and in our decision-making processes. We must do the hard work to create pipelines that include women actively in church life and ministry. Jesus esteemed, valued, and affirmed women, and I believe that if the church reflects these values, women would reengage dramatically.

BARNA
TAKES

To Reach Young People, Reach Families

Kara Powell,
Jake Mulder, and
Brad Griffin

If your church is like many, you have bare spots: holes created by the younger generations missing from your congregation. According to 2015 U.S. Census Bureau projections, adults ages 18 to 29 comprised 17 percent of the adult population. Yet that same age group represents less than 10 percent of church attendees nationwide, according to the U.S. Congregational Life Survey. In other words, the generation gap is all too real in too many of today's churches.

In the midst of this age gap, there are hundreds of "bright spot" congregations that are effectively loving and serving young people in their twenties as well as their teens. Some of them quietly and without flash. Others with great magnetism and fanfare. At the Fuller Youth Institute (FYI), we call these churches "growing young" because:

1. They are engaging young people ages 15–29, and
2. They are growing—spiritually, emotionally, missionally, and sometimes also numerically.

Four years ago, the FYI team launched an investigation into what these innovative churches are doing right. We studied over 250 growing young churches because we wanted to give leaders and parents access to what's actually working. These churches are diverse in age, size, denomination (or lack thereof), ethnicity, and geographical region, but in the midst of their variety, they hold several core commitments in common.

One of these core commitments is that they prioritize young people. More accurately, they *disproportionately* prioritize young people. Their choice to place young people at the center of their life together is the inflection point that separates them from those churches that are growing old.

In all candor, until we began gathering data from churches, we didn't anticipate how much prioritization would surface in the research. But when we asked pastoral leaders to name up to three characteristics of their churches that account for their success at engaging young people, the top response category—tied with leadership—was making young people and their interests a priority.

Often that translates into budget. Sometimes that has implications for staffing and facility. But always it means that as the church makes major decisions or plans, young people are front and center. As Easter Sunday approaches, one of the first questions becomes, What role will young people play in our Easter service? As churchwide short-term mission trips are being planned, a key initial question is, How does this fit with the momentum and calendar of our youth and young adult ministries?

These wise churches have also recognized it's impossible to prioritize young people well without also prioritizing their families. The best data across disciplines confirms that parents still carry the most important weight in their kids' faith development. This is true not only in childhood but also through adolescence, according to Christian Smith and the National Study of Youth and Religion team. That means the role of ministry leaders who care about kids must also include the care, equipping, and formation of parents and families.

My (Kara's) church realized we had become good at the rhetoric of partnering with families, but had not put that rhetoric into practice. Resolving to blend

words with action more consistently, the student ministry team devised a plan for parent engagement that includes daily, weekly, monthly, and yearly touch points.

Daily: Each day from Monday through Friday, the staff members set calendar reminders to stop and pray for five minutes for parents. Five minutes may not sound like much, but our leaders confessed that before the cues, they hardly prayed for parents at all.

Weekly: The team agreed to communicate with all parents directly once each week in some way—most often through a weekly email to parents—and to communicate with various parents individually through occasional calls, texts, and meetings. This commitment included a promise to respond to parent emails and phone calls within 48 hours.

Monthly: Parent training had been scattered and inconsistent at our church, so the team built a monthly rhythm of resourcing parents directly. Using a variety of means, they offered training parents could access more readily: an online article one month, a parent book club another, and occasionally an in-person training seminar.

Yearly: Taking a cue from schools, our innovative ministry leaders set up annual parent-leader conferences. They scheduled 30-minute blocks over the course of a couple of weeks, and the staff or volunteer team member most connected with a student would meet with that student's parents for an intentional conversation. The leader shared highlights of the student's growth, the gifts they saw emerging, and the ministry's vision of better partnering with parents to nurture teenagers' spiritual formation. Perhaps most importantly, they asked seven golden words: How can we pray for your family?

It took time to establish all of these rhythms, but the hard work has paid off over the past several years. Today, parents at our church feel more connected and cared for than ever, and the ministry leaders benefit from greater parent buy-in and support.

Churches are making these decisions to prioritize young people and their families not just for the sake of pleasing young people, but because the whole church benefits. As one pastor of over 40 years put it, "Everybody rises when you focus on children and teens." Adults in another church reflected, "Young people are like salt. When they're included, they make everything taste better."

Adapted from Growing Young *by Kara Powell, Jake Mulder, and Brad Griffin. Used by permission. (Baker Books, a division of Baker Publishing Group, 2016). For more information about this research and free resources, visit churchesgrowingyoung.com.*

Millennials Are Looking for More from Church 💬🧑

Millennials have come of age at a time when many of the institutions and structures that undergird North American society have faltered. And with the myriad voices competing for Millennials' attention and their skepticism about institutions, many are not sure where to place their trust—a cynicism that extends to the church. Among those who grew up in church, nearly six in 10 have dropped out at some point.

Why have so many closed the door on church involvement? Why have more than half been absent from church for the past six months? Why do three in 10 Millennials say church is not at all important while an additional four in 10 feel ambivalent?

Research for the Barna FRAME *Sacred Roots* asked Millennials why they do or don't think church is important. Their answers reveal a general feeling that church is simply not necessary—and, for some, that it is harmful.

Among those who say church is not important, most are split between two reasons: Two in five say church isn't important because they can find God elsewhere (30%), and one-third say it's because church is not personally relevant to them (35%). One in three simply find church boring (31%) and one in five say it feels like God is missing from church (20%). Only 8 percent say they don't

attend because church is "out of date," undercutting the notion that all we need to do for Millennials is to make church "cooler."

A significant number of young adults have deeper complaints about church. More than one-third say their negative perceptions are a result of moral failures in church leadership (35%). Almost half—44 percent—feel church people are hypocritical. Nearly one in three say Christianity is anti-science (29%) and one in four call it anti-intellectual (24%).

In a national survey conducted by Barna and Cornerstone Knowledge Network, respondents were asked to rate how well each statement in a series describes the Christian community in America. Fewer than half of respondents agree a lot or somewhat that the statement "The people at church are tolerant of those with different beliefs" describes the church (46%). About the same proportion say that "The church seems too much like an exclusive club" is an accurate description (44%). Taken together, a significant number of young adults perceive a lack of relational generosity within the U.S. Christian community.

More worrisome are the two-thirds of Millennials who believe American churchgoers are a lot or somewhat hypocritical (66%). To a generation that prides itself on the ability to smell a fake at 10 paces, hypocrisy is the mother of all indictments.

Open Windows

If those are the closed doors of negative views on the church, positive perceptions are windows that show Millennials' openness to connecting with the Jesus community. What do they find valuable in church? Their answers can give insights for what to prioritize in ministry to and with Millennials. A plurality say they attend church to be closer to God (54%) and three in 10 go to learn more about God (31%). Getting outside the humdrum of their everyday lives to experience transcendence—in worship, in prayer, in teaching—is a key desire for many Millennials when it comes to church.

Two-thirds of survey participants say a good description of church is "a place to find answers to live a meaningful life" (a lot + somewhat = 65%). Over half say "church is relevant for my life" (54%), and about half "feel I can 'be myself' at church" (49%). Three out of five survey respondents say it is not true that "the faith and teaching I encounter at church seem rather shallow" (not too much + not at all = 62%), and about the same number would not agree with the statement "the church is not a safe place to express doubts" (60%).

Millennials are, on the whole, skeptical about the role churches play in society. This is the closed door. But their hope for the role churches could play? That's an open window.

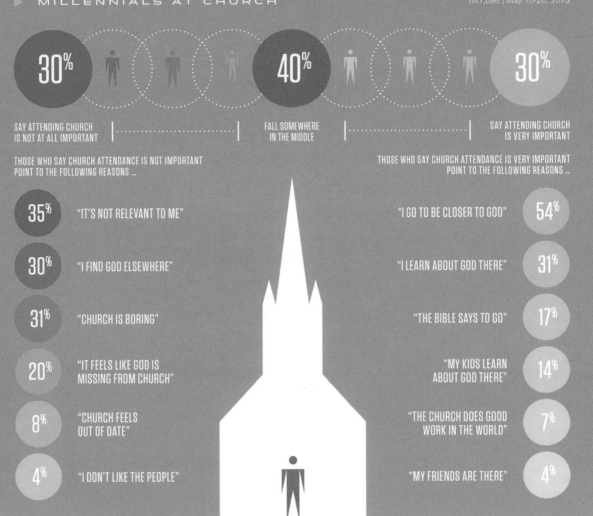

30%

SAY ATTENDING CHURCH
IS NOT AT ALL IMPORTANT

40%

FALL SOMEWHERE
IN THE MIDDLE

30%

SAY ATTENDING CHURCH
IS VERY IMPORTANT

THOSE WHO SAY CHURCH ATTENDANCE IS NOT IMPORTANT
POINT TO THE FOLLOWING REASONS ...

35% "IT'S NOT RELEVANT TO ME"

30% "I FIND GOD ELSEWHERE"

31% "CHURCH IS BORING"

20% "IT FEELS LIKE GOD IS MISSING FROM CHURCH"

8% "CHURCH FEELS OUT OF DATE"

4% "I DON'T LIKE THE PEOPLE"

THOSE WHO SAY CHURCH ATTENDANCE IS VERY IMPORTANT
POINT TO THE FOLLOWING REASONS ...

"I GO TO BE CLOSER TO GOD" **54%**

"I LEARN ABOUT GOD THERE" **31%**

"THE BIBLE SAYS TO GO" **17%**

"MY KIDS LEARN ABOUT GOD THERE" **14%**

"THE CHURCH DOES GOOD WORK IN THE WORLD" **7%**

"MY FRIENDS ARE THERE" **4%**

Life-Shaping Relationships

Young adults who continue their involvement in a local church beyond their teen years are twice as likely as those who don't to have a close personal friendship with an older adult in their faith community (59% vs. 31% among church dropouts). They're also twice as likely to have had a mentor other than a pastor or youth minister (28% vs. 11%). That means, conversely, that seven out of 10 Millennials who dropped out of church did not have a close friendship with an older adult, and nearly nine out of 10 never had a mentor at their church. Of course, correlation does not equal causation. But if Jesus' discipling style is any indication, consistent, deepening friendship over a long period of time and through life's hills and valleys is an (if not *the*) essential element of lasting spiritual formation within the community of faith.

Vocational Discipleship

Work is very central to the Millennial identity—as well as a great source of stress; half (49%) of Millennials worry about choosing the wrong career. Helping young adults connect the dots between faith and work makes a difference to their lifelong pursuit of Jesus. Millen-

MILLENNIALS ARE HESITANT TO SHARE MUCH INFORMATION WITH A CHURCH WHEN THEY VISIT FOR THE FIRST TIME:

WELCOME!
PLEASE PROVIDE THE FOLLOWING INFORMATION:

FIRST NAME	82%
LAST NAME	53%
EMAIL ADDRESS	33%
PHYSICAL ADDRESS	19%
PHONE NUMBER	12%
SOCIAL MEDIA	6%
I DON'T WANT TO SHARE ANYTHING	15%

SUBMIT

nials who remain active in church are: more than twice as likely as dropouts to have learned how Christians can positively contribute to society (46% compared to 20%); nearly four times as likely to say they better understand their purpose in life through church (45% compared to 12%); three times more likely to say they learned to view their gifts and passions as part of God's calling (45% compared to 17%); and four times more likely to have learned how the Bible applies to their field or career (29% compared to 7%). A similar gap exists when it comes to having received helpful input from a pastor about education (21% compared to 5%).

Drawn to Serve

Serving is not incidental for the next generation. Barna partnered with Compassion International to assess Americans' attitudes toward and perceptions of extreme global poverty. The study found that, among the general population, there is broad agreement that Christians have a unique obligation; two-thirds of U.S. adults agree strongly or somewhat that

Christians should play a strong role in alleviating poverty (66%). The proportion of practicing Christians under 40 who agree is even higher, nearly nine in 10 (86%). About half of young practicing Christians say their church should be more involved in fighting extreme poverty (47%), and almost the same number say they would give more if their church were more involved with poverty alleviation (45%). Among Millennials who attend church, one in six say it's important to them because the church is God's hands and feet in the world (16%).

Millennials have a reputation for being concerned about social justice, even though their record as effective, long-haul activists is spotty thus far. They share an expectation that communities of faith should lead the charge on justice issues like poverty. And when a church's resources are channeled inward instead of outward, they don't hesitate to criticize.

When mobile focus groups in Chicago and Atlanta visited suburban megachurches, participants in both locations commented that such facilities must require a lot of financial resources to build and maintain. "It feels like a really big business," said one. "There's a lot of money here," another observed. Participants in both groups expressed skepticism and mistrust of a church that spends too much on itself instead of on serving others. (To be fair, the churches visited have generous outreach and missions budgets, but these programs were not front and center to counteract the groups' impression of extravagance.) To Millennials, sacrificial generosity is non-negotiable when it comes to communities that claim to follow Jesus.

There is an aspirational element involved in this high standard. Many in the younger generation express a desire to make the world a better place. Their desire is a faint echo of God's intention to remake the heavens and the earth into a whole, healed place where he will dwell forever with his people (see Rev. 21:5). What would it look like for your church to mentor Millennials to live in the new creation? If young adults aspire to be sacrificially generous but don't know how, their mentoring friendships should incorporate clear teaching on and rigorous practice of the Christian virtue of charity.

More of Jesus

Serving with a godly, trustworthy older friend isn't the only thing a young adult needs to stay connected to a family of faith. She should also be able to seek and find Jesus.

When presented with four images and asked to select which most feels like present-day Christianity American Millennials from all regions were likely to pick a negative image: a pointing finger with a Bible.

n=843 ages 18–29 | October 10–15, 2013; n=1,086 | May 10–20, 2013; n=784 ages 18 to 29, with a Christian background | January 7-23, 2011

Sadly, one in five Millennials with a church background report, "God seems missing from my experience of church" (20%). (This includes dropouts and regular church attenders.) Among young adults who drop out of church involvement, one in four believes Jesus speaks to them in a personal and relevant way, compared to seven out of 10 of those who remain in a Christian community.

It's a chicken-or-egg question to identify if people drop out of church because they haven't heard from Jesus, or if they haven't heard from Jesus because they're disconnected from church (or if the correlation of these two factors is merely coincidental). The fact remains that eight out of 10 young adults say growing closer to or learning about God are the two most important reasons to attend church. And with all the other options open to Millennials, it's safe to conclude that, when they show up at church for a worship or learning opportunity, they do so hoping there is Someone present to worship or learn about.

There is no simple, one-size-fits-all blueprint for an institutional culture, ministry program, leadership structure, or building that is guaranteed to reach Millennials. But the data shows that cultural discernment, intergenerational friendships, vocational discipleship, and an experience of and connection with Jesus are just some of the reasons Millennials go to—and stay in—church.

Design with Millennials in Mind

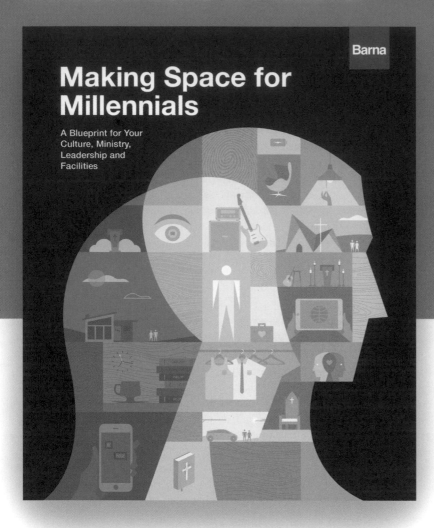

Making Space for Millennials

A Blueprint for Your Culture, Ministry, Leadership and Facilities

Barna

Use this book to

- Discover how churches are impacted by the values, allegiances, and assumptions of Millennials

- Hear Millennials' perspectives on worship and community spaces

- Learn from practitioners in culture, ministry, leadership, and facilities

- Gain valuable insights about how this generation views and relates to form and function

Faith communities and Christian organizations are struggling with how to make space for Millennials—not just appealing space in their buildings and gathering places, but also space in their institutional culture, ministry models, and leadership approach. This groundbreaking report, produced in partnership with Cornerstone Knowledge Network, is a handbook for turning information about Millennials into connections with Millennials in your church, school, or organization.

Whether you're a pastor, educator, youth or young adult ministry leader, nonprofit or business leader, or a parent, *Making Space for Millennials* is designed to help you make the most of your current and future partnerships with Millennials.

Order at
**barna.com
/makingspace**

A Single-Minded Church

Joyce Chiu,
Barna Group,
Research Associate

There are more married people in church than single people. You probably already know this just from looking around every Sunday—but here's some data to prove it. According to a recent Barna study, less than a quarter of active churchgoers are single (23%). Comparing to the national average, the 2014 U.S. census estimates that more than half of Americans (54%) between the ages of 18 to 49 are single (either never married or divorced). Young adults are also getting married later in life. This means that your church should be filling up at least half of your pews with single people. So what will get them there?

The same Barna study found the majority of singles who are not active in or committed to a church are searching for meaning and purpose in life (55%). These single Americans say they have emotional pain or frustration they would like to resolve (50%) and that something feels missing from their life (45%). There is a real sense of awareness that they have a spiritual vacuum needing and waiting to be filled, especially among older singles.

In fact, almost two-thirds of these singles (65%) are looking for ways to improve themselves and nearly one out of six (15%) would be motivated to go to church for the opportunity to find out more about God. Christians are called not only to be educators of biblical principles, but more importantly, to be disciple-makers. Here is a group of people, willing and ready to follow. How can the church, as the body of Christ, better reach these singles?

I believe we can reach them by imitating what Jesus did with his disciples—by going as a loving community to reach those who are hurt and lonely. One in five (21%) singles who are not active in or committed to a church are interested in going to church to have support during difficult times. One-quarter of singles (23%) would be motivated to go to church if they simply knew that anyone would be welcomed into the church community.

We who are active in and committed to the church—married or not—must come up with better ways to incorporate singles into leadership in the church, better ways to integrate marrieds and singles, and better ways to notice and serve the lonely. The church is not made up of husbands and wives, but sinners and seekers. Therefore, let us call on the entire Church to love better and more effectively through caring for the singles we already know, as well as the ones we don't.

Racial Differences Concerning Discipleship

Striving for unity within the Church does not mean striving for a kind of multi-cultural homogeneity. On the contrary, it requires recognizing racial differences in how Christians worship, grow spiritually, and so on. To that end, Barna has examined the different ways in which black and white Christians approach discipleship, individually and collectively.

What Is Spiritual Progress?

Black Christians are more likely to describe the process of spiritual progress as "spiritual maturation" (31%). White Christians prefer the phrase "spiritual growth" (21%). Barna found that this slight difference in word choice—maturation versus growth—encapsulates key differences between black and white Christians. The language of "maturation" implies an internal transformation and the development of wisdom through life experience, whereas the word "growth" suggests reaching milestones.

A majority of both groups believe "discipleship" is a concept that is relevant to spiritual growth: 65 percent of white Christians and 74 percent of black Christians agree that discipleship is relevant to spiritual growth. Black Christians are more likely to agree that it is "very relevant" (47% compared to 25%).

However, when black and white Christians were asked how they define "discipleship," they tended to choose different answers. White believers were more likely to define it as a "process of learning to follow Jesus Christ as Savior and Lord, seeking to observe all that Jesus commanded, by the power of the Holy Spirit and to his glory." Black Christians instead prefer this answer: "The process of transformation that changes us to be increasingly more like Christ through the Word, the Spirit, and *circumstance*" (italics added for emphasis).

For black Christians, spiritual progress is tied to experiences and life's circumstances. It is not just about meeting certain faith-based goals, but about maturing into a Christ-like character as one weathers life's seasons.

The greater emphasis on experience is also evident when one examines the reasons why black and white Christians want to grow spiritually. Although both groups share similar reasons, black Christians are more likely to select the answer, "I have been through a lot, and growing spiritually will help me" (34% compared to 27%). Life experiences can be a two-sided coin; they can hinder as well as foster the process of discipleship. Black pastors are more likely than white pastors to state that "guilt about things in the past" poses a major obstacle for their congregation's spiritual maturation (64% compared to 42%). Perhaps because of the disparity in experiential stakes, black disciples are much more likely to say that it is "very important" to them to see progress in their spiritual lives (82% compared to 59%).

How Is Discipleship Pursued?

According to Barna's research, there were plenty of similarities in how both groups define the primary goals of discipleship, but black Christian leaders were more likely to select as a goal of discipleship "deepening one's faith through education and fellowship" (85% compared to 70%).

1. Fellowship

A crucial part of "fellowship" for black Christians is mentorship. Black Christians are more likely to currently be mentored and discipled by another Christian (38% compared to 19%) and to be discipling others themselves (28% compared to 17%). Black church leaders are more likely to believe that having "regular one-on-one conversations about discipleship issues with a more mature believer" will make a significant impact on someone's spiritual development (93% compared to 81%). The prioritization of mentorship as a means of discipling, wherein the old pass on their wisdom to the young, makes sense in light of how black Christians frame spiritual progress as a kind of maturation shaped by their experiences.

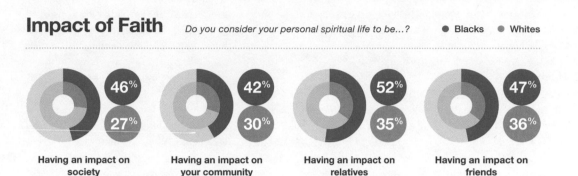

Impact of Faith
Do you consider your personal spiritual life to be...? ● Blacks ● Whites

Having an impact on society — 46% / 27%

Having an impact on your community — 42% / 30%

Having an impact on relatives — 52% / 35%

Having an impact on friends — 47% / 36%

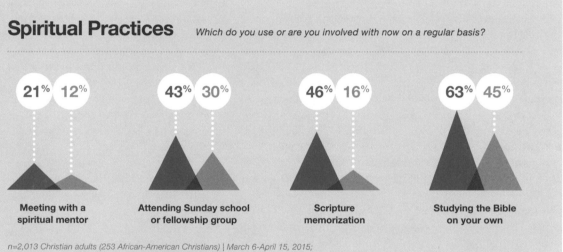

Spiritual Practices
Which do you use or are you involved with now on a regular basis?

Meeting with a spiritual mentor — 21% / 12%

Attending Sunday school or fellowship group — 43% / 30%

Scripture memorization — 46% / 16%

Studying the Bible on your own — 63% / 45%

n=2,013 Christian adults (253 African-American Christians) | March 6-April 15, 2015;
n=833 church leaders (702 white congregations, 68 black congregations) | April 7-May 30, 2015 | The Navigators

White Christians are more likely than black Christians to prefer being discipled on their own (39% compared to 31%), whereas black Christians show a greater preference for group-based discipleship (32% compared to 22%). Group-based discipleship is not just about small groups, although both black and white church leaders hold that to be the most effective means of discipleship. Large groups and family networks are also prime settings for spiritual maturation. Black church leaders are more likely to list large group study or discussion groups (18% compared to 4%) and family members (71% compared to 61%) as "very important" in aiding spiritual development.

Given that black communities tend toward communal rhythms of spiritual development while white communities prefer more individualistic settings, it is not surprising that white Christians are more likely to view their spiritual life as "entirely private" (42% compared to 32%). Black Christians, on the other hand, are much more likely to believe their personal spiritual life has an impact on others—whether they are relatives, friends, community, or society at large.

This sense of impact is tied to the different ways that each group approaches evangelism. Four in ten white Christians tend to be more likely to disagree that they have a responsibility to tell others about their religious beliefs (39% compared to 28%), whereas half of black

Christians believe it is their responsibility to tell others (50% compared to 34%). The ways in which we grow in our faith—communal or individualistic—seem to shape the ways—public or private—in which we live it out.

2. Education

Another crucial way by which both communities grow spiritually is through studying the Bible. Black Christians, however, generally demonstrate a higher regard of and deeper devotion to Scripture. They are more likely to believe that the Bible is "totally accurate in all of the principles it teaches" (59% compared to 48%), a belief that translates into more consistent and frequent study of the Bible (63% compared to 45%) and memorization of Scriptures (46% compared to 16%).

Unsurprisingly, black Christians consistently rate the personal spiritual impact of many forms of biblical study—including memorizing or meditating on Scriptures, studying the Bible in a group or on one's own, or following Bible study curriculums—at higher levels than white Christians. This starts with leadership; black church leaders are also more likely than their white counterparts to believe that "teaching the Word in weekly services" (90% compared to 80%) and "memorizing Scripture" (75% compared to 63%) will have a "significant impact on developing disciples."

In addition to the emphasis that black Christians place on their life experiences, it is also important to recognize the high esteem that they have for the Bible, as it indicates that the Bible is likely a very important authority and guide for navigating their life experiences. The integration of experience and Scripture is most likely an activity that regularly happens in community, whether with a mentor or a larger group.

3. Friendships

One of the more significant differences that Barna found in its research is the role that friendships play in the lives of white and black Christians for their spiritual growth.

Black Christians were more likely to rate their relationships with family members, mentors, church members, Christian communities outside of church, and small group members as "valuable" for their spiritual journeys. Whites and blacks were just as likely to rate friendships as valuable; 43 percent of white Christians deemed their friendships as valuable for their spiritual journey, compared to 41 percent of black Christians. Only 14 percent of white Christians thought their friends were "not too valuable" or "not at all valuable," in contrast to one-quarter (26%) of black Christians. Barna also found that white Christians are slightly less likely to feel that the fact that their "friends are not as interested in

spiritual things" poses a major obstacle to their spiritual growth (8% compared to 11%). Black church leaders were much more likely to believe that "navigating peer relationships" poses a major obstacle for people's growth as disciples (73% compared to 48%).

While black communities may have robust formal networks for spiritual development, such as mentorship structures, family networks, or small groups, it seems that their informal relational networks, such as friendships, might be more likely to be a source of spiritual hindrance. It is also telling that, even though black Christians are more likely to be mentors or be mentored, it is white Christians who are more likely to list being inspired by another person and wanting to be more like them as a reason for their desire to grow spiritually (13% compared to 5%). This statistic may indicate a greater prevalence of positive role models for white Christians among their peers, further confirming the overall statistics on friendship between black and white Christians.

Critical Gaps

Aside from the weak role of friendships, it seems that, overall, black Christians have developed strong mechanisms of fellowship and education for spiritual maturation, perhaps even more so than white Christians. This distinctive culture translates to a sense of greater spiritual devotion and commitment within black communities.

These healthy signs of faith do not mean that they are satisfied or complacent with their spiritual progress. In fact, black Christians are slightly less likely to say that they are happy with where they are in their spiritual life than white Christians (31% compared to 39%). This might be the result of heightened

Markers of Faith

● Blacks
● Whites

Qualify as practicing Christian

75%
62%

"My religious faith is very important in my life today"

90%
75%

"I have attended church service in the past week"

62%
55%

"I made a lot of spiritual progress in the past year"

55%
26%

n=2,013 Christian adults (253 African-American Christians) | March 6-April 15, 2015 | The Navigators

Overall, Christian adults believe their churches are doing well when it comes to discipleship. Fifty-two percent of those who have attended church in the past six months say their church "definitely does a good job helping people grow spiritually."

expectations for where they should be spiritually, but it might also be tied to the fact that black church leaders are much more likely to believe that there are not enough discipleship programs and resources out there (42% compared to 19%).

"Discipleship resources" include curriculums and programs, which often cost money to purchase. Material gaps in resources, then, may be a real obstacle in discipleship for black Christians, an unfortunate reality given their clear desire and hunger for spiritual development.

Beyond material resources, "discipleship resources" includes people—specifically, leaders to facilitate discussion groups or mentor others. Black church leaders believe that having a spiritual mentor is a more essential resource for discipling others (85%) than studying the Bible (82%) or having a comprehensive discipleship curriculum (69%). The fact that every single black church leader who was surveyed said that they were actively discipling members of their church (100% compared to 94% of white church

n=2,013 Christian adults (253 African-American Christians) | March 6-April 15, 2015; n=833 church leaders (702 white congregations, 68 black congregations) | April 7-May 30, 2015 | The Navigators

leaders) may indicate a shortage of experienced spiritual leaders. Moreover, black Christians are more likely to judge that they are not doing well at discipling new and young believers (47%) than to say that they are doing well (35%), even if their overall evaluations of their discipleship are higher than those of white church leaders.

Celebrating Differences

Our different communities of faith undoubtedly shape the ways in which we experience God. The focus on modes of discipleship, rather than styles of worship or preaching, is significant because it asks fundamental questions around what it means to be a Christian, as well as how to develop a Christian identity in others.

In looking over Barna's research, it is safe to say that a theology that is detached from experience and can be privately practiced will likely be foreign to a black Christian. Likewise, a church that relies heavily on robust social mechanisms (such as mentorship structures or large groups) to disciple others will likely be unfamiliar to a white Christian. So how do we respond to these differences?

As the Church at large seeks to bridge racial divides, it would be helpful to begin by recognizing that there is not a monolithic understanding and practice of spiritual development. There is room to celebrate and learn from each other's unique practices and beliefs.

BARNA
TAKES

What Keeps Christians from Integrated Worship?

Brooke Hempell,
Barna Group,
Vice President of
Research

I volunteer with a ministry in an extremely disadvantaged neighborhood in Atlanta. Like others in the city, the area has experienced decades of economic and social decline, despite the increasing prosperity of the city at large. It's a neighborhood desperately in need of restoration and hope.

This kind of ministry is hard work—but not just for the obvious reasons of trying to bring the hope of the gospel to drug dealers, prostitutes, and neglected children. It is hard work because the neighborhood is almost entirely African American, and the ministry's leadership is primarily white—and a truly integrated church, with white and black Christians worshiping and living in community together, is fraught with hidden assumptions and communication challenges that divide rather than unite.

Why is the Christian Church—the most global religion, and one which should be a banner of unity through the reconciling power of Jesus—so innately segregated? Few churches—even in the 21st century—have managed to integrate successfully.

A hidden culprit: We are unaware of our own biases. As a white, educated woman who grew up in the suburbs, this was (and is) my blind spot. I have the privilege of confidence that comes from growing up in a "majority culture." When I speak, I do not wrestle with feelings of anxiety that I won't be heard or respected or understood. I have rarely felt unwelcome, undervalued, or disrespected in a social or professional setting. Meanwhile, many of my minority brothers and sisters in Christ still wrestle with these notions.

In my experience with this inner city ministry, specifically with their afterschool program, I have realized just how oblivious I am to the basic struggles that produce such perspectives. The problems these kids face are structural and outside their control. For example, they are not allowed to bring schoolbooks home (which makes practical sense for schools without a budget to replace frequently lost books), but how can already disadvantaged kids catch up academically without books to study? These are uphill battles I never knew of—nor took the time to learn about—coming from a place of comfort and convenience.

Another barrier: relationships. Barna data reveals what many in ministry have discovered anecdotally: that the African American experience of faith—and many aspects of life—is far more communal than it tends to be among whites. This is important not only to the way people *live out* their faith, but also to the way they *define* it.

A friend of mine in campus ministry observed that when college students come to ministry activities, white students come alone, while African American students always come with a friend or two or three. Upon inquiring, she learned that not only did the students desire moral support and not want to be alone, or stand out, but they also had a stronger desire for community, connection, and relationship in ministry activities. The natural expression of their faith was significantly more communal.

Inherently, many Christians see their faith as an individual belief or conviction—one adopted personally; a salvation gratefully accepted ("Jesus is my personal Savior"). But this concept of personal accountability can spill over into cultural norms, like an individualistic, versus communal, expression of faith. (Michael Emerson and Christian Smith delve into this in their book *Divided by Faith*.)

African American culture, on the other hand, is rooted in community and family in a way that is foreign to many of European heritage. Further, the persecution and injustices many African Americans still suffer today, and the structural challenges they face, necessitate a communal, rather than individualistic, social structure.

Is it any surprise that we struggle to worship together? And what can we do about it?

A first step is to become *aware* of one's unconscious biases, or blind spots. In April 2016, the *New York Times* reported on a study of racial biases in the National Basketball Association in which the authoring economists measured the impact of self-assessment and resulting behavioral adjustments and found that simply being aware of one's innate biases eventually reduces bias in their *behavior*.

Scripture goes further, calling Christians to both repent and rebuild, or restore. For example, as pastor Walter Henegar pointed out in a sermon on race, Nehemiah started with *collective* repentance—taking personal responsibility for the injustices committed by others—and sought forgiveness on behalf of Israel (Nehemiah 1:4–7). Then he began the hard work of rebuilding. Another example in 2 Chronicles 28:15 shows the leaders of the tribe of Ephraim taking personal responsibility for a group of captives, modeling the extraordinary lengths to which Christians are called to go to restore those who have been victims of injustice.

For me, coming to a place of personal responsibility required a great deal of introspection and humility. I have dear friends of color and enjoyed learning about and participating in their cultural activities. But when it came to making personal sacrifices to help those failing to thrive, my selfish nature said, "I didn't create this problem!" In time, however, I realized, just as Nehemiah did, that "my fathers" did in fact create this problem, and while I may not be held accountable for those past actions, I *will* be held accountable for failing to help a brother or sister in Christ.

The Church's Online Future

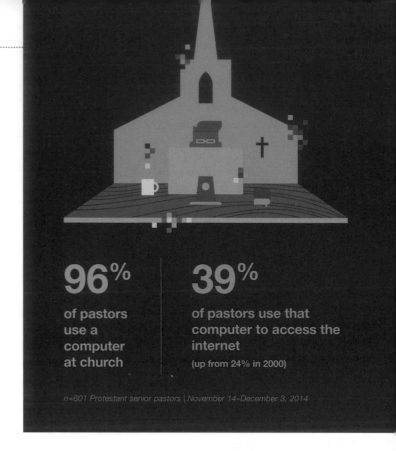

96%
of pastors use a computer at church

39%
of pastors use that computer to access the internet
(up from 24% in 2000)

n=601 Protestant senior pastors | November 14–December 3, 2014

While pastors are using the internet for personal and pragmatic reasons, how likely are they to see it as a useful tool for doing ministry and facilitating religious experiences among their congregants?

In a recent study of U.S. Protestant church leaders, Barna looked at pastors' use of the internet and their attitudes toward it today compared to at the turn of the century.

Today, nearly nine in 10 pastors say they believe it is theologically acceptable for a church to provide faith assistance or religious experiences to people through the internet (87%). This is up from about three-quarters of pastors in 2000 (78%). Similarly, nearly nine in 10 pastors today say they think people in their area would find it acceptable for their church to provide faith assistance or religious experiences to people through the internet (86%), compared to only seven in 10 who would have said so in 2000.

Compared to 2000, pastors are somewhat more likely to agree that, within the next decade, some people will have all of their faith experiences through the internet. Today, just about half of pastors affirm this (11% believe this is definitely true, up from 7% in 2000, while 36% say people probably will, up from 20% in 2000). Of course, this means that just over half of pastors believe this will not be the case (17% say this definitely will

not occur—down from 26% in 2000—while 34% say it probably won't—down from 44% in 2000).

Pastors show increasing openness to people experiencing religion online and an increased willingness to see the church as a conduit for those online experiences. They are more than willing to acknowledge that the internet is playing a key role in how people engage with religion, yet they remain skeptical about those online interactions representing the entirety of faith activities.

The Internet as a Ministry Tool

When asked questions to gauge their overall feelings toward the internet as a good tool for ministry, a more neutral tool, or as something more negative, the majority of pastors agree with the positive statements and few of them agree with any of the negative statements. Both their agreement with positive statements and their disagreement with negative statements are more pronounced than they were in 2000, indicating that pastors increasingly believe in the internet's effectiveness as a tool for ministry.

More than half of pastors today agree that the internet is a powerful tool for effective ministry (54%, up from 35% in 2000). A similar percentage say that for a church to be effective in the future, it will need to have a significant website or presence on the internet (55%).

Additionally, more than half of pastors agree that developing a significant presence on the internet is a good investment of their church's money (54%). Though these percentages have grown, it's interesting that substantial numbers of pastors do not agree strongly with these statements.

As might be expected, most of the resistance to digital ministry comes from older pastors. Younger pastors are more likely to agree with these positive statements than are older pastors. For example, 72 percent of Millennial pastors agree that the internet is a powerful tool for effective ministry, while only 56 percent of Gen-Xers, 54 percent of Boomers, and 39 percent of Elders agree.

Money is a factor, too. Pastors who make $60,000 or more a year are more likely to see the internet as a powerful ministry tool (63%) than are those who make less than $40,000 (49%). This trend is particularly true when asked whether developing a significant presence on the internet is a good investment of church resources: 69 percent of pastors making $60,000 or more a year say yes, while only 44 percent of those making $40,000 to $60,000 and even fewer (40%) of those making under $40,000 a year agree. One way to interpret this is that pastors of smaller churches are trying to stretch their financial resources, so digital initiatives such as websites are more likely to be deemed nonessential.

Pastors are less likely to agree with some of the more neutral—or contextualized—views on the internet. Only 2 percent of pastors agree that the internet is a passing fad and won't continue to be a significant factor in people's lives. One in nine pastors thinks the ministry potential of the internet is overrated (11%, down from 19% in 2000). About four in 10 pastors believe the internet is a ministry tool that will be important for some age groups but not important for others (42%, up from 37% in 2000).

Very few pastors agree with any of the more negative statements regarding the internet and ministry. Only 3 percent say that small churches are better off not trying to have a website or a presence on the internet as part of their ministry (down from 10% in 2000). Less than one in 10 pastors believes websites and internet activities are a distraction from doing significant ministry (8%, down slightly from 12% in 2000). And about one in seven pastors believes that the chances of the internet being used to spread spiritual heresy and to distort Christianity outweigh the potential of the internet to spread authentic Christianity (13%, edging down from 17% in 2000).

The Role of Presence

"No matter the church's size, location, or demographic, the internet has become and will continue to be a vital tool for connection, outreach, and even spiritual formation," Barna's editor-in-chief Roxanne Stone says. "Even so, most pastors aren't ready for the internet to be people's only means of spiritual growth or religious experience. Much of a pastor's role—and the role of a local church—is about presence: presence in a community of believers, presence in the taking of communion, presence in the service of others, presence in communal prayer and worship. The internet can offer an important and accessible supplement to these physical activities, but pastors are reluctant to say it can fully replace them or duplicate them."

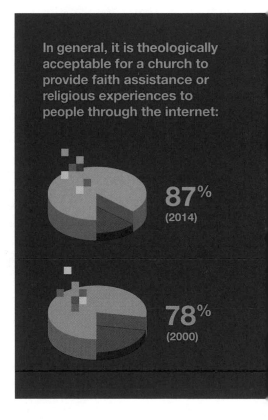

In general, it is theologically acceptable for a church to provide faith assistance or religious experiences to people through the internet:

87% (2014)

78% (2000)

n=610 Protestant senior pastors | December 7–28, 2000; n=601 Protestant senior pastors | November 14–December 3, 2014

THE CHURCH AND PORN: WHO LOOKS AND HOW OFTEN

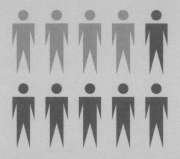

Practicing Christians are less likely than their peers to look at porn, Barna research in partnership with Josh McDowell Ministry shows. However, practicing Christian males between the ages of 13 and 34 are still the third most likely group to view porn; four in 10 actively seek out porn at least once or twice a month. This number could even be under-reported since porn use within the Christian community is less socially acceptable than in wider culture. Christian leaders, especially those who regularly minister to teen/young adult males, can't underestimate the role of porn among this group.

AGE, GENDER, AND FAITH PRACTICE ARE THE THREE BIGGEST FACTORS IN FREQUENT PORN USE

% combined of those who report seeking out porn daily, weekly, and monthly

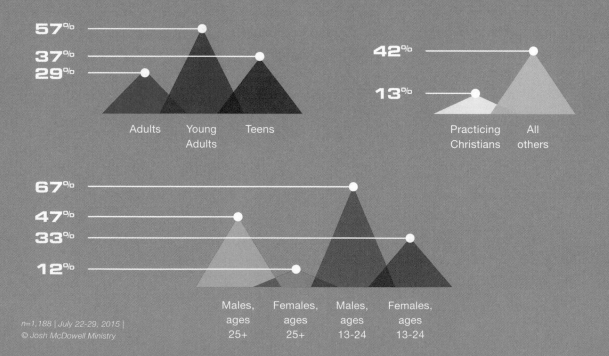

57%

37%

29%

Adults | Young Adults | Teens

42%

13%

Practicing Christians | All others

67%

47%

33%

12%

Males, ages 25+ | Females, ages 25+ | Males, ages 13-24 | Females, ages 13-24

n=1,188 | July 22-29, 2015 |
© Josh McDowell Ministry

1 OUT OF 3 AMERICANS SEEK OUT PORN AT LEAST ONCE A MONTH

6% Daily

14% Weekly

13% Once or twice a month

18% Less often

49% Never

IN OTHER WORDS, IF YOU'RE A YOUNG MAN WHO IS NOT A PRACTICING CHRISTIAN, YOU PROBABLY USE PORN REGULARLY...

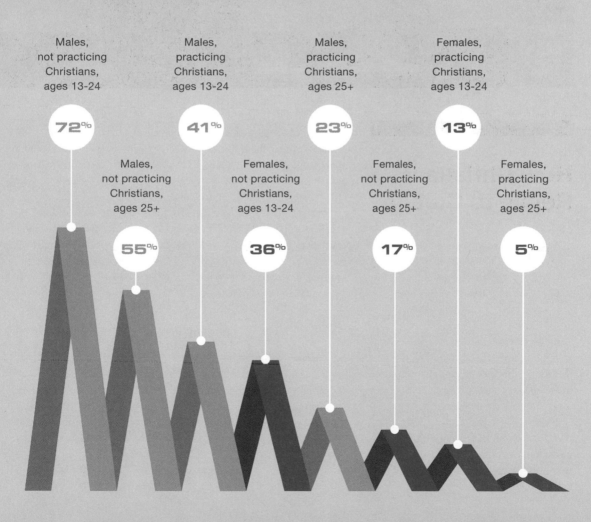

Males, not practicing Christians, ages 13-24 — 72%

Males, not practicing Christians, ages 25+ — 55%

Males, practicing Christians, ages 13-24 — 41%

Females, not practicing Christians, ages 13-24 — 36%

Males, practicing Christians, ages 25+ — 23%

Females, not practicing Christians, ages 25+ — 17%

Females, practicing Christians, ages 13-24 — 13%

Females, practicing Christians, ages 25+ — 5%

BARNA
TAKES

How Christians Relate to Culture

Cory Maxwell-Coghlan,
Barna Group,
Senior Writer &
Managing Editor, Web

How do Christians relate to the culture around them? This perennial question has found new life among the devout as they feel increasingly misunderstood and marginalized in a secularizing American context. We are now witnessing profound shifts in the way Christians— particularly evangelicals—imagine their relationship not only to politics, but also to the broader American culture.

Ever since the sexual revolution, the church's ability to influence real, sustained cultural change in the United States has been on the decline. The recent Supreme Court decision on same-sex marriage, growing concerns about religious freedom, and the steady decrease in church attendance all point to the waning power of Christianity—and evangelicals—in American public life.

How does the Church engage a culture that increasingly perceives it as irrelevant? Throughout history, in times of cultural tension, the Church has a handful of reactions to broader culture: retreat, accommodate, seek to transform, or wage war. Let's look at each response in detail:

Retreat

This group represents those who are resolute in their view of culture as corrupted by sin. They believe real devotion to Christ requires an outright rejection of culture because it stands in stark contrast to the pure and unstained Church. This group thrives on opposition: light vs. darkness, good vs. evil, Church vs. culture. For "retreatists," there is a clear demarcation between the Church and the world. Therefore, in the tradition of the peace churches (Mennonites, Amish, etc.) and monasticism, this group seeks to withdraw from the culture they condemn. This is also exemplified in the building of parallel Christian institutions to compete with those of secular society, an emphasis on practices like home schooling and most recently the Benedict Option (the belief, according to Rod Dreher, that creating strong, thick communities within which traditional Christian life and formation can thrive requires some separation from the broader culture).

Accommodate

Other Christians recognize God at work in culture and look for ways to affirm it. They don't feel the great tensions that exist for the retreatists, and believe in seeking harmony and finding common ground with culture. This group feels, as H. Richard Niebuhr says, "equally at home" within the Church and the culture. Christ represents the embodiment of all that is good in human achievement; therefore no tension exsits between loyalty to one's faith and the very finest expression of their culture. This is exemplified in liberal Protestantism, a theological approach that seeks to incorporate modern ideology, particularly scientific thought, into Christianity. A more recent example is the "relevant" church model.

Transform

Some Christians approach culture by seeking to transform it. They see culture as initially good, but subsequently corrupted by sin and the fall. Culture for this group is not inherently evil, but simply perverted good. Although they believe sin pervades culture, all is not lost. Because Christ is redeeming all of creation, this group remains optimistic that Christians can—and should— seek to renew and transform culture. They affirm what is good, but look to transform that which is corrupted by sin, actively seeking to take part in God's redemptive work as co-laborers. This is typically the most popular view among evangelicals, and is the default position for the Reformed tradition.

Wage War

And finally, this group represents those who seek to convert culture primarily through political and issue-based activism. Similar to the "transformationists," this group aims to change culture through intentional engagement, but like the retreatists, their view is more fatalistic and sectarian, perceiving culture as more inherently evil than inherently good. They see Christ and culture in deep tension, and seek to overcome that tension through waging war against a sinful and corrupt culture, a war in which Christian values prevail. Birthed largely out of a response to liberal Protestantism (the "accommodationists"), this group sought to return to the "fundamentals" of the faith and were labeled accordingly as fundamentalists (or more recently as the Religious or Christian Right), anchored to conservative politics.

These approaches are not new, but if we follow any of them exclusively, we will have failed in some sense to adequately address the tension between our faith and culture. Unlike retreatists, we cannot withdraw from culture as if uncorrupted by sin ourselves; unlike accommodationists, we cannot allow the desire for harmony to trump our theology; unlike transformationists, we cannot be naive about the challenges we face and the temptations of power; and unlike the warring group, we cannot place too much hope in politics and ideology as a way to transform culture. As Niebuhr himself claims, the problem is enduring, and the answers remain "unconcluded and inconclusive." The responses are partial, incomplete, and fragmentary, and rarely does anyone fit neatly into a single group or embody a single response.

But as problematic as each response may be, together they hint at a greater truth. Living in exile means encountering complexity, ambiguity, and irony. Incorporating the insights and critiques of each approach allows us to form a more complete picture of what it means to live faithfully in a pluralistic, multicultural, postmodern culture. Like the retreatists, we must consistently understand our posture as "set-apart;" like the accommodationists, we must affirm, celebrate, and build upon what is genuinely good about culture; like the transformationalists, we must be hopeful about our place as co-laborers in the renewal of all things; and like the warring group, we must remember and cling to the fundamentals of our faith. As we consider what it means to relate to culture in this unique moment, let us be more acutely aware than ever of the need for critical discernment.

Beliefs

Doubts, doctrines, and other
contemporary spiritual points of view

5 Popular Beliefs About Jesus

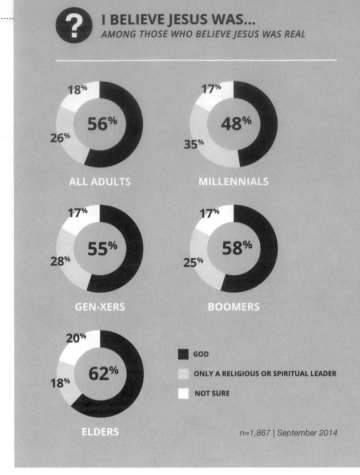

ALL ADULTS — 56% / 18% / 26%

MILLENNIALS — 48% / 17% / 35%

GEN-XERS — 55% / 17% / 28%

BOOMERS — 58% / 17% / 25%

ELDERS — 62% / 20% / 18%

■ GOD
ONLY A RELIGIOUS OR SPIRITUAL LEADER
NOT SURE

n=1,867 | September 2014

Jesus Christ remains a central figure and perennial person of interest in the American religious landscape. But what do Americans *believe* about Jesus? Who do they say he is? Here are five popular perceptions Barna has observed:

1. The Vast Majority of Americans Believe Jesus Was a Real Person

Although the character of Jesus has certainly been fictionalized, satirized, and mythologized over the centuries, the vast majority of Americans still maintain that he was a historical figure. More than nine out of 10 adults say Jesus Christ was a real person who actually lived (92%). While the percentages dip slightly among younger generations—only 87 percent of Millennials agree Jesus actually lived—Americans are still very likely to believe the man, Jesus Christ, once walked the earth.

2. Younger Generations Are Increasingly Less Likely to Believe Jesus Was God

People are much less confident in the divinity of Jesus. Most adults believe Jesus was God (56%), while about one-quarter say he was only a religious or spiritual leader like Mohammed or the Buddha (26%). The remaining one in six say they aren't sure if Jesus was divine (18%).

Millennials are the only generation among whom fewer than half believe Jesus was God (48%). About one-third of young adults (35%) say instead that Jesus was merely a religious or spiritual leader, while 17 percent aren't sure what he was.

In each older generation, the belief in Jesus as divine is more common—55 percent of Gen-Xers, 58 percent of Boomers, and nearly two-thirds of Elders (62%) believe Jesus was God.

3. Americans Are Divided on Whether Jesus Was Sinless

Perhaps reflective of their questions about Jesus' divinity, Americans are conflicted on whether Jesus committed sins during his earthly life.

About half of Americans agree, either strongly or somewhat, that while he lived on earth, Jesus Christ was human and committed sins like other people (52%). Just less than half disagree, either strongly or somewhat, that Jesus committed sins while on earth (46%), and 2 percent aren't sure.

Millennials are more likely to believe Jesus committed sins while he was on earth—56% of Millennials believe so. Gen-Xers, Boomers, and Elders are all similar to the national average—almost evenly split—when it comes to beliefs about Jesus' fallibility.

4. Most Americans Say They Have Made a Commitment to Jesus Christ

On the whole, America is still committed to Jesus. More than six in 10 Americans say they have made a personal commitment to Jesus—often seen as the "first step" in becoming a Christian—and, moreover, that commitment is still important in their life today.

While the majority of Americans report such a commitment, some groups are significantly more likely to have done so than others. Women, for example, are more likely than men to have made a personal commitment to Jesus (68% compared to 56%, respectively). White Americans are the least likely ethnic group to have committed to Jesus: Only six in 10 white Americans report having done so (60%), compared to eight in 10 black Americans (80%) and nearly two-thirds of all nonwhite Americans (65%). The more money people make, the less likely they are to have committed to Jesus: Those making more than $100K per year are significantly less likely (53%) to have made such a commitment than those making between $50K and $100K (63%) or less than $50K (65%).

And, of course, Millennials are much less likely than any other group to have made a personal commitment to Jesus that is still important in their life today. Fewer than half of Millennials say they have made such a commitment (46%), compared to six in 10 Gen-Xers (59%), two-thirds of Boomers (65%), and seven in 10 Elders (71%).

Overall, roughly two out of five Americans have confessed their sinfulness and professed faith in Christ (a group Barna classifies as "born again Christians").

5. People Are Conflicted Between "Jesus" and "Good Deeds" as the Way to Heaven

Among adults who have made a personal commitment to Jesus, most also believe that Jesus is the way to heaven. When given several beliefs about the afterlife to choose from, nearly two-thirds of those who have made a personal commitment to Jesus say they believe they will go to heaven because they have confessed their sins and accepted Jesus Christ as their Savior (63%). Only 2 percent of adults who report a personal commitment to Jesus say they will not go to heaven. About one in seven admit they don't know what will happen after they die (15%).

Millennials are less likely than other generations to believe that Jesus is the path to heaven. Among Millennials who have made a personal commitment to Jesus, only

Southeastern states tend to have higher population percentages that report a personal commitment to Jesus. Mississippi has the highest percentage (90%) of residents who have made such a commitment.

n=1,036 | September 2–10, 2014; n=1,001 | August 25– September 10, 2014; n=1,000 | February 3–11, 2015; n=1,010 | January 8–20, 2015

56 percent say they believe they will go to heaven because they have confessed their sins and accepted Jesus as their Savior. This percentage climbs to two-thirds of Gen-Xers (64%), six in 10 Boomers (62%), and nearly seven in 10 among Elders (68%).

Many adults believe, however, that they will go to heaven as a result of their good works. This is the most common perception among Americans who have never made a commitment to Jesus—and it is also quite common among self-identified Christians. In this category, people believe they will go to heaven because they have tried to obey the Ten Commandments (5%), as a result of being basically a good person (8%), or because God loves all people and will not let them perish (7%).

A Mile Wide, an Inch Deep

Barna president David Kinnaman says, "There isn't much argument about whether Jesus Christ actually was a historical person, but nearly everything else about his life generates enormous, and sometimes rancorous, debate.

"This study also shows the extent of Christian commitment in the nation. More than 150 million Americans say they have professed faith in Christ. This impressive number provokes the question of how well this commitment is expressed. As much of our previous research shows, Americans' dedication to Jesus is, in most cases, a mile wide and an inch deep."

Most Christians View Their Faith as a Force for Good

In research conducted for Barna president David Kinnaman and Q founder Gabe Lyons's book *Good Faith*, Barna looked at how people of faith feel in society today. Though large numbers believe they are misunderstood, persecuted, and marginalized, most feel as though their faith is not only essential, but a force for good in today's world.

The Tension of Being a Person of Faith

Barna asked those who consider themselves a "person of faith" how they feel, personally, in society today. Looking at the broadest segment of practicing Christians, a group that includes Catholics, evangelicals, and mainline churchgoers, a majority say they feel misunderstood (54%) and persecuted (52%), while many others use terms like "marginalized" (44%), "sidelined" (40%), "silenced" (38%), "afraid to speak up" (31%), and "afraid to look stupid" (23%) to describe living their faith in today's world.

Millennial practicing Christians, in particular, are getting hit from all sides as they seek to live out their faith in an increasingly secularized context. They are more likely than other practicing Christians to feel the negative repercussions

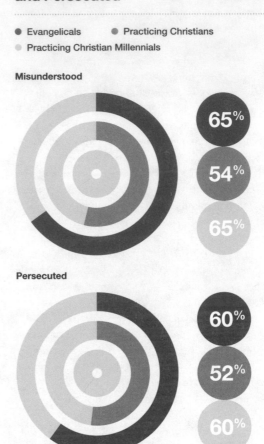

Christians Feel Misunderstood and Persecuted

● Evangelicals   ● Practicing Christians
● Practicing Christian Millennials

Misunderstood

65%
54%
65%

Persecuted

60%
52%
60%

n=767 adults who describe themselves as a "person of faith" | August 17-21, 2016

of their faith. Many feel persecuted (60%), misunderstood (65%), and "afraid to speak up" (47%). Evangelicals are just as likely to perceive their experience of faith in culture in these negative terms. They feel equally misunderstood (65%) and persecuted (60%) as Millennial practicing Christians, and even feel slightly more silenced (50% compared to 46%) than their younger counterparts. Both groups report relatively higher than average numbers compared to the rest of the faith segments represented.

Good Faith in Society

Even though they feel misunderstood, persecuted, and marginalized—and, as Barna has reported recently, are increasingly viewed as extreme—most people of faith believe their faith is not only a force for good, but a primarily positive contribution to society. Large majorities of practicing Christians, especially Millennials and evangelicals, report two confident attitudes: They feel they are a force for good, and they feel they are essential.

Among each faith segment represented here, even the lowest percentage of those who believe their faith is a force for good is nine in 10 (91%). Almost all evangelicals (98%) believe their faith is a force for good, and more than nine in 10 (93%) believe they are essential.

However, evangelicals consistently report scores that differ from the other faith groups, providing valuable insight into this segment. For instance, evangelicals report the lowest levels of acceptance among all people of faith. A mere 57 percent feel they are accepted, 24 percent lower than all those who consider themselves a person of faith. In addition to that, only seven in 10 (71%) feel they are empowered, the second lowest percentage. Though these numbers are still fairly positive, they are relatively low among the various faith groups.

Evangelicals also feel their faith is distinctive at a rate much higher than average (86% compared to 60% among all people of faith). So although evangelicals appear confident about their faith and its potential as a force for good in the world, they feel more marginalized (less empowered, or accepted) than any other group. This is consistent with evangelicals' higher-than-average feelings of persecution and marginalization. It appears that evangelicals are more likely than any other faith segment to perceive they are losing cultural capital.

Practicing Christian Millennials are another standout group for similar reasons. They are the group most likely to feel as though their faith is countercultural, at over six in 10 (62%), a rate 20 percentage points higher than any other group. Coming of age in a more secular American context, it's not hard to imagine younger generations feeling more countercultural about their faith than the broader Christian population. Interestingly, though, they are also more likely to feel empowered (81%, compared to 69% among all people of faith) than the rest of the faith segments.

The Path Forward

"Believers are feeling significant pressure," says Kinnaman, lead designer and analyst on the study. "There is a shared sense that the cultural tide is turning against religious conviction, and people of faith are starting to feel the effects of this growing antagonism in tangible ways.

"It's encouraging to see how many Christians still feel optimistic about the positive role their faith can play in society today," continues Kinnaman. "So it makes sense that Christians feel frustrated when they possess something they feel is so good for the world, that ends up being marginalized.

"We see an inclination among Christians to respond either by forcing their beliefs on others or by shrinking back from offering them, but living with good faith is the true way forward into an uncertain future," concludes Kinnaman. "This means being the people of God who, through the power of the Holy Spirit at work in us, help the world and the people in it to flourish."

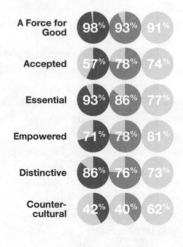

Good Faith in Society

Think about your faith; how do you feel, personally, in society?

● Evangelicals
● Practicing Christians
○ Practicing Christian Millennials

	Evangelicals	Practicing Christians	Practicing Christian Millennials
A Force for Good	98%	93%	91%
Accepted	57%	78%	74%
Essential	93%	86%	77%
Empowered	71%	78%	81%
Distinctive	86%	76%	73%
Countercultural	42%	40%	62%

n=767 adults who describe themselves as a "person of faith" | *August 17-21, 2015* | *Conducted for* Good Faith *(Baker Books, 2016)*

Meet Today's Skeptic

Barna spends a considerable amount of time studying the religious population in America. But what about the growing irreligious population? Who are they? While many who don't attend church still claim a faith identity (in fact, most do), there has also been an uptick in atheism and agnosticism in America. What do we know about this group—and how do today's skeptics differ from those in the past?

Who Are the Atheists?

Barna often combines atheists and agnostics into one group, which we call skeptics. Skeptics either do not believe God exists (atheists) or are not sure God exists, but are open to the possibility (agnostics). Skeptics represent 38 percent of all unchurched adults. One in six skeptics (16%) have never attended a Christian church service in their lives. That's nearly double the proportion of those who are not skeptics but have never attended church (17%).

Today's skeptics, like their counterparts from two decades ago, are defined by their denial of or doubts about God's existence. But that is about the only thing they have in common with the unchurched atheist or agnostic of yesteryear. Below are five demographic shifts among skeptics in the past two decades.

Five Demographic Shifts among Skeptics

They are younger. Skeptics today are, on average, younger than in the past.

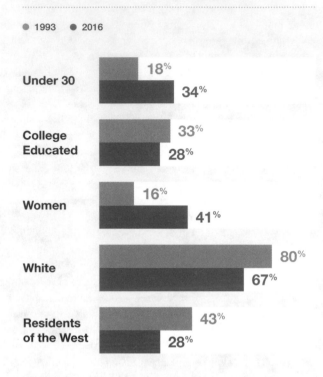

The Evolving Profile of the Skeptic

● 1993   ● 2016

Under 30
18%
34%

College Educated
33%
28%

Women
16%
41%

White
80%
67%

Residents of the West
43%
28%

n=1,025 | February 1993; n=2,005 | January 20–February 16, 2016

Twenty years ago, 18 percent of skeptics were under 30 years old. Today that proportion has nearly doubled to 34 percent. By the same token, the proportion of skeptics who are 65 or older has been cut in half, down to just 7 percent.

They are less educated. Today's skeptics tend to be slightly less educated than in the past. Two decades ago, one-third (33%) of skeptics were college graduates, but today 28 percent of the group has a college degree.

More of them are women. Perhaps the biggest transition of all is the entry of millions of women into the skeptic ranks. In 1993, only 16 percent of atheists and agnostics were women. By 2016, that figure had nearly tripled to 41 percent. This enormous increase is not because the number of skeptic men has declined. In fact, among men skepticism has steadily increased over the last two decades—but not nearly as rapidly as among women.

They are more racially diverse. Religious skepticism has become more racially and ethnically inclusive. While whites represented 80 percent of all skeptics 20 years ago, that figure had dropped to

67 percent by 2016. This is largely a reflection of the increasing Hispanic and Asian adults among the skeptic cohort. Asian Americans, the least-Christian ethnic demographic in the United States, especially tend to embrace skepticism. While a growing number of skeptics are Hispanic, they still remain, along with blacks, less likely than other ethnic groups to accept the idea of a world without God. White Americans, who constitute two-thirds of the country's total population, are well above average in their embrace of atheism and agnosticism; they comprise three-quarters of the skeptic segment.

They are more dispersed regionally. In decades past, the Northeast and West were seen as isolated hotbeds of atheism and agnosticism. They still remain the areas where skeptics are more likely to live, but the skeptic population is now broadly dispersed across all regions.

In many ways, skeptics resemble the rest of America more than they once did. And their numbers are growing more quickly than anyone expected 20 years ago.

Three Components of Disbelief

Just as believers arrive at their belief in God by amassing a variety of information and experiences, skeptics piece together different inputs to draw conclusions. According to Barna research, however, it seems the three primary components that lead to disbelief in God's existence are 1) rejection of the Bible, 2) a lack of trust in the local church, and 3) cultural reinforcement of a secular worldview.

Skeptics dismiss the idea that the Bible is holy or supernatural in any way. Two-thirds contend that it is simply a book of well-known stories and advice, written by humans and containing the same degree of authority and wisdom as any other self-help book. The remaining one-third is divided between two groups: those who believe the Bible is a historical document that contains the unique but not God-inspired accounts of events that happened in the past, and those who do not know what to make of the Bible but have decided it deserves no special treatment or consideration.

Given their indifference toward the Bible, it is remarkable that more than half of skeptics (56%) own at least one copy. Most have read from it in the past, and a handful (5%, mainly agnostics) still read it at least once a month. Most skeptics have some firsthand experience with or regular exposure to the Bible during their youth.

Churches have done little to convince skeptics to

Looking at cities around the country, San Francisco has the highest percentage of residents defined as skeptics (24%). Augusta-Aiken, Georgia, falls at the bottom of the list, with less than 1 percent of its population being skeptics.

n=60,808 post-Christian adults | January 2008-2015

reevaluate. In fact, because more than two-thirds of skeptics have attended Christian churches in the past—most for an extended period of time—their dismissal of God, the Bible, and churches is not theoretical in nature.

Can Christians Reach Beyond Christians?

"Our research suggests that most of the efforts of Christian ministries fail to reach much beyond the core of 'Christianized' America," says David Kinnaman, Barna president and coauthor of *Churchless* (Tyndale, 2014), a book about the unchurched.

"It's much easier to work with this already-sympathetic audience than to focus on the so-called 'nones.' And it's no mystery why: Figuring out how to effectively engage skeptics is difficult.

"One of the unexpected results we uncovered is the limited influence of personal relationships on skeptics. They are considerably less relational and less engaged in social activities than the average American. Christians for whom 'ministry is about relationships' may be disappointed when they find that many skeptics are not as enamored of relational bonds as are those who are already a part of church life.

"But in giving his followers the Great Commission, Jesus didn't mention anything about doing what is easy. New levels of courage and clarity will be required to connect beyond the Christianized majority."

More than Four in Ten Americans Now Post-Christian

Is America, home to the largest Christian population in the world, actually becoming a "post-Christian" nation? While the increasing cultural prominence of self-identified atheists and agnostics is one belief trend, the much-examined "rise of the 'nones,'" it is also important to look at actual faith practices and attitudes among the general populace.

To measure a person's level of irreligion, Barna tracks 15 metrics related to faith that can be used to measure an individual's level of Christian identity, belief, and practice. They include whether individuals identify as atheist, have never made a commitment to Jesus, have not attended church in the last year, or have not read the Bible in the last week.

Compared to simply ticking the "Christian" box in a census, such questions get beyond how people loosely identify themselves (affiliation), and get to the core of what people actually believe and how they behave as a result of their belief (practice).

To qualify as "post-Christian," individuals had to meet 60 percent or more of the factors (nine or more out of 15 criteria). "Highly post-Christian" individuals meet 80 percent or more of the factors (12 or more of these 15 criteria).

Based on Barna's aggregate metric, more than four in 10 (44%) of the nation's adult population qualifies as post-Christian. This includes 12 percent of Americans who are highly post-Christian—lacking engagement in 80 percent or more of the measures of belief, practice, and commitment. Another one-third is moderately post-Christian (32%), refraining from at least 40 percent of the factors.

While self-described atheism and agnosticism may be on the rise in America, the post-Christian metric reminds observers that most Americans remain connected in some way with Christianity.

Barna's Post-Christian Metric

"Post-Christian" individuals meet 60 percent or more of the following factors (nine or more).
"Highly post-Christian" individuals meet 80 percent or more of the factors (12 or more of these 15 criteria).

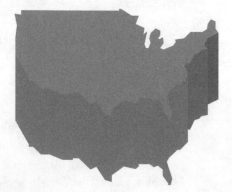

- Do not believe in God
- Identify as atheist or agnostic
- Disagree that faith is important in their lives
- Have not prayed to God (in the last year)
- Have never made a commitment to Jesus
- Disagree the Bible is accurate
- Have not donated money to a church (in the last year)
- Have not attended a Christian church (in the last year)
- Agree that Jesus committed sins
- Do not feel a responsibility to "share their faith"
- Have not read the Bible (in the last week)
- Have not volunteered at church (in the last week)
- Have not attended Sunday school (in the last week)
- Have not attended religious small group (in the last week)
- Do not participate in a house church (in the last year)

A Q&A on Ministry in a Post-Christian Context

with Jon Tyson

Tyson is a church planter, lead pastor of Trinity Grace Church in New York City, and author of the Barna FRAME Sacred Roots: Why the Church Still Matters. *He is on the board of City Collective, a network of incarnational churches committed to multiplying missional church networks in urban centers.*

What do you think is unique about Millennials' criticisms of church, compared to the way a generation of Boomer skeptics approach church?

I think for Boomers—and this is a massive generalization—it was about making church credible intellectually, and relevant culturally. I think those were the two great challenges post-WWII. There was a lot of apologetics and trying to make the Christian faith credible in light of history. Millennials wrestle with completely different things. They are wrestling with issues of authority; a distrust of authority has basically leaked into everything. I think consumerism is a default. Millennials want access, not ownership. They tend to use things rather than own things. Marketing has been telling them their life has to be exceptional—so they're always on that journey of attempting to be exceptional. I think that's a very, very real generational shift. I would say this: The culture of distraction we wrestle with is unprecedented in human history. And the implications of getting people to focus, to be still, to walk with God, to hear from God, to think and read and have convictions on any sort of deep level are just incredibly hard.

How do you see people using, rather than owning, faith?

One of the great challenges that we have in being disciples of Jesus is that our culture pushes individual projects which I would call "Project Self," which means that we think the whole world exists to build our lives—maximum pleasure and maximum expression for the individual. So when it comes to following Jesus, we end up just dabbling with the teachings of Jesus and importing what

he offers to simply make our lives better. The problem with that is that we never actually get to the heart of what Jesus is talking about. He framed up discipleship as self-denial, taking up our cross, loving one another, being servants, washing feet, giving ourselves away. So we live with that tension of wanting to use Jesus for Project Self, rather than following Jesus on behalf of others.

What does the Church offer in an increasingly post-Christian climate?

Charles Taylor said that, in the 1950s, we lived in a culture of belief, and people were tempted to doubt—but in a secular culture [like we have today], it's a culture of doubt, and people are tempted to believe. So when people [in today's culture] see the Church as a compelling counterculture, they're tempted to move out of secularism and embrace something that's true, and beautiful, and hopeful, and resonates with the things that they're wrestling with. We can't give up on the Church because Jesus won't give up on the Church.

Leadership

The obstacles and opportunities
of life behind the pulpit

Financial Myths & Realities of Church Planters 💬👤

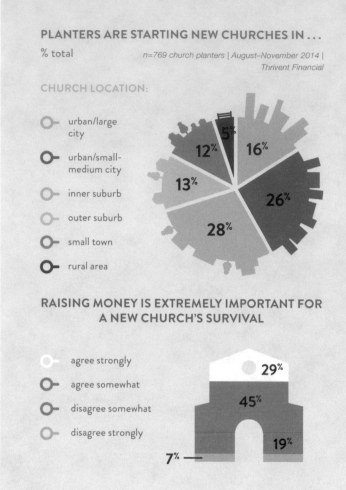

PLANTERS ARE STARTING NEW CHURCHES IN . . .

% total

n=769 church planters | August–November 2014 | Thrivent Financial

CHURCH LOCATION:

○— urban/large city

○— urban/small-medium city

○— inner suburb

○— outer suburb

○— small town

○— rural area

5%
12%
16%
13%
26%
28%

RAISING MONEY IS EXTREMELY IMPORTANT FOR A NEW CHURCH'S SURVIVAL

○— agree strongly

○— agree somewhat

○— disagree somewhat

○— disagree strongly

29%
45%
19%
7%

How many ministry leaders dread talking to potential supporters about their financial needs? How much time do they spend trying to line up the resources they need for basic operations, all while longing to get on with their "real" work?

According to a 2007 study by the Center for Missional Research of 12 denominations and church planting networks, one-third of church plants do not survive past four years (32%). Among those that do survive, financial self-sufficiency and a proactive stewardship development plan are among the top four factors with the greatest impact on success. Having a solid financial foundation increases the odds of survivability by 178 percent.

In order to address this financial reality for church planters, Barna and Thrivent Financial undertook a research project to promote healthy conversations about money and ministry. The research shows the heavy financial burdens on today's church planters. For example:

- Three-quarters of church planters say finances are one of the top two or three things they are concerned about (73%).
- The typical church planter spends 21 percent of his or her time on finances.

- More than one-third says their church startup's income is inadequate (37%) and half report it is "just sufficient" (51%). Only 12 percent say the church's income is "more than sufficient."
- One-third says they have considered quitting their ministry because of finances.
- One-third reports considerable friction in their marriage due to finances.
- Three-quarters believe finances will play a major role in the survival of their ministry (74%).

In statistical models, Barna found that church stability—defined by typical weekly church attendance and the percent of the budget comprised by tithes and offerings—is correlated with higher salaries and less personal debt for pastors, a location with a population that is less dense, and sustained funding sources (i.e., those without an end date). New churches in rural and suburban areas tend to be more stable, and those where the pastor is more amply compensated are more likely to become self-sustaining than those in urban areas or where the pastor subsidizes the ministry with his or her own money.

But these indicators of stability are not as common as they should be in order for new churches to become self-sustaining communities of faith.

One in five church planters (21%) report an annual household income of less than $35,000. This would qualify a family of four for food stamps in most states. Thirty-nine percent are in the $35,000–50,000 bracket and 41 percent bring in more than $50,000 annually.

When asked to choose a description of their finances, 8 percent of church planters say they are surviving—that is, they require financial assistance to get by. Twenty-four percent say they are struggling to keep up with day-to-day expenses, which is twice the norm of 12 percent among all U.S. adults.

Among church planters with less than $30,000 in household income, 69 percent say either that they are struggling or surviving. Conversely, among those earning $50,000 or more, half consider their financial situation as sufficient to cover their needs and leave at least some money left over (47%).

A final area of concern is that church planters carry a significant amount of personal debt, including 39 percent with credit card debt. Half say their debt is a significant problem (47%), and 4 percent consider their debt a "huge" problem. This is higher among those with income less than $30,000: 68 percent say their debt is a "significant" or "huge" problem.

There are four implications of church planters' financial situation to be highlighted from this research:

First, money equals time. This is true for anyone but is especially salient for church planters because they tend to have a scarcity of both resources. Scarcity of money leads to scarcity of time—because more time must be invested in fundraising or administrative tasks.

Second, time equals ministry. A lack of time reduces a church planter's ability to nurture relationships, prepare messages and teaching, develop innovative ministry practices, and maintain a healthy margin in their personal lives. One church planter describes complex financial and administrative duties taking "time from what I can be doing in the community, to be building relationships,

Church planters' self-assessment of their personal financial situation is bleak in urban areas. Thirty-nine percent in large cities say they are "struggling" or "surviving." In small or medium-sized cities, almost half (48%) describe their financial situations with these terms.

n=769 church planters | August–November 2014 | Thrivent Financial

to be developing the core team, seeking out worship leaders and youth leaders."

Third, money equals stress. The greater the financial burden on a church planter, the greater his or her emotional burden. The data show a correlation between financial stress and marital and emotional stress. One church planter describes the challenge of "learning how to handle the emotional stress of being a church planter without taking that home and allowing it to affect my relationship with my wife or my kids."

Fourth, ministry finances affect personal finances. While legally and technically the finances of the ministry and of the church planter are separate, in practice the distinctions are often theoretical for many planters. This does not mean Barna discovered ethical violations. Rather, money flows from the ministry to the church planter via salary, allowances, and reimbursements, and from the planter to the ministry via personal tithes, offerings, and operational subsidies. The health of one impacts the other.

Barna's vice president of research Brooke Hempell says the goal of this study is to "promote healthy conversations about money and ministry" with the hope that "those conversations will lead to innovative ideas that advance the church planting movement into a season of unparalleled health and growth."

Do Pastors Feel Their Religious Rights Are Threatened?

When national faith leaders from a variety of denominational and non-Christian segments were asked to define "religious freedom," the most popular definition is "freedom to practice religion without interference from government." A majority of Catholics (90%), non-mainline Protestants (89%), African-American Protestants (69%), mainline Protestants (75%), and non-Christians (58%) also favor this definition.

Although many see the government as central in the battle over religious liberty, at least two-thirds of all Christian pastors believe that atheists/secularists have a very or somewhat negative impact on religious liberty in America; but only one-third of non-Christian clergy share that view. Regardless of their faith, a majority of American clergy say both Christian and non-Christian religious extremists have a very or somewhat negative impact on religious freedom.

The majority of clergy members have given at least some thought to the possible ramifications for their ministry of restricted religious freedoms. Among the most common possibilities are the likelihood he or she would receive criticism for preaching the truth; the possibility that he or she would be pressured or required to perform gay marriages; a loss of tax-exempt status; more difficulty evangelizing; and declines in church attendance and commitment. Although not all clergy members agree on the likelihood of various outcomes or consequences of a decline in religious freedoms, at least one out of 10 in every denominational segment says "society in general would be less moral"; "people would have less ability to practice their faith without interference"; "other kinds of freedoms, not just religious, would also be at risk," and "the government would have too much control over religious institutions."

Level of Concern About Restrictions to Religious Freedoms

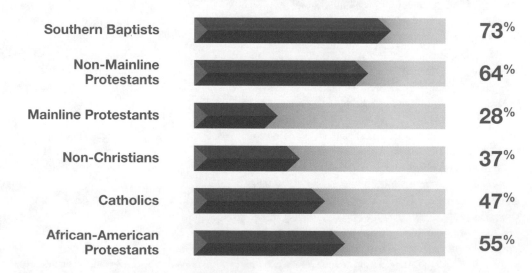

Southern Baptists	73%
Non-Mainline Protestants	64%
Mainline Protestants	28%
Non-Christians	37%
Catholics	47%
African-American Protestants	55%

n=1,608 American clergy (1,286 Protestant pastors, 163 Catholic priests, 159 non-Christian faith leaders | June–July 2014 | Maclellan Foundation

What Does It Mean to Be Faithful in Public?

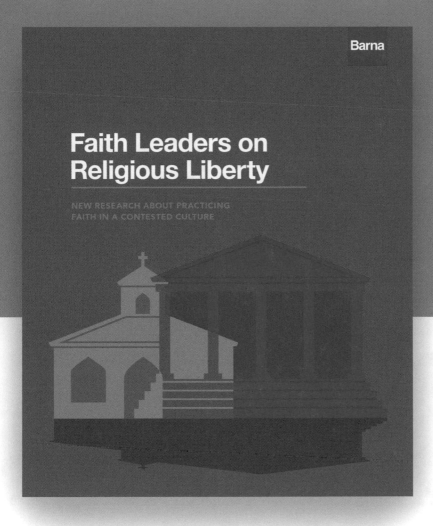

Barna

Faith Leaders on Religious Liberty

NEW RESEARCH ABOUT PRACTICING FAITH IN A CONTESTED CULTURE

You will learn

- The redefinition of religious liberty in the context of cultural change

- Perceptions of the place faith should occupy in culture and threats to religious freedom

- Faith leaders' expectations regarding the consequences of limited liberty

- How faith leaders approach religious freedom and other contentious social issues

The future of public life for faith communities and religious organizations hinges on how leaders—religious, political, community, and beyond— understand and advance a healthy vision for religious expression in the public square. *Faith Leaders on Religious Liberty* is the culmination of a project commissioned by the Maclellan Foundation to examine faith leaders' views on matters of religious liberty. The data represent the broadest study Barna has yet undertaken on the ways faith in general and Christianity in particular are perceived, expressed, and limited in the public square. Faith leaders are uniquely positioned to help their communities of faith find sure footing in the days ahead, and the insights in this report will help them renew their confidence to lead in uncertain times.

Order at
**barna.com
/religiousliberty**

Pastors and Porn

In anonymous surveys conducted for Barna's *The Porn Phenomenon* report, in partnership with Josh McDowell Ministry, one in five youth pastors (21%) and one in seven senior pastors (14%) admitted they currently use porn. About half of those who use porn do so at least a few times per month, and the vast majority feels guilt or shame when they do so. More than half of youth pastors who use porn (56%) and one-third of senior

pastors who use porn (33%) believe they are addicted.

Porn use by any church leader is a problem, but senior pastors' responses are cause for particular concern. Senior leaders are more likely than their youth leader counterparts to say that their job makes it easy to use porn in secret and that neither their spouse nor a trusted friend is aware of their struggle. There also seems to be a tendency among senior leaders to underestimate or downplay the impact of porn use on their ministry and relationships. And although a majority says they feel guilt or shame related to their porn use, senior pastors are less likely than youth leaders to say so.

These data combine to paint a portrait of senior leaders in isolation, too many of them unaware of or in denial about the spiritual risks and the potential to harm not only themselves but others. Recent years have presented ample evidence that, for some pastors and priests, wielding spiritual power can too easily lead to sexual coercion and abuse. If, as some experts suggest, porn is implicated in sexual violence, the Christian community and its leaders must bring these struggles into the light.

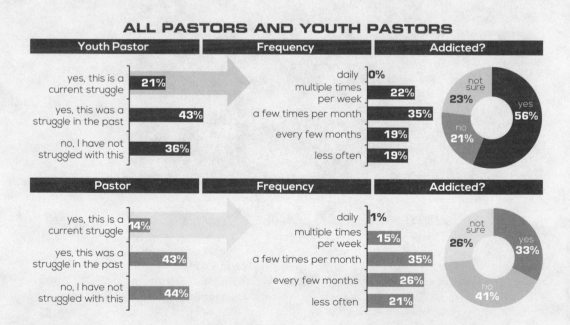

ALL PASTORS AND YOUTH PASTORS

Youth Pastor		Frequency		Addicted?
yes, this is a current struggle	21%	daily	0%	not sure 23%
		multiple times per week	22%	yes 56%
yes, this was a struggle in the past	43%	a few times per month	35%	no 21%
no, I have not struggled with this	36%	every few months	19%	
		less often	19%	

Pastor		Frequency		Addicted?
yes, this is a current struggle	14%	daily	1%	not sure 26%
		multiple times per week	15%	yes 33%
yes, this was a struggle in the past	43%	a few times per month	35%	no 41%
no, I have not struggled with this	44%	every few months	26%	
		less often	21%	

n=432 Protestant senior pastors | July 13-July 23, 2015; n=338 youth pastors | July 28–September 14, 2015 | © Josh McDowell Ministry

PASTORS AND YOUTH PASTORS WHO CURRENTLY USE PORN

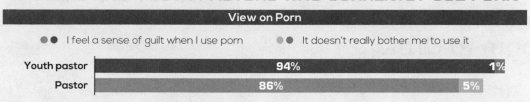

View on Porn

● ● I feel a sense of guilt when I use porn   ● ● It doesn't really bother me to use it

Youth pastor	94%	1%
Pastor	86%	5%

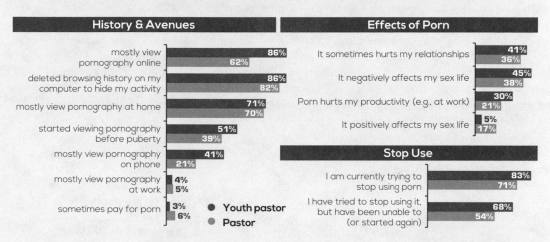

History & Avenues

	Youth pastor	Pastor
mostly view pornography online	86%	62%
deleted browsing history on my computer to hide my activity	86%	82%
mostly view pornography at home	71%	70%
started viewing pornography before puberty	51%	39%
mostly view pornography on phone	41%	21%
mostly view pornography at work	4%	5%
sometimes pay for porn	3%	6%

● Youth pastor
● Pastor

Effects of Porn

	Youth pastor	Pastor
It sometimes hurts my relationships	41%	36%
It negatively affects my sex life	45%	38%
Porn hurts my productivity (e.g., at work)	30%	21%
It positively affects my sex life	5%	17%

Stop Use

	Youth pastor	Pastor
I am currently trying to stop using porn	83%	71%
I have tried to stop using it, but have been unable to (or started again)	68%	54%

The nature of my job makes it easier to use pornography secretly

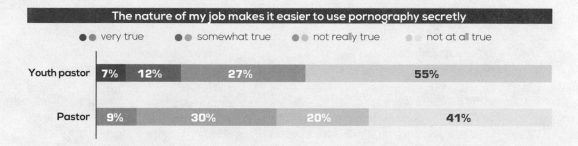

● ● very true   ● ● somewhat true   ● ● not really true   ● ● not at all true

	very true	somewhat true	not really true	not at all true
Youth pastor	7%	12%	27%	55%
Pastor	9%	30%	20%	41%

The use of porn negatively impacted my ministry

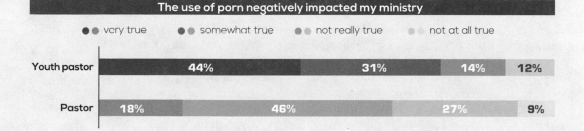

● ● very true   ● ● somewhat true   ● ● not really true   ● ● not at all true

	very true	somewhat true	not really true	not at all true
Youth pastor	44%	31%	14%	12%
Pastor	18%	46%	27%	9%

Discipleship: Room to Grow

Effective approaches to Christian discipleship become even more important in a world that is increasingly polarized around spiritual issues. What is the current state of discipleship in the U.S.? Is the church effective in its efforts? Are churchgoers involved in discipleship activities, and, if so, which models do they prefer? Do investments in discipleship actually affect spiritual growth?

To answer these questions, Barna, in partnership with The Navigators and NavPress, conducted a comprehensive, multiphase research study among Christian adults, church leaders, exemplar discipleship ministries, and Christian educators. Here's a sampling of what the research uncovered.

How Well Are We Doing?

Christian adults believe their churches are doing well when it comes to discipleship: 52 percent of those who have attended church in the past six months say their church "definitely does a good job helping people grow spiritually" and another 40 percent say it "probably" does so. Additionally, two-thirds of Christians who have attended church in the past six months and consider spiritual growth important say their church places "a lot" of emphasis on spiritual growth (67%); another 27 percent say their church gives "some" emphasis.

Church leaders tend to believe the opposite is true. Only 1 percent say "today's churches are doing very well at discipling new and young believers". A majority—six in 10—feels that churches are discipling "not too well" (60%).

At their own church, only 8 percent say they are doing "very well" and 56 percent "somewhat well" at discipling new and young believers. Thus, pastors give their own church higher marks than churches overall, but few believe churches—their own or in general—are excelling in discipleship.

Not surprisingly, emphasis on discipleship is correlated with higher faith engagement. Three-quarters of practicing Christians—self-identified Christians who have attended church in the past month and who consider their faith very important—say their church places "a lot" of emphasis on spiritual growth (73%), while only 40 percent of non-practicing Christians say the same.

Breaking Down Discipleship

Despite believing their church emphasizes spiritual growth, engagement with the practices associated with discipleship leave much to be desired. For example, only 20 percent of Christian adults are involved in some sort of discipleship activity; this includes a wide range of activities, such as attending Sunday school or fellowship group, meeting with a spiritual mentor, studying the Bible with a group, or reading and discussing a Christian book with a group.

Practicing Christians are more likely to be involved in a variety of spiritual growth activities than are non-practicing Christians. Yet, even among practicing Christians, fewer than half are engaged in these four types of spiritual development. Only 17 percent say they meet with a spiritual mentor as part of their discipleship efforts.

To Grow or Not to Grow?

It is difficult for researchers to analyze accurately the degree to which people are changing spiritually. From the point of view of self-perception, most people perceive they are growing and say they want to develop spiritually. Yet, self-perceptions also show that Christians tend to be quite satisfied in their spirituality, perhaps edging toward complacency. Most Christians express satisfaction with their spiritual lives: Thirty-eight percent of Christian adults say they are "happy with where they are in their spiritual life" and another 36 percent are "almost to where they want to be."

Some good news is that people firmly assert that they want to grow spiritually. Indeed, three-quarters of practicing Christians (77%) believe it is "very important to see growth in their spiritual life." Even among non-practicing Christians—people who rarely or never

What Is Standing in the Way?

n=2,013 Christian adults |
March 26–April 15, 2015 |
The Navigators

ONLY 1 IN 5 CHRISTIANS ARE INVOLVED IN SOME SORT OF DISCIPLESHIP ACTIVITY

TOP BARRIERS TO SPIRITUAL GROWTH

● PRACTICING CHRISTIANS ● NON-PRACTICING CHRISTIANS

4% 6%	5% 6%	5% 7%	5% 8%	11% 8%	8% 10%

I HAVEN'T FOUND ANYONE WILLING TO HELP ME	IT'S HARD TO FIND GOOD RESOURCES OR INFORMATION	I DON'T KNOW WHERE TO START	MY FAMILY MEMBERS ARE NOT SUPPORTIVE	MY FRIENDS ARE NOT AS INTERESTED IN SPIRITUAL THINGS	I HAVE OTHER MORE IMPORTANT PRIORITIES RIGHT NOW

10% 12%	16% 13%	9% 15%	9% 16%	6% 16%	23% 22%
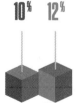		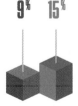			
I DON'T WANT TO THINK ABOUT MISTAKES I'VE MADE IN THE PAST	SPIRITUAL GROWTH WILL REQUIRE A LOT OF HARD WORK	I DON'T WANT TO GET TOO PERSONAL WITH OTHER PEOPLE	I'VE HAD BAD PAST EXPERIENCES WITH GROUPS OR INDIVIDUALS	I CAN'T FIND A GOOD CHURCH OR CHRISTIAN COMMUNITY	GENERAL BUSYNESS OF LIFE

attend church and who are mostly inactive spiritually—37 percent say it is very important to grow spiritually.

Yet the research reveals little correlation between activity and perceived growth, further revealing the disconnect between how people think about their spirituality and what's actually happening in their lives. For example, most practicing Christians feel they have made "a lot" (40%) or "some" (51%) progress in their personal spiritual growth in the past year. However, among respondents who are currently involved in at least one discipleship activity, their self-reported growth was not much higher than these levels. Even among non-practicing Christians, a majority believes they have made spiritual progress in the last year.

One of the implications of these findings is that church leaders must be diligent in finding tools that help people examine the reality of their spiritual growth, not merely how they perceive it.

Motivations for Discipleship

What motivates people to cultivate their spiritual lives? Practicing and non-practicing Christians report different motivations for seeking spiritual growth. Practicing Christians see discipleship as intimately tied with their faith, saying they are most motivated by "a general desire to know Jesus, or God, more" (46%); "a general desire to be more like Jesus" (41%); and because "the Bible instructs us to be more like Jesus" (34%).

Non-practicing Christians, on the other hand, see discipleship as a part of a broader project of self-improvement, saying they "think it is important to be improving or growing in all things" (51%); "have been through a lot, and growing spiritually will help me" (41%); and "have a general desire to know Jesus, or God, more" (36%).

TERMS USED TO DESCRIBE SPIRITUAL GROWTH	ALL CHURCH LEADERS	SENIOR PASTORS	DISCIPLESHIP LEADERS	ALL CHRISTIANS
Q: WOULD YOU USE ANY OF THESE WORDS TO DESCRIBE THE PROCESS OF SPIRITUAL GROWTH? *(TWO ANSWERS ALLOWED)*				
BECOMING MORE CHRIST-LIKE	51%	51%	49%	43%
DISCIPLESHIP	46	45	46	17
SANCTIFICATION	26	25	28	9
SPIRITUAL GROWTH	21	20	22	31
SPIRITUAL FORMATION	17	18	16	5
SPIRITUAL JOURNEY	16	17	15	28
SPIRITUAL MATURATION	14	14	14	16
NONE OF THESE	1	1	1	8
NOT SURE	0	0	0	1

n=833 Protestant senior / discipleship pastors | April 7–May 30, 2015 | The Navigators

The research examines differences between various demographic segments, and many differences emerged based upon generation. For instance, when it came to motivations, Millennial Christians are more likely than average to be motivated to grow spiritually because "I have been through a lot and growing spiritually will help me" and "I am inspired by others and want to be more like them." Younger believers are also more likely than average to say they grow in peer groups and when reading the Bible with others. Millennial Christians are less likely to say that "my church encourages spiritual growth."

One of the implications of the research, then, is for churches to rethink what is working in connecting with today's younger Christians, particularly when it comes to relational and mentoring forms of spiritual development.

Can Discipleship Be a Solo Activity?

When it comes to their preferred methods of discipleship, Christian adults are split among small group, one-on-one mentorship or self-discipleship. Among Christians who say spiritual growth is important, more than one-third say they prefer to pursue spiritual growth on their own (37%). Similarly, two in five of all Christian adults consider their spiritual life to be "entirely private" (41%). This is a greater proportion—though only slightly—than Christians who believe their faith, rather than being private, has an impact on relatives (37%), friends (36%), and their community (33%). In other words, one of the problems revealed by this research is that millions of Christians believe that discipleship is a solo affair, with only personal and private implications.

Even when it comes to what Christians are experiencing in the churches they attend, there does not seem to be much emphasis conveyed about the communal, relational nature of spiritual growth. Just one-third of Christian adults report that their church recommends meeting with a spiritual mentor; half of their churches publicly endorse studying the Bible with a group; and half recommend studying the Bible independently.

Among Christian adults, one-quarter prefers a small-group setting for discipleship (25%). Another one in five prefers a combination of group and one-on-one discipleship (21%) and 16 percent prefer one-on-one only. Thus, in total, about one-third of those pursuing spiritual growth prefers some element of one-on-one, person-to-person discipleship.

However, not all of those who prefer discipleship "pairs" are currently involved in a one-on-one discipleship relationship: less than one-quarter of Christian adults (23%) are currently being discipled by someone (29% of practicing vs. 12% of non-practicing Christians), and 19 percent are discipling someone else (25% of practicing vs. 9% of non-practicing Christians).

One-on-one discipleship relationships are established in various ways: Of those currently being discipled by another person, one-quarter say that person invited them (27%), one in five invited their mentor (20%), and about one-quarter were paired by the church (23%)—but the largest proportion, 28 percent, were matched "some other way."

The View from the Pulpit

When asked to choose the single method of discipleship they believe is most effective, church leaders tend to select small group formats (52%) nearly two-to-one over discipleship pairs (29%). For good or ill, small groups are the disciple-making format preferred by most of today's church leaders.

Do church leaders engage in discipleship themselves?

Somewhat. Fully 94 percent are currently discipling at least one other Christian. However, only six in 10 are being discipled themselves. Discipleship pastors (72%) are somewhat more likely than senior pastors (59%) to have a spiritual mentor.

A compelling finding of the study is that personal discipleship relationships are more common among leaders of larger churches: Eight out of 10 church leaders of 500+ member churches report being currently discipled by someone else (78%), compared with 64 percent of those with 100 to 499 members and 55 percent of those who lead in churches with fewer than 100 members.

According to pastors, the most critical elements of discipleship are matters of the heart rather than of structure. Aside from prayer and time with God, the top three spiritual disciplines pastors believe are essential to discipleship are "personal commitment to grow in Christlikeness" (94%), "attending a local church" (91%), and "a deep love for God" (90%). Having "a comprehensive discipleship curriculum" is by far the least important element of effective discipleship according to pastors, 44 percent of whom select it as essential.

When asked how they want to improve in their discipleship programs, a plurality of church leaders says they would "develop a more clearly articulated plan or approach to discipleship" (27%). Additionally, churches need to develop assessment criteria to track the effectiveness of their discipleship efforts. Less than 1 percent of leaders report using a survey or other evaluation instrument to assess the results of their programs. This underscores the previous conclusion that church leaders and congregants need better methods of thinking about and evaluating their discipleship efforts.

n=2,013 Christian adults | March 26–April 15, 2015;

n=833 Protestant senior and discipleship pastors |

April 7–May 30, 2015 | The Navigators

Discipleship in the 21ST Century

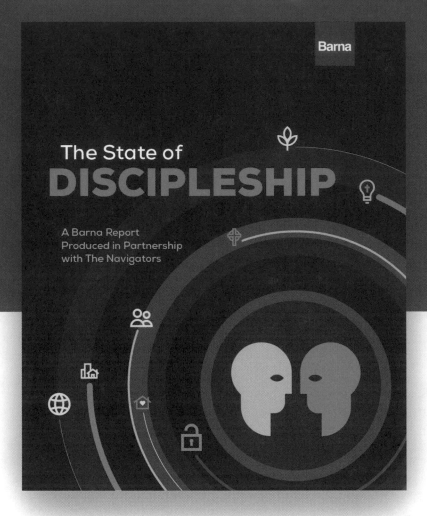

Barna

The State of
DISCIPLESHIP

A Barna Report
Produced in Partnership
with The Navigators

In this report you will find

- Statistics on discipleship activities, methods, and outcomes

- An examination of various terms, definitions, and objectives related to discipleship

- Insights from leaders whose churches exemplify excellence in discipleship

The Great Commission is an audacious undertaking, all the more so given the fast and sweeping changes taking place in the broader culture. Effective approaches to discipleship are more important than ever in a world that is increasingly polarized concerning spiritual issues. What is the current state of discipleship in America? What are the hallmarks of transformative discipleship and how do we measure its outcomes? What resources and models are necessary for effective discipleship? How do The Navigators' discipleship methods and resources align with the needs of the Church? The Navigators commissioned Barna Group to design a comprehensive, multiphase study of American churches, leaders and Christian adults. *The State of Discipleship* evaluates how effectively the Church is creating disciples and where there is need for better models or mind-sets—or both.

Inside the Minds of Pastors

There are 322,000 Christian clergy in senior positions and an estimated 73 million practicing Christians (people who say their faith is very important in their life, who identify as Christian, and who attend a church at least once a month) in the United States. Taking into account those two data points, the ratio of clergy to practicing Christians would be about 1 to 227.

In partnership with Pepperdine University, Barna conducted a study on the current state and future prospects of these spiritual leaders in the United States. The study explored the role of these pastors from three different angles: Self-leadership (individual), which relates to the personal lives and souls of today's pastors—that is, how they lead themselves, how their personal lives influence their leadership, and how they care for and develop their own souls; Congregational leadership (organizational), which relates to how they perceive themselves as church leaders and organizational leaders—how their leadership of a local church is expressed and lived out; and finally, Cultural leadership (systemic), which relates to how outside influences are reshaping what it means to be a faith leader, including both the ministry ecosystem, such as denominations and seminaries, and cultural currents.

Self-Leadership

When asked how satisfied they are with their vocation as a pastor, the vast majority (72%) of pastors say "very satisfied." But when it comes to their ministry at their current church specifically, only about half (53%) are very satisfied. Six in 10 (59%) say it is "completely true" that their vocation has deepened their relationship with Christ, and the vast majority (91%) say it is either "completely" or "somewhat true." They were also asked whether it had increased their passion for ministry (86% completely and somewhat true), been difficult on their family (48%), and been a disappointment (27%). The latter are less likely to be true, but these numbers are cause for concern.

In addition, most married pastors say they are satisfied right now in their relationships with their spouse (70%), and among parents, with their kids (60%). These numbers are fairly high, though when it comes to respect from the community, less than one-quarter are satisfied (22%). One-quarter (24%) say they are satisfied with their physical well-being. Mental and emotional health came in higher, at four in 10 (39%), as well as having true friends (34%), which points to the isolation of a pastoral role.

When asked about their first response to a ministry crisis, the majority (58%) say they pray or turn to Jesus. The next most frequent response is calling a mentor or spiritual advisor (26%), or talking with a spouse or partner (9%). Reading Scripture is less popular (2%). The responses are very similar when asked about their first response to a personal crisis. Again, the majority (52%) turn to God in prayer, but their likelihood to talk to a spouse or partner more than doubles (23%) when compared to ministry crisis. The likelihood of calling a mentor follows at 15 percent, and, again, reading Scripture is low at only 2 percent.

Pastors were asked whether, during their ministry, they had struggled with depression (46%), significant marital problems (26%), major parenting difficulties (27%), or addiction (19%). Nearly half of pastors reporting experience with depression is a fairly significant number, but perhaps most troubling is that almost one in five pastors say they have struggled with addiction.

Following up on the addiction question, Barna asked how pastors have sought help, and the most frequent answers are an accountability partner or group (60%), spiritual disciplines or practices (51%), and counseling or psychotherapy (25%). Almost one-fifth (18%) say they have not sought treatment or recovery. Those who have struggled with addiction are torn about whether honesty or concealment is the best way forward. Forty-six percent say disclosure of their addiction would have a negative impact on their ministry, while 41 percent say being honest about their struggles would have a positive impact.

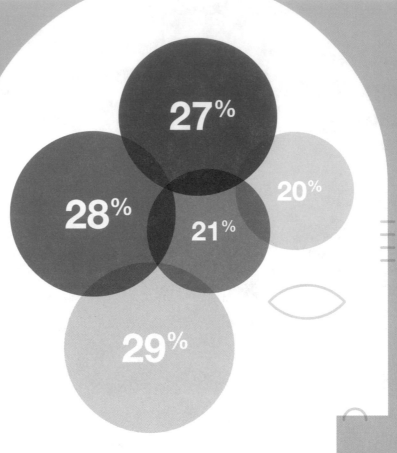

What is an area of ministry that you wish you had been better prepared for?

- Handling conflict
- Importance of delegation / training people
- Balancing ministry and administration
- Administrative burden
- Counseling

27%
20%
28%
21%
29%

n=1,300 Protestant pastors | April–December 2015 |

Pepperdine University

Asked to describe their financial condition, half (50%) say they are able to make ends meet and have some left over. One-fifth (19%) say they have more than they need for themselves and their family, and another quarter (23%) say they are just making ends meet. Only a few say they are either struggling to keep up with day-to-day expenses (7%) or require assistance to get by (1%). Do they have a trustworthy, knowledgeable person to turn to for financial advice? Forty-one percent say that is completely true, and 35 percent say it is somewhat true, a total of 76 percent.

When asked if they were confident that they will be financially secure when they retire, only 23 percent say this is completely true, and 49 percent say it is somewhat true. And finally, a majority say they are financially prepared for unforeseen expenses such as a health crisis, 18 percent say completely true, and 46 percent say somewhat true.

Pastors' answers to questions about intellectual humility show 37 percent of pastors agree strongly with the statement "I'm willing to change my mind once it's made up about an important topic." A vast majority (82%) agree strongly with the statement "I am willing to hear others out, even if I disagree with them," and two-thirds (62%) with "I welcome different ways of thinking about important topics." When compared to all adults (19%, 44%, and 34% respectively), pastors certainly appear much more intellectually humble than the general population.

Substantial minorities report feeling threatened when others disagree with them on topics close to their heart (29%), feeling their ideas are better than other people's ideas (37%), and fearing the chance they are wrong when they are really confident in a belief (12%). These

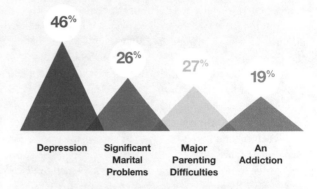

During your ministry, have you struggled with any of the following?

46% Depression
26% Significant Marital Problems
27% Major Parenting Difficulties
19% An Addiction

Of the following aspects of serving as a pastor, which one do you most enjoy?

66% Preaching & Teaching

10% Developing Other Leaders
8% Discipling Believers
5% Pastoral Care
6% Evangelizing or Sharing the Gospel
2% Organizing Church Events, Meetings, or Ministries

n=1,300 Protestant pastors | April–December 2015 | Pepperdine University

numbers confirm a moderately strong sense of intellectual humility among pastors.

Congregational Leadership

When asked to describe the positive aspects of the pastor-elders relationship in their church, almost seven in 10 (67%) say elders are hugely supportive, six in 10 say there is healthy accountability (60%) and clear, shared vision and values (57%). A little under half (44%) say it is a powerful partnership. One-third (34%) say the relationship is characterized by frequent prayer together. These are mostly encouraging findings, except for the noteworthy rarity of group prayer. When describing the negative aspects of the pastor-elders relationship in their church, the numbers are significantly lower but are dominated by unclear areas of decision-making authority (18%), power struggles (12%), and feeling underappreciated by the board (11%).

In an attempt to get a sense of the psychographic profile of pastors, Barna asked them to choose between symbolic roles when it comes to describing the experience of being a pastor. For instance, pastors choose leader over administrator (81% vs. 19%), doctor over referee (83% vs. 22%), coach over counselor (60% vs. 40%), and manager over entrepreneur (60% vs. 40%). To further build the profile, pastors were asked which aspects of their job they most enjoyed, and two-thirds (66%) say preaching and teaching. This is by far the most common enjoyable aspect, followed by developing other leaders (10%), discipling believers (6%), evangelizing (6%), and pastoral care (5%). The popularity of preaching and teaching compared to other aspects of the role of pastor is certainly notable.

Counter to this, Barna also asked pastors which ministry challenges cause them the most frustration. Lack of commitment among lay people (35%) and the low level of spiritual maturity among churchgoers (27%) are the top two, followed by financial and/or administrative duties (19%), church politics (18%), implementing change in the church (16%), and, finally, relational difficulties (11%).

Pastors were asked to indicate how someone who knows them well might rate them on various aspects of pastoral ministry on a typical day. Preaching, knowledge of Scripture, and practical theology are given top ratings, and mentoring young people, evangelizing people, and mobilizing volunteers are the bottom three. These map fairly well onto the other answers in the psychographic profile, with a higher priority and enjoyment placed on preaching and teaching as opposed to evangelizing and discipleship.

Cultural Leadership

To look at their perceptions of cultural leadership, Barna asked pastors about the qualities that make a good pastor or effective leader in today's culture. Their top two choices by far are "love for people" and "a desire to help people" (30%). "Love for God, Jesus" (21%), "zeal, passion, commitment" (17%), "leadership, vision" (16%), "faithfulness, obedience" (10%), and "insight, wisdom, discernment" (9%) all followed.

Surprisingly, only 5 percent of pastors believe Bible knowledge is a top quality that makes a good pastor. Also, in almost every case except for "leadership, vision" and "zeal, passion, commitment," pastors rate traits as less important than the general population did.

Pastors are ambivalent about the effect of pervasive social media. Almost half (46%) of pastors say social media has affected the amount of time and effort they might have previously given to other aspects of ministry, with only 16 percent saying social media has been a "huge benefit" to ministry.

Thinking about the next generation of leaders, almost one-quarter of pastors (21%) believe that large church facilities built by older leaders will be a burden on the younger generation. Slightly more than two-thirds (68%) at least somewhat agree. Twenty-two percent agree strongly that their church puts a significant priority on training and developing the next generation of church leaders, with a total of seven in 10 (68%) agreeing at least somewhat. One-quarter (24%) agree strongly that it is becoming harder to find mature young Christians who want to become pastors, with seven in 10 (69%) at least somewhat agreeing. Almost one in five (18%) agree strongly that a lot of young leaders seem to think other kinds of work are more important than vocational ministry, again with seven in 10 (70%) at least somewhat agreeing. When it comes to recommending ministry careers, 63 percent of pastors nationwide would encourage a young person who is considering a career as a pastor.

Finally, when it comes to ministry preparation, about half of pastors rate their ministry training as good, with around one in four rating it as either excellent or average. Pastors wish they had been better prepared for handling conflict (27%), delegating and training people (20%), balancing ministry and administration (21%), administrative burden (28%), counseling (29%).

Again, this aligns with the rest of the research, suggesting pastors have a higher competence and preparation in theology and teaching, but less preparation and competence in broader organizational leadership.

n= 1,300 Protestant pastors | April–December 2015 |

Pepperdine University

Pastoring in an Age of Complexity

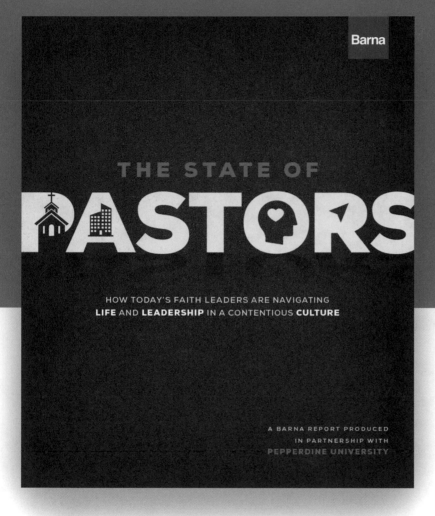

Barna

THE STATE OF

PASTORS

HOW TODAY'S FAITH LEADERS ARE NAVIGATING
LIFE AND **LEADERSHIP** IN A CONTENTIOUS **CULTURE**

A BARNA REPORT PRODUCED
IN PARTNERSHIP WITH
PEPPERDINE UNIVERSITY

Examines church leaders' perceptions of

- Their own mental, physical, financial, emotional, and spiritual well-being

- The health of their relationships with family and church members

- How they are received as a leader in their local community

- How well their skills, gifts, and calling align with their pastoral responsibilities

In the broader culture today, Christian ministers are as likely to be ignored as they are to be admired. But despite the challenges they face, called and committed pastors are essential to lead and shepherd an increasingly shrinking and marginalized Christian community through the wilderness ahead. But how are these leaders doing? Commissioned by Pepperdine University, *The State of Pastors* contains the findings of a comprehensive, whole-life assessment of American pastors. The study reveals where church leaders are most in need of healing and encouragement and offers hopeful counsel for pastors (and those who love them) who are seeking greater health as they continue to answer God's call.

Order at
**barna.com
/stateofpastors**

BARNA TAKES

Pastoring in a New Reality

David Kinnaman,
Barna Group,
President

Many industries and sectors of culture are undergoing tremendous change as digital tools and other factors produce an effect so powerful it needs seven syllables: *disintermediation*.

This word describes, among other things, how people are renegotiating their relationships with institutions and how the flow of goods is continually shifting to find an unobstructed (or *unmediated*) path to consumers. Along with everyone else, pastors are impacted by disintermediation. Clergy are, almost by definition, *mediators*—representatives of God's kingdom on earth—yet what has been their traditional role within culture is subjected to greater skepticism today. Pastors once held a position of esteem in the public eye, but people are renegotiating their relationships with spiritual authority. Likewise, pastors historically mediated the transmission of knowledge to spiritual seekers, but now people consult Twitter, search Google, or ask Siri.

Technology is not the only factor at work. An era of overscheduled busyness and compulsive distraction means even regular attenders go to church less often than churchgoers in the past. The Bible is losing traction as a formative text for our broader culture, replaced by self-fulfillment as the interpretive grid for life, love, and faith. Radical secularism is pushing tolerant pluralism to the margins, squeezing people of faith and their leaders out of the public square and into a box of private belief and practice.

Barna research shows growing skepticism of churches, of Christianity, and of Christians. But people are also skeptical that Christian ministers are reliable guides through life. One-third of U.S. adults say pastors are "very reliable" when it comes to offering wisdom about God's will and about how the church can help people live according to God's will. Not bad, right? But on issues that are not obviously "spiritual," pastors are trusted less. Only one in six adults says ministers are very reliable guides for how Christianity should inform the U.S. justice and political systems. And just one in four says they are very reliable when it comes to helping people live out their convictions publicly and privately.

In the past, a career in ministry might have appealed to any leader who sought recognition and respect. Today, however, Christian ministers are as likely to be ignored and insulted as they are to be admired and revered. It's not a job for the thin-skinned or the weak of heart.

Yet despite these daunting challenges, called and committed pastors are absolutely indispensable. A society moving at full speed, oblivious to the cliff's edge, needs all the help it can get, even if it scoffs at the worker in the orange vest waving SLOW and CAUTION signs. And the shrinking, increasingly marginalized Christian community needs wise, humble guidance through the twists and turns ahead. If they are to navigate the effects of disintermediation and effectively lead God's people, pastors must rise to three challenges:

1. **Practice humble self-leadership in an age of distraction and celebrity.** How well pastors lead themselves may be more important, in the long run, than how effectively they lead others. "I focus on this one thing," Paul wrote to the church he pastored in Philippi. "I press on to . . . receive the heavenly prize for which God, through Christ Jesus, is calling us" (3:13-14). That level of focus is more urgent now than ever, given the potential distractions clamoring for leaders' attention—not least of which is today's cult of celebrity that prioritizes image and reputation over transformation into Christ's likeness. The church needs pastors who are single-minded, not about seeking the false worship lavished on celebrities, but about finding themselves in Jesus.

2. **Provide congregational leadership that turns consumers into the body of Christ.** The cultural elevation of individual self-fulfillment as the highest moral good has countless downsides, including the widely accepted assumption that church is a service to consume. Some church leaders buy into or even promote this idea. Yet the New Testament paints a very different picture: "We are many parts of one body, and we all belong to each other. . . . Love each other with genuine affection, and take delight in honoring each other. . . . When God's people are in need, be ready to help them" (Rom. 12).

For today's congregations to embody the biblical vision of church, pastors must empower God's people to serve one another rather than enabling them to be mere consumers of spiritual goods and services.

3. **Offer cultural leadership to a society in search of wisdom.** Dallas Willard wrote in his book *Knowing Christ Today*, "The task of Christian pastors and leaders is to present Christ's answers to the basic questions of life . . . in the public arenas of a world in desperate need of knowledge of what is real and good." Thanks to the internet, information is cheap but wisdom is at an all-time premium—and this complex, uncertain age demands clarity and courage from Christian ministers. It is a tall order to communicate with truth and grace in today's fragmented, contested culture, but pastors can trust our Lord's promise: "I am with you always, even to the end of the age" (Matt. 28:20).

There are two main responses to the powerful cultural changes all around us. The first option is to search for easy, simplistic answers that promise a return to the status quo. The second requires that spiritual leaders acknowledge that there's no going back and commit to moving forward into the unknown.

In other words, for pastors to master the art of leading in an era of disintermediation, they must find new tools and new techniques in order to bring the truth of the unchanging gospel to today. Pastors, then, must be adaptive leaders, willing to be formed in new ways. The challenges of pastoring are significant. So, too, are the opportunities.

Global Religion

Studies focused on the state of the
Christian faith in other countries

The Francis Effect: Views of the Pope

Photo: Jeon Han

Since taking over the papacy in 2013, Pope Francis has won wide acclaim across generational lines and among Protestants and Catholics. His approach has marked a break with the tone of past popes—and it's a tone that has resonated deeply with Americans.

Pope Francis' widespread popularity has only increased; American adults reporting favorable views of the Pope grew from 54 percent in 2014 to 60 percent in 2015. Growth is most notable among younger generations, with the Pope's favorability among Millennials and Gen-Xers increasing by 14 (41% to 55%) and 20 (51% to 71%) percentage points in one year, respectively. Among the older generations, favorability drops slightly from 64 percent to 54 percent for Boomers, and 66 percent to 58 percent for Elders.

Some of Francis' harsher critics are within his own tradition; favorability dipped slightly among Catholics since 2014. Protestants overall report a 10-point increase (from 48% to 58%), but Catholics' favorable impressions dropped 6 percentage points. Still, Catholics overall report highly favorable views—at 79 percent, the highest among all segments.

When asked whether Pope Francis has improved their view of the church, Protestants and younger generations are the most persuaded. The Pope's appeal to younger generations is hard to ignore. Half of Millennials agree that the Pope has positively influenced their view of the Catholic Church (49%), almost twice as many as 2014 (27%). It's the same story among Gen-Xers, with half affirming that he's improved their view of the church; this also represents an increase from 2014 (36% to 50%). More Protestants since 2014 also report the Pope's positive influence on their views of the church—from one-quarter (27%) to nearly four in 10 (39%). More than half of Catholics (52%) report an improved view of the church.

Pope Francis is often touted as the "everyman" Pope, and this clearly resonates with—and inspires—Americans, Catholic and non-Catholic alike. But has inspiration turned into imitation?

In just a single year, the proportion of American adults who say Pope Francis has caused them to make changes to their spiritual life quadrupled, from five percent to 21 percent. The most significant shifts have been among Millennials (up 23 points) and Gen-Xers (up 25 points). The story is slightly different among older generations, with Boomers reporting a 6-percentage-point increase, and Elders remain unchanged. There is a 10-percentage-point increase in Catholics who report the Pope's influence on spiritual life. Interestingly, Protestants report a dramatic 19-percentage-point increase from 2014, emphasizing the influence of Pope Francis on those outside his tradition and age groups.

Pope Francis and the Big Issues

Though many have wondered if he is a liberal reformer, Pope Francis has neither officially changed nor challenged any traditional, orthodox Catholic beliefs. For the most part, Americans—regardless of age and religion—say that Pope Francis is taking the right stance on today's big issues.

When it comes to divorce and marriage, most adults believe Pope Francis is doing pretty well, with 40 percent agreeing he has the "right stance" regarding issues surrounding the mariage covenant. The major differences are between generations, with more Millennials believing he is too conservative (28%) than other generations (18% of Gen-Xers, 11% of Boomers, and 16% of Elders).

The issue of birth control garners the most controversy. Even though a plurality says the Pope has the right stance, a higher proportion of adults view his position as being "too conservative" (23%) than on other issues. Again, Millennials are the generation most likely to say so (29% of Millennials, compared to 22% of Gen-Xers, 20% of Boomers, and 25% of Elders).

As with the issue of birth control, a high percentage of respondents claim the Pope is "too conservative" on abortion (21%)—with Millennials most likely to feel this way (27%). This is the issue for which the lowest proportion of adults claims he is "too liberal" (9%), and the highest percentage choosing "unsure" (37%). Although abortion remains a contentious and complicated political issue, few adults appear to believe Pope Francis is too liberal on the issue. Catholics were more certain of the Pope's position than Protestants: 55 percent vs. 36 percent, respectively believe the Pope has the "right stance" on this issue.

On the other end of the spectrum, the largest proportion of adults to report "too liberal" (15%) is on the issue of same-sex marriage—though an almost equal number claim his stance is "too conservative" (17%). Additionally, an equal one-third of adults believe he has the "right stance" or say they "don't know." This diversity of opinion

The most self-identified Catholic state in the U.S. is Rhode Island, where 43 percent of the population identifies with the faith. However, in terms of the population that qualifies as practicing Catholic, Louisiana slightly exceeds Rhode Island (20 percent and 19 percent, respectively).

n=1,026 | February 20–24, 2014; n=1,000 | August 24– 26, 2015

on same-sex marriage reflects Barna's research on the issue, which shows that Americans remain deeply divided.

Francis has made climate change and global warming a priority for his papacy, and it appears that he is making an impact. The Pope scores high for "right stance" on the environment (41%), alongside the 40 percent who affirm his view on marriage and divorce, and just behind the nearly half (47%) who say he has the right perspective on poverty and social issues.

Cardinal Jorge Mario Bergoglio chose "Francis" as his papal name in honor of St. Francis of Assisi, a 13th-century saint known for his commitment to serving the poor. This was an early indiciation of the nature of Pope Francis. Among all of the policies surveyed, the highest proportion of U.S. adults regard the Pope's policy on poverty and social issues as the "right stance" (46%). This opinion is particularly high among Catholics at 67 percent, the highest among any group on any issue.

"Pope Francis remains hugely popular, and his favorable impact seems to be growing within the U.S. population," Barna president David Kinnaman says.

"Whether one agrees with his perspectives or not, Pope Francis continues to be a fascinating case study in spiritual leadership. People respond positively to a leader who, among many other things, prioritizes the poor and believes Christian convictions matter in society."

Spiritual Lessons from Scotland 💬🧍

Scotland is a nation divided. A yearlong Barna study conducted in partnership with the Maclellan Foundation found that half of all Scots describe themselves as Christian (51%) while the other half identify with another faith or none (49%). The cultural trend to identify as Christian is in decline. Younger adults are much less apt than older adults to describe themselves as Christian.

For many, the label alone is enough. The power of Christendom's cultural legacy remains strong, especially among older Scots. Seven out of 10 self-identified Christians are "legacy Christians" who do not believe basic elements of Christian doctrine or express personal faith in Jesus (69%). This translates to more than one-third of the total population (36%). Interestingly, a legacy Christian is more likely than the average Scot to say "a Christian nation" is the best way to describe the country (44% vs. 31%), a view which also demonstrates a more cultural than personally transformational view of their religious affiliation.

At the opposite end of the belief spectrum among self-identified Christians are evangelicals. For the purposes of this research, Barna adopted a definition of "evangelical" based on David Bebbington's four-part rubric, known as the "Bebbington quadrilateral." (*See infographic for details.*) Only those who meet all four of the standards qualify as "evangelical" under this definition.

Between legacy Christians and evangelicals are self-identified Christians, who might be categorized as "non-evangelical born again" Christians. They do not qualify as evangelical under the Bebbington rubric, yet, in contrast to legacy Christians, they express personal faith in Jesus. Non-evangelical born again Scots report having made a commitment to Christ that is still important in their life today and having confessed their sins and accepted Jesus as Savior. One-quarter of self-identified Christians fits this category (26%), about 15 percent of the total Scottish population.

Even more interesting are the Scots who do not self-identify as Christian but who report having made a personal commitment to Jesus Christ that is still important in their life today and say they have accepted him as their Savior (2%). In combined percentages that reflect real numbers, this means that more than 800,000 adults in Scotland (17%) have a significant connection to Jesus.

Beyond Belief

Another lens through which we can view Scottish Christianity is that of religious practices. In the Barna study, "practicing Christian" is a self-identified Christian who attends church at least once a month and says her faith is very important in her life. About one in eight among all Scots (12%)—one in four self-identified Christians (23%)—is in this category. By contrast, a "non-practicing Christian" is a self-identified Christian who either does not attend church at least once a month or says faith is not important, or both. Non-practicing Christians represent 40 percent of the total adult population or 77 percent of self-identified Christians.

Nearly half of practicing Christians say their faith has "transformed" their lives (47% compared to 16% among all adults) and another 43 percent say their faith has been "helpful" but not necessarily transformative (compared to 36% among all adults). Similarly, a majority of practicing Christians strongly agree that their faith is relevant to their life (52%). That is more than eight times the number of non-practicing Christians who say the same (6%). A majority of non-practicing Christians report that faith has not made much of a difference in their life (57%); just 5 percent say their life has been transformed by faith and one-third say their faith has been helpful but not transformative (33%)—on par with the national average (36%).

Nine out of 10 non-practicing Christians are unchurched (93%), including 86 percent who are "dechurched," meaning they attended church at some point in their lives but not in the past six months. Among non-practicing Christians who have not attended a church service in the past year, one-third feels that church does not have anything to offer them (32%), 29 percent say they are simply not interested in religion, and 16 percent feel they simply

SCOTLAND & BEBBINGTON'S "EVANGELICAL" RUBRIC

Principle 1

Biblicism
A perception of the Bible as totally accurate or authoritative in all of its teachings

Principle 2

Crucicentrism
A focus on Christ's atoning work on the cross. Individuals who are crucicentric have confessed their sins and accepted Jesus as their Savior.

Principle 3

Activism
A belief that the gospel must be shared with others. Someone who holds this conviction believes that he has a personal responsibility to share his faith with others.

Principle 4

Conversionism
A belief that conversion to Christianity is imperative for every person. These Christians strongly disagree that "everyone goes to heaven when they die, because God loves all people" or that "if a person is generally good, or does enough good things for others during their lifetime, they will go to heaven."

n=1,019 Scottish adults | June 2014 | Maclellan Foundation

don't have time to get involved with church. One-third of practicing Christians reports reading the Bible on at least a weekly basis (34%), not including while at church or in group study. On the other hand, nearly six in 10 non-practicing Christians say they never read the Bible (56%).

Perceptions of Christianity and Churches

According to census data, Scotland has seen a precipitous drop in church involvement during the past few decades. Between 1966 and 2006, membership in the Church of Scotland, still the largest denomination, declined from 1.2 million to 504,000. By the end of 2013, membership had dropped below 400,000. In 2011, those who registered as having "no religion" (37%) outnumbered, for the first time, those registered as "Church of Scotland" (32%).

Overall church involvement in Scotland fell, but the more dramatic decrease in Church of Scotland membership skews the numbers. From 2005 to the end of 2015 (predicted by Peter Brierley in 2010) membership will have fallen 35 percent overall, from about 934,000 to 633,000; when the Church of Scotland is excluded, the drop is 8 percent, from 382,000 to 349,000.

What has precipitated such declines? One clue may lie in the ways adults describe present-day Christianity in Scotland. Presented with a list of possible descriptors, respondents were asked to rate each on a scale from "very accurate" to "not at all accurate." The phrase most frequently chosen as "not at all accurate" was "relevant to my life" (42%). "Not compatible with science" was most commonly considered "very accurate" (23%). Even so, a majority reports either a very favorable (12%) or fairly favorable (42%) impression of the faith. Even wider majorities—more than eight in 10—believe the presence of a church is very (24%) or fairly (59%) favorable for a community.

Why Church? Why Not Church?

If Scots hold favorable views of Christianity and churches, what could motivate them to make a personal connection to

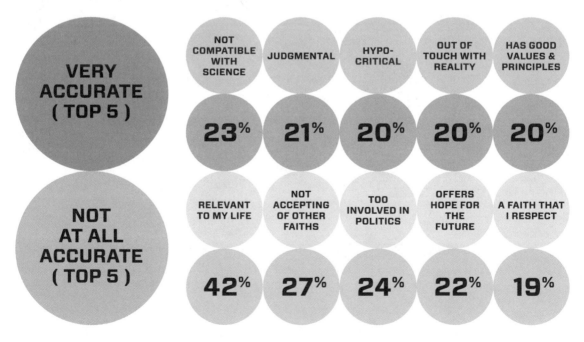

PERCEPTIONS OF CHRISTIANITY IN SCOTLAND

	NOT COMPATIBLE WITH SCIENCE	JUDGMENTAL	HYPO-CRITICAL	OUT OF TOUCH WITH REALITY	HAS GOOD VALUES & PRINCIPLES
VERY ACCURATE (TOP 5)	23%	21%	20%	20%	20%

	RELEVANT TO MY LIFE	NOT ACCEPTING OF OTHER FAITHS	TOO INVOLVED IN POLITICS	OFFERS HOPE FOR THE FUTURE	A FAITH THAT I RESPECT
NOT AT ALL ACCURATE (TOP 5)	42%	27%	24%	22%	19%

n=1,019 Scottish adults | June 2014 | Maclellan Foundation

either? Adults were asked to rate a variety of possible reasons to attend church from "very convincing" to "not at all convincing." Seven in 10 find meeting others from the community a very or fairly convincing motivation. Six in 10 consider finding out more about God very or fairly convincing. More than half say religious teaching for their children or improving their own understanding of the Bible might be convincing reasons to attend church.

A lack of personal experience with church plays a significant role in young adults' absence from church involvement. Contrasted with the majority of all adult non-attenders whose parents practiced Christianity when they were youngsters (52%), just two out of five Scots ages 18 to 24 who do not attend church say their parents practiced Christianity (40%). Fewer than half of young-adult non-attenders went to church as children (45%, compared to 61% among all non-attenders), and more than half say they have never in their lives regularly attended church (54%, compared to 30% among all non-attenders).

When asked to describe their reasons, eight out of 10 people who do not attend religious services say, "I am just not interested in religion" (50%) or "the church really does not have anything to offer me" (32%). In that vein, although a majority of Scots views the presence of a Christian fellowship as beneficial (or benign) for a local community, there are substantial differences between the priorities of ministers/pastors and the needs that outsiders believe the church should prioritize.

For example, ministers/pastors of Scottish churches report their top three ministry priorities are preaching and teaching (67%), worship (44%), and discipleship and spiritual growth (42%). Scottish adults, meanwhile, believe that a church's top priorities should be to provide a place where everyone is accepted (50%), to offer activities to keep local teens out of trouble (44%) and to feed the needy (40%). (A majority of churches in Scotland offers programs to meet some of these needs: Two-thirds have programs for youth or teens, and half provide a food bank.)

Sizable majorities of ministers/pastors agree on the factors that are "extremely important" to transform people's lives for the sake of the gospel. Unfortunately, not many ministers/pastors would rate their church as "extremely effective" on these factors. Most dramatically, for example, nearly nine out of 10 say that "bringing people who are not Christian to relationship with Jesus" is extremely important to transform people's lives (86%)—but just two percent of ministers/pastors would rate their church as extremely effective in this area.

Against a receding tide of Christian faith and practice in Scotland advance a fervent few whose lives have been transformed by faith. Scots under the age of 45 are twice as likely

(23%) as those 45 and older (12%) to say faith "has transformed my life." Younger adults are significantly less likely than older adults, by a margin of nine percentage points, to say faith "has not made much of a difference" (39% vs. 48%) or that faith "has been helpful but has not greatly transformed me" (34% vs. 43%). As it is comparatively rare for young Scots to have been raised in church, it may be that a greater proportion of young adults are Christian by choice, rather than by cultural default.

Noteworthy, as well, are the 36 percent of young adults ages 18 to 24 who hold to an orthodox view of the Bible, compared to 29 percent of all adults. Conversely, young adults are somewhat more likely than the national average (32%) to understand Jesus as "just a moral teacher or prophet and not God" (37%), and twice as likely as the average (7%) to say that Jesus "was not an actual historical person" (12%). Such generational cognitive dissonance may be the natural result of few formative church experiences.

Barna president David Kinnaman hopes this data will "inform leaders in Scotland as well as pastors, church planters, and leaders in other post-Christian contexts by showing both the significant headwinds facing and unexpected tailwinds aiding Christian communities."

Go to barna.com/scotland to learn more about this landmark multi-phase research project or to purchase the full Transforming Scotland report.

n=1,019 Scottish adults | June 2014 | Maclellan Foundation

Behind the U.K.'s Mixed Feelings About Christianity

Jesus remains a central figure in the American context—but cross the pond to the United Kingdom, and you'll find a more secular environment, even though the Church of England is the established state church there. So, what do U.K. adults know and believe about Jesus Christ? What do they think of his followers? Do U.K. Christians talk about their faith in Jesus? How do both Christians and non-Christians feel about those conversations? The Church of England, Evangelical Alliance, and HOPE partnered with Barna to ask more than 4,000 U.K. adults these and other questions.

Jesus: Man, Myth, or God?

You don't have to be a Christian to believe Jesus actually walked the earth 2,000 years ago, and among the general population of U.K. adults, this historical reality is a common assumption. Six in 10 U.K. adults believe Jesus was a real person (61%). Age plays a minor role in that belief—adults 35 and older (63%) are slightly more likely than those 18 to 34 (57%) to believe Jesus actually lived. Younger adults (26%) are also more likely than those over 35 (20%) to believe Jesus was a "fictional character from a book and not a real, historical person."

But even though most U.K. adults believe Jesus was a historical person, they are much less convinced of his divinity.

In fact, belief in Jesus' divinity is not common at all. Only about one in five adults among the general population holds the belief that Jesus was "God in human form who lived among people in the first century" (22%). The most common belief about Jesus is that he was "a prophet or spiritual leader, not God" (29%).

When we look closely at some of the racial demographics, the story is somewhat different. For instance, most ethnic minorities believe Jesus was a real person but are divided on whether or not he is God. Four out of five believe "Jesus was a real person who actually lived" (79%)—20 points higher than among white adults (59%)—but only 25 percent believe Jesus was "God in human form," only slightly more than among whites. This is likely due to the fact that a majority of ethnic groups in the U.K. belong to a religion—but not always Christianity. For instance, almost all Pakistani and Bangladeshi U.K. adults are Muslim, and their religion teaches Jesus was a prophet but not God.

When it comes to the resurrection of Jesus, not quite half of U.K. adults believe the event actually happened (44%). One in six believes "the resurrection happened word-for-word as described in the Bible" (17%) while one-quarter believes the story "contains some content which should not be taken literally" (26%).

An Outsider Perspective on U.K. Christians

A majority of U.K. non-Christians knows a Christian. Two-thirds of non-Christians say they personally know someone who is a follower of Jesus—that is, someone they perceive to be a "practicing Christian" (68%). Most of these Christians are either family members (35%) or friends (38%). But one in three U.K. adults does not know a practicing Christian (33%). Many of these individuals are under the age of 35 (29%) or between 35 and 44 (41%).

The good news is that most non-Christians in the U.K. enjoy the company of the Christian they know (61%). Three out of five say they enjoy being around their Christian friend or family member always (28%) or most of the time (33%). And overall, non-Christians attribute more positive than negative qualities to the Christian they know. The most common positive perceptions are that he or she is friendly (64%), caring (52%), or good-humored (46%), while the most common negative perceptions are that he or she is narrow-minded (13%), hypocritical (10%), or uptight (7%).

How Do Non-Christians Experience Evangelism?

Although U.K. adults have generally positive perceptions of Christians, they don't always share enthusiasm for Christian beliefs when evangelized. More than half of U.K. non-Christians who know a Christian (57%) have had a conversation with them about Jesus. Younger adults 18 to 34 (60%) are somewhat more

COMFORTABLE WITH EVANGELISM

% among Christians who shared about Jesus in the past five years

● U.K. practicing Christians   ● U.K. non-practicing Christians

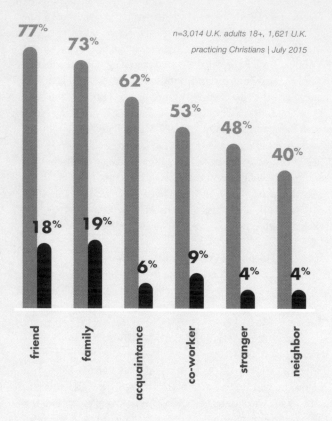

n=3,014 U.K. adults 18+, 1,621 U.K. practicing Christians | July 2015

	friend	family	acquaintance	co-worker	stranger	neighbor
practicing	77%	73%	62%	53%	48%	40%
non-practicing	18%	19%	6%	9%	4%	4%

likely than adults over 35 (54%) to report having had such a conversation. Two out of every five non-Christians say evangelism made them glad not to be a Christian (43%). Another two in five don't know how they felt about it (41%), while only 16 percent felt sad after the conversation about Jesus, that they did not share the Christian's faith.

When Christians talk about Jesus, the response is mixed. One in five non-Christians says that after such a conversation, they felt open to an experience or encounter with Jesus. But almost half say they were not open to such an experience (49%) and six in 10 didn't want to know more about Jesus (60%). One in six did want to know more (18%); 16 percent felt sad that they did not share the

Christian's faith; about one-quarter felt more positive about Jesus (22%) or felt closer to the Christian with whom they had the conversation (27%).

How Do Christians Experience Evangelism?

Despite the mixed responses from non-Christians, practicing Christians feel a strong responsibility to evangelize (85%). Nearly half strongly agree that "it is every Christian's responsibility to talk to non-Christians about Jesus Christ" (46%), and another two in five tend to agree (39%). One out of ten tends to disagree with the statement (10%). Non-practicing Christians, however, do not feel the same responsibility for evangelism. Two-thirds of non-practicing Christians disagree that they have a responsibility to evangelize (63%) while just 19 percent agree—about the same proportion as those who don't know (18%).

This strong sense of responsibility among practicing Christians to evangelize is backed up by their actions. For instance, most practicing Christians have recently talked about Jesus with a non-Christian. Two-thirds have talked about their faith in Jesus within the past month (68%), and eight in 10 have talked with a non-Christian about Jesus in the past six months (82%). Belief and action also align for non-practicing Christians, who, feeling little obligation to share their faith, overwhelmingly do not, with almost half having talked about Jesus to a non-Christian either more than 6 months ago (30%) or never (18%). Most also feel confident about those conversations (71%).

Further, practicing Christians also report seeking out opportunities to share about Jesus and their faith. Over half of practicing Christians actively look for opportunities to talk to non-Christians about Jesus (53%) and seven in 10 are comfortable sharing their faith (71%). Just more than one-quarter of practicing Christians says they feel unable to take up opportunities to talk about Jesus (26%).

A significant minority are "afraid of causing offense when talking to non-Christians" (29%); "think others are better suited to talking with non-Christians about Jesus" (33%), or "do not know how to talk to non-Christians about Jesus" (22%).

Relationships matter a lot when it comes to evangelism. The level of comfort among practicing Christians who share about their faith is likely related to the fact that these conversations happen primarily in the context of an established relationship. For instance, practicing Christians are most likely to share about their faith with friends (77%), family (73%), acquaintances (62%), or a co-worker (53%).

Younger Christians appear to be leading the charge when it comes to evangelism. Nearly twice as many younger adults 18 to 34 (practicing and non-practicing combined) say they talked about their relationship with Jesus in the past month (33%) compared to adults 35 and older (18%).

There also appears to be a certain optimism among practicing Christians about the impact of their evangelism efforts. More than half say the impact of their faith-sharing conversation on the other person's opinion of Jesus was very or fairly positive (59%).

Reflecting on their experiences of evangelism, both non-Christians and practicing Christians were asked to describe what happened after having a conversation about Jesus. After talking to a non-Christian about Jesus, one in four practicing Christians recall asking if they could pray for the non-Christian (25%). Slightly fewer non-Christians remember being asked this (19%). A similar proportion of non-Christians remember being invited to a church service (18%), although fewer practicing Christians actually recall doing this (14%).

Practicing Christians perceive varied responses from non-Christians after speaking with them about Jesus. Top answers include "want to experience the love of Jesus Christ for themselves" (20%); "request prayer on behalf of themselves, or a friend or family member" (18%); "they are looking into Christianity more broadly" (18%); "express an interest in going to church" (17%); "ask to have another conversation" about Jesus (10%); and ask how

Even though a majority of U.K. adults (61%) believe Jesus was a real person who actually lived, adults in the U.S. are still much more likely to hold this belief. Ninety-two percent of American adults say he was a human who walked the earth.

n=3,014 U.K. adults 18+, 1,621 U.K. practicing Christians | July 2015

they could "find out more about Jesus" (6%).

A Renewed Sense of Mission

Gareth Russell, Barna's Vice President for U.K. and Europe (Barna Global), has presented these findings to a number of church groups and helped launch the online resource talkingJesus.org. He explains that "this research has generated healthy discussion among church leaders about what's working and what's not working in evangelism. Leaders have been pleasantly surprised to learn that many practicing Christians in the U.K. are not only sharing their faith regularly but they are confident in doing so. It was also encouraging that one in five non-Christians who know a Christian are open to faith and a conversation about Jesus with that person.

"Leaders have been stunned to see that only six in 10 U.K. adults believe that Jesus was a real historical person, although belief in the resurrection amounts to about four in 10 adults. Still, people seem to be disconnected from the significance of the resurrection for their own lives. Finally, people have favorable views of Christians; the vast majority of assigned characteristics were positive. We have been encouraged to see the response and the renewed sense of mission among leaders in the U.K. context as a result of this data."

Learn more about Barna Global at barna.com/global.

BARNA TAKES

The Urgency of Biblical Literacy

Gareth Russell,
Barna Global, Vice
President for
the U.K. and Europe

The *Transforming Scotland* study was an important project for me personally. Not only was it the first major project I worked on for Barna Global, but it was based in my homeland.

Being Scottish, I grew up in a culture that has had a tumultuous relationship with faith, the Church, and Scripture. There is a growing dichotomy between the historical values of our nation that are rooted in the Bible, the rise of secularism, and the desire to be in the progressive *avant garde*.

So when Barna came to me with the idea of launching this study and asked me to be part of it, I jumped at the idea.

I could finally get some clarity on what the relationship between God, the Bible, and faith was in my country. It was a project that could have a lasting impact on the Scottish church and equip leaders to better engage with their communities.

At the study's outset, I viewed Scotland as a post-Christian nation, and a nation without a desire to explore faith in a higher being and without a felt need for the local church.

Much of that is true.

Scotland is certainly no longer an active Christian nation (5 percent were found to be practicing evangelicals), but there are signs of hope. The green shoots of recovery are becoming more clearly visible.

We have to be realistic. Most people in Scotland are far from living an active and transformational faith, and that challenge is no more accurately seen than in the average Scot's relationship with the Word of God.

Fewer than three in 10 Scots believe the Bible is the actual or inspired Word of God, 42 percent disagree that the Bible is totally accurate in all of the principles it teaches, and nearly nine in 10 Scots are neutral (44%) or skeptical (42%) toward the Bible.

As someone who is passionate about the Word of God—not only about people reading it, but engaging with it and allowing it to transform their lives—I could easily be disheartened. But the study has also highlighted where we could be.

One church leader in our qualitative survey described Scotland as a "pre-Christian" country. Given the years of historical impact that the Church has had on our nation, that could feel like a terrible blow.

I don't agree.

If we are, in essence, a pre-Christian country, we get to start from scratch. If we are a pre-Christian country, people don't come with wounds caused by ungracious church experiences. If we are a pre-Christian country, we don't have to "unteach" poor theology. If we are a pre-Christian country, we can point people to the person of Jesus and allow God to do the rest.

But the Word of God has to be central to any transformation that we are to experience in Scotland (and for that matter, any other nation on earth).

I was encouraged that when we identified the key characteristics of those churches that are experiencing growth in Scotland, one of the major factors was expository teaching of the Scriptures.

These churches don't dilute the gospel in order to appeal to the masses; in fact, they are doing the opposite. They are teaching the Bible as it should be taught: prioritizing solid theology, thinking about engaging delivery, and encouraging individual study.

Millennials (those aged 18-30 years old) are searching for a level of depth in understanding Scripture—not only to understand God, but to receive the appropriate guidance for the various decisions that life presents them with. Eighteen to 24-year-olds are more likely to look to the Bible when confronted with issues of illness or death, family conflict, money and finances, careers, and romance and sexuality.

That same age group wants to explore the Word of God in community. Seventy-two percent of Millennials say they find the Bible most useful when discussing it with others.

These Millennials are zealous. They are passionate. They are motivated and eager to learn. Many of them will be first-generation Christians, coming from families who rarely attend church, if at all.

But Millennials aren't the only ones who will benefit from solid biblical teaching; this is an issue across the generations. We found that, among all growing churches, expository teaching was one of the key drivers for transformation.

There is a need for strong Bible mentorship. There is a need for discipleship grounded in good theology. This will take time, energy, and resources.

Biblical engagement should not be about how we water down the message to be a "consumer-friendly" marketing piece. What our churches require is robust, deep teaching and understanding. People want to grapple with the mysteries of God and come to a real, authentic, and meaningful relationship with him through his Word.

Investing in biblical literacy, in both our Millennial leaders and the wider Church, will provide a strong foundation from which to give Scotland—and the global Church—the best chance it has to experience the spiritual transformation we so desperately need.

Barna | Global

Around the world, Barna is studying issues that affect the local and global Church

In 2014, Barna expanded its operations into the global market, taking on projects covering a variety of topics, including:

- The state of the Christian church in Scotland
- Perceptions of Jesus, Christians, and evangelism in England
- Vocation and the workplace in Australia
- Attitudes toward biblical financial stewardship in Australia
- Faith and science in Brazil
- New product research in the Philippines
- Christian higher education in the United Kingdom
- A multi-language program study spanning 11 countries and five continents

Contact us to explore faith in your part of the world
Find out how at barna.com/global

Barna Trends Presenter's Pack

Includes data about

- Faith and culture
- The New Moral Code
- Millennials
- The Bible and Jesus
- Ministry
- Church planting
- Politics and religious liberty
- Technology
- Pornography
- Education
- Discipleship

Take full advantage of Barna's data through our presenter's slides—a convenient way to utilize the vast amount of data in Barna Trends to enhance your own sermon or presentation.

Special Offer for Barna Trends Purchasers
Make the most of your *Barna Trends* purchase by adding the Presenter's Pack, normally $29, for just $9. Go to barna.com/barnatrends and use code **PRESENTER** at checkout for your discounted download.

Order at
barna.com /barnatrends

Generational Faith

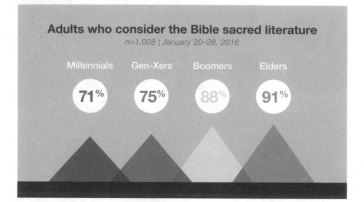

Adults who consider the Bible sacred literature

n=1,008 | January 20–28, 2016

Millennials	Gen-Xers	Boomers	Elders
71%	**75**%	**88**%	**91**%

Younger Adults Less Likely to Esteem Sacred Texts

According to American Bible Society's annual "State of the Bible" survey, performed in partnership with Barna, most American adults believe that the Bible is sacred literature (80%) and that it contains everything a person needs to know to live a meaningful life (66% strongly or somewhat agree). Among Elders aged 70 and older and Boomers 51 to 69, the percentages are even higher: nine out of 10 Elders (91%) and Boomers (88%) consider the Bible sacred. More than two-thirds of Elders (65%) and more than half of Boomers (56%) agree the Bible's contents are sufficient for living a meaningful life.

Generally, American adults under 50 tend to be more skeptical, or at least more ambivalent, about the Bible than older adults, and this is especially true of Millennials aged 18 to 31. Fewer young adults consider the Bible sacred literature (71% of Millennials and 75% of Gen-Xers, compared to 88% of Boomers and 91% of Elders), and Millennials (22%) are three times more likely than Elders (7%) to say that none of the books considered sacred literature by many religions—including the Torah, the Koran, the Book of Mormon, and "other"—are holy books.

Similarly, smaller percentages of younger adults agree that the Bible contains everything a person needs to know in order to live a meaningful life (27% of Millennials and 40% of Gen-Xers).

"One of the significant challenges of this [Millennial] generation is actually financial. They haven't experienced a lot of prosperity. And while large institutions have failed in the course of their lifetimes, they also see stories of individuals who have changed and shaped the world as we know it. There is a sense that people have the ability to change things that are wrong with the world and I think that's a big part of what makes them so optimistic. From a Christian perspective it's not just naiveté. There's a reason for optimism, even despite the brokenness that we see in our world today. And I think this generation really embodies the hope that the gospel presents to us."

—*David H. Kim, executive director for the Center for Faith & Work, author of the Barna FRAME* 20 and Something

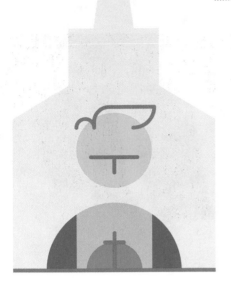

Elders Love Their Local Church

When asked what they love most about their city, 10 percent of adults first acknowledge church. Elders are the most likely generation to do so: 15 percent of them point to church as the thing they most appreciate about where they live. Yet, even for Elders, church is outranked by several other factors—friendships (18%), weather (17%), and like-minded people (17%)—and it ties with work. Among both Boomers and Gen-Xers, 11 percent say church is their favorite thing about their community. Millennials are the least attached to church, with just 3 percent saying it is what they love most about their home.

Discipling at Every Age

The relationships that seem to be most influential in Millennials' spiritual growth are somewhat distinct from other generations, Barna research conducted in partnership with The Navigators reveals.

More Millennials say "friends" have been "very helpful" to their spiritual growth (47%, vs. 33% of Gen-Xers and 39% among Boomers who say spiritual growth is important). In addition, 39 percent of spiritually growing Millennials say a "Christian community other than a church" has been "very helpful" to their spiritual growth, compared with 31 percent among Gen-Xers, 30 percent of Boomers, and 25 percent of Elders. Online social networks are considered "very helpful" by 14 percent of Millennials who consider spiritual growth at least somewhat important, compared with 11 percent of Gen-Xers and 9 percent of Boomers among the same segment.

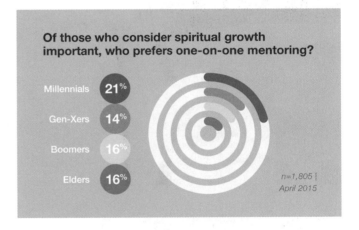

Of those who consider spiritual growth important, who prefers one-on-one mentoring?

Millennials **21%**
Gen-Xers **14%**
Boomers **16%**
Elders **16%**

n=1,805 | April 2015

Despite these propensities for social interaction, Millennials are more likely than other generations to prefer one-on-one or solitary discipleship structures. Forty percent of Millennials who consider spiritual growth very or somewhat important prefer on-their-own discipleship, compared with 36 percent among Gen-Xers and 32 percent of Elders (and 39 percent of Boomers, who are more like Millennials in this respect).

Twenty-one percent of Millennials who consider spiritual growth important prefer one-on-one mentoring models, compared to 14 percent of Gen-Xers and 16 percent of Boomers and Elders. A greater percentage of Millennials are currently in a one-on-one discipleship relationship. Twenty-eight percent of Millennials who consider spiritual growth important are currently being discipled, contrasted with 25 percent of Gen-Xers and 22 percent of Boomers.

BARNA TAKES

What's the Point of Church?

Roxanne Stone,
Barna Group,
Editor-in-Chief

You've gotten the message by now, but here's the recap: Millennials, mostly twentysomethings, are famously saying they no longer need church.

Fifty-nine percent of Millennials who grew up in the church have dropped out, 52 percent have not been to church in the last six months, and one-third don't see church as important.

Perhaps just as telling are the insights of Millennials who do say church is important (20%). Barna asked them: What's the point? Why is church still important to you? And it is in asking that question that we began to clearly see some of the reasons Millennials are no longer seeing much need for church.

The majority—54 percent—said the reason they go to church is to be closer to God. A close second, 31 percent, said it was to learn more about God. Sixteen percent said it was because the church is God's hands and feet in the world. Somewhat alarmingly, only 14 percent said they go to church to be part of a community, and only 8 percent say it is because the church does good work in the world.

These top two answers—ranked far above the others, and both quite focused on the personal relationship with God—reveal that there is something missing from an understanding of the purpose of church. (Of course, this isn't just among Millennials; these expectations are learned expectations from parents and older generations who answered in almost the same way.)

Let's take a look at why Millennials who no longer attend church stopped going in the first place:

The top three answers:

- 35 percent say it's because the church is not relevant to them personally.
- 30 percent say they find God elsewhere.
- 17 percent say they can teach themselves what they need to know.

When I see these three answers, I see a close parallel to their reasons for attending church.

If people believe the most important reasons to attend church are to be closer to God and learn more about him, why would they keep going when they can find God elsewhere and teach themselves what they need to know? And, if they no longer need the church to achieve their spiritual goals, it's no wonder the church is not personally relevant to them.

Millennials have a plethora of resources at their disposal to help them find God and to learn what they need to know. This is by far the most resourced Christian generation. There are podcasts, blogs, books, worship albums, and concerts. They can download a Bible commentary app, read daily devotions in their inbox, and retweet inspiring quotes from Christian celebrities. What happens when—as is the case—fewer than one in 10 people say they learned something about God or Jesus the last time they went to church? What happens when the vast majority of people—61 percent—say they did not gain any significant or new insights regarding faith when they last went to church?

If you believe the most important reason to attend church is to get closer to God and to learn more about him, why would you keep going?

Of course, this is not the whole story. There are many reasons Millennials—or anyone—decide not to go to church. Barna's research over the years details many of these reasons: because the church discourages doubt, because of the church's treatment of gay people, because the church seems "anti-science," because of church wounds, because of hypocrisy, because of moral failures in leadership, because they simply "don't like the people." All of those are documented reasons Millennials say they dislike church.

It's important for leaders to understand what deters Millennials from going to church. And it's important to evaluate how to fix those things—not simply so we can draw in Millennials, but because these are critical things that need to be fixed in the church.

However, as a Millennial who longs for my generation (and all generations) to be part of the Church, it's not enough to change church. It's also time to start fundamentally making a case for church. Not only asking what is broken, but beginning to remember again what is right. To remember why church is worth it.

If you ask what the point of church is, and the best answer is effective teaching, or worship—or even a very good purpose like helping people get close to God—then we've lost our imagination. We've lost something significant in our understanding of the breadth and depth of a living, complex, responsive, self-sacrificing body of Christ that is bringing God's kingdom to earth.

The Church does not simply exist to make individuals better followers of Jesus. That's part of it. It also exists for reasons that stretch far beyond the personal, in both space and time. The Church exists to testify to a greater story than the world's: through traditions and symbols and sacraments—like baptism and marriage and communion—that point to a mysterious Presence and a grace beyond our everyday experience. The Church exists to renew the world: to unite holy saints in a battle that has spanned millennia as we continue to labor and pray for "thy will to be done on earth as it is in heaven."

Can the Church reclaim those spiritual practices that reflect such a grand communal vision? And will Millennials (and every other generation) embrace it?

The State of the Church 2017

A snapshot of faith in America today

n= 5,137 | January–April 2016
See glossary for a full definition of all terms in bold.

How Americans Affiliate and Practice Their Faith

A majority of Americans identifies as Christian and more than half (52%) say that faith is very important to their life ...

73% Identify as Christian

20% No faith

6% Other faith

1% Not sure

*... However, the nation is increasingly post-Christian (see page 184 for a summary of Barna's post-Christian metric). Nearly half of Americans qualify as such, and there are more **non-practicing Christians** than **practicing Christians**.*

48% Post-Christian

41% Non-practicing Christians

31% Practicing Christians

How Americans Express and Experience Faith

Despite the cultural impact of mega-churches, most churchgoers attend services in a more intimate context

- attend a church of 100 or fewer attendees
- attend a church of 100–499 attendees
- go to a church of 500-999 attendees
- attend a church of 1,000 or more attendees

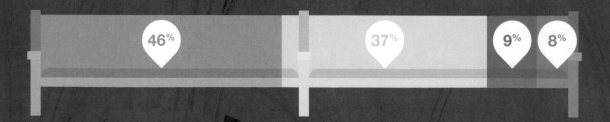

46%   37%   9%   8%

*Most Americans are considered **"churched"**—that is, they have attended a religious service (other than a wedding or funeral) in the past six months*

55% Churched

45% Unchurched

In the past year ...

54% of Americans gave any money to a church

22% of Americans gave any money to a non-profit, other than a church

What does a week in the (spiritual) life of an American look like? Here are the ways people report engaging their faith in a given week:

1	2	3	4	5	6	7
75%	**35**%	**34**%	**19**%	**18**%	**17**%	**16**%
Pray to God	Attend a church service	Read the Bible	Volunteer at a nonprofit	Volunteer at church	Attend adult Sunday school	Attend small group

What Americans Believe

*An **orthodox view of God**—that he is all-powerful, all-knowing, creator of the universe, and ruling the world today—remains the most common among Americans*

35% Born again Christians

7% Evangelical Christians

23% Bible-minded

10% "There is no such thing as God."

26% Strongly agree "Christians have a responsibility to evangelize others."

33% Other view of God

55% Agree strongly or somewhat "Good works result in going to heaven."

57% "God is all-powerful, all-knowing, creator of the universe, and ruling the world today."

Barna

Knowledge to navigate a changing world

Understanding Culture

Barna specializes in studying the junction between faith and culture, helping both faith-based and secular organizations better understand their audience, mission, and goals. In the past decade alone, Barna has interviewed more than 500,000 people in hundreds of projects for nearly 450 client organizations that are working to change the world for good.

. . . and Equipping the Church

Barna's work on the Millennial generation, discipleship, vocation, biblical education, church planting, generosity, relationships, and the well-being of pastors helps leaders and laypeople think about these topics in new ways. Fresh insights breed innovative, transformative solutions that will help the Church flourish in the 21st century.